Alvino, James
   Parents' guide to raising a gifted
toddler; recognizing and developing
the potential of your child from
birth to five years.   Little, Brown,
1989.
   288 p.
   Bibliography: p. 276-179.

1. Gifted children.   I. Title.

Parents' Guide to Raising a Gifted Toddler

Also by James Alvino and the Editors of *Gifted Children Monthly*

Parents' Guide to Raising a Gifted Child:
  Recognizing and Developing Your Child's Potential

For information about subscribing to *Gifted Children Monthly*,
please contact the Subscription Department,
Gifted Children Monthly, P.O. Box 115, Sewell, NJ 08080.

Parents' Guide to Raising a Gifted Toddler

Recognizing and Developing the Potential of Your Child from Birth to Five Years

James Alvino
and the Editors of *Gifted Children Monthly*

Little, Brown and Company
Boston   Toronto   London

FIRST EDITION

Much of the material in this book was
previously published in *Gifted Children Monthly*.

The author is grateful for permission to reprint the following copyrighted materials:

Excerpt from "The Greatest Love of All" by Linda Creed. Copyright © 1977 by Gold Horizon Music Corp. and Golden Torch Music Corp. c/o Filmtrax Copyright Holdings Inc. International Copyright Secured. Made in U.S.A. All Rights Reserved.

"What Do You Do for Fun?" by Bernard DeKoven. Copyright © 1986 by Bernard DeKoven. Reprinted by permission.

Excerpt from "April Rain Song" by Langston Hughes, published in *Selected Poems of Langston Hughes*. Copyright 1932 by Alfred A. Knopf and renewed © 1960 by Langston Hughes. By permission of Alfred A. Knopf, Inc.

"It's You I Like" song lyrics by Fred Rogers. Copyright © Fred M. Rogers, 1970. Reprinted with permission.

Excerpts from *A Parent's Guide to the First Three Years* by Burton L. White. Copyright © 1980 by Burton L. White. By permission of Prentice-Hall, Inc.

Page 7 illustration. Copyright © 1978 by J. A. Renzulli. Reprinted by permission.

Page 195 illustration by Csikszentmihalyi. Reprinted by permission of Jossey-Bass Inc., Publishers.

Library of Congress Cataloging-in-Publication Data

Alvino, James, 1947–
    Parents' guide to raising a gifted toddler : recognizing and
developing the potential of your child from birth to five years / by
James Alvino and the editors of Gifted children monthly. — 1st ed.
      p.   cm.
    Bibliography: p.
    Includes index.
    ISBN 0-316-03636-6
    1. Gifted children. 2. Child rearing. 3. Gifted children —
Identification. 4. Gifted children — Education (Preschool)
5. Toddlers. I. Gifted children monthly. II. Title.
HQ773.5.A59 1989
649'.155 — dc19   88-28582
                           CIP

10 9 8 7 6 5 4 3 2 1

MV-PA

Published simultaneously in Canada
by Little, Brown & Company (Canada) Limited

PRINTED IN THE UNITED STATES OF AMERICA

For little Oruchi Salerno, and others like him,
who, if given half a chance and a whole lot of caring,
will do even better the next time around

Contents

Preface

Parents' Guide to Raising a Gifted Toddler is for *all* parents interested in recognizing and developing their children's potential. Whether or not your child has been formally identified as "gifted," the information presented here can help you. Expanding your knowledge about what's best for your child — right from the beginning — is what this book is all about.

This volume is a sequel and companion to *Parents' Guide to Raising a Gifted Child* (Little, Brown, 1985). As such, it is similar to the latter in that it is a compilation of several recent years' worth of the best articles, research, parenting advice, and other material gleaned from *Gifted Children Monthly*, the multiaward-winning publication "for the parents of children with great promise."

This new *Parents' Guide* is unlike its predecessor in that it contains original work by the principal author in the areas of emotional needs, perfectionism, and gender-specific issues pertaining to growing up gifted.

Both books are committed to the notion that parents make a tangible difference in the growth and development of their children in those everyday areas in which they interact, guide, admonish, teach, provide for, and otherwise rear their children to the best of their knowledge.

Precious little information exists on gifted toddlers/preschoolers, and you will not find more breadth or depth on the subject than in these pages. Moreover, because of the continuity in childhood development, and the general applicability of the book's themes regardless of age level, many of the discussions and suggestions herein pertain to older children as well. In some cases the chapters deliberately project developmental stages beyond the first five years to give you a holistic view — either of where you're heading, or what could happen down the road.

Parents' Guide is a resource that provides highly practical and specific parenting advice, consumer tips, troubleshooting techniques, and enjoyable and educational family activities offered by experts in education for the gifted and by parents who have "been there." Not everything will fit your situation or work for you, but many of these time-tested ideas and suggestions certainly will.

Special features include essays by David Elkind, today's most celebrated proponent of turning childhood back to children; and Fred Rogers of *Mister Rogers' Neighborhood*. Among the cutting-edge topics covered are mothering in the United States versus Japan; how to discipline and how to praise; the real connection between healthy bodies and healthy minds; the pros and cons of the Suzuki method; stress management for kids; "hothousing" children; and the value of play for social, emotional, and intellectual growth.

Early childhood has been described as "the magical years." Welcome to a Magical Tour of the formative years of your child's life. Enjoy the ride!

Acknowledgments

MANY PEOPLE have contributed to this book and deserve a special thank-you for their help.

Robert Baum, managing editor of *Gifted Children Monthly*, edited several key chapters, skillfully weaving this thread and that into a completed tapestry. He was also instrumental in challenging and helping to resolve issues of a sensitive nature that crop up from chapter to chapter in a project like this.

Carolyn Baker, *GCM*'s office manager, meticulously prepared the manuscript through several revisions to its final form, and secretly admitted that it was easier the second time around.

A good number of authors and educators have contributed to this book by virtue of their previously published material in *Gifted Children Monthly*. Their special insights add a depth and variety to each chapter and a richness of perspective that otherwise would have been impossible to achieve. They are Steve Allen, Nancy Alvarado, Ruth Arent, Alexinia Baldwin, Bruno Bettelheim, Rita Haynes Blocksom, Janet Brady, Carolyn Callahan, Patricia Lund Casserly, Jack Cassidy, David Cheetham, Alice Chen, Barbara Clark, Carol Copple, Barbara Davis, Bernard DeKoven, James R. Delisle, Jim Dieringer, Kathy Dieringer, Carol S. Dweck, Virginia Ehrlich, David Elkind, Barbara Elleman, Mary Candice Evans, Jay Falls, Kathryn Ferner, Max Fogel, Virginia L. Fortner, Julian Fountaine, Lynn Fox, Sandra Fujita, Judy Galbraith, Tricia Garwood, Ray Gottlieb, Beverly Tucker Graham, Tom Greenspon, Claire Grubich, Frank Hajcak, Betsy Hearne, Stan Heck, Hazel Hohn, J. Kent Hollingsworth, Johanna Houck, Tanya Houseman,

Robert Leland Johnson, Stephen Jordan, Merle B. Karnes, Patricia C. Kenschaft, Barbara Kerr, Kathryn A. Knox, Dolores Kozielski, Anne Lewis, Michael Lewis, Cathy Lifeso, Anni Lipper, Deirdre V. Lovecky, Signe Lundberg, Connie Anderson Merrihew, Michael K. Meyerhoff, Patricia Bruce Mitchell, Jane Navarre, Jana Pantazelos, Donna Lugg Pape, Susan Perry, Leslie Renee Ravenstein, Sandford Reichart, Joseph Renzulli, Susanne Richert, Gina Ginsberg Riggs, Fred Rogers, Charles Rosenberg, Phyllis Rosser, John Roth, Ruth Roufberg, Ronald L. Rubenzer, Lee Salk, Suzanne Schneider, June Scobee, Bruce Shore, Betty Siegel, Dorothy Sisk, Judy Sizemore, Wood Smethurst, Nancy Stuart, Bess Tittle, E. Paul Torrance, Cynthia Turnock, Priscilla Vail, Burton White, Joanne Whitmore, Jerome Wieler, Phil Wiswell, Ferida Wolff, and Judith Wurtman.

And finally, once again, a very special thank-you goes to Arthur Lipper III, founder and chairman of *Gifted Children Monthly,* and the country's leading private-sector proponent of gifted-child advocacy.

J.A.

Parents' Guide to Raising a Gifted Toddler

How to Tell
If Your Child Is Gifted

B Y ALL outward appearances, little Susie, just two-and-a-half years old, looks like any other bright and healthy toddler. She's active, full of energy, and happy. Her language development *does* appear to be a little advanced, her mother thought to herself recently, after Susie exclaimed one afternoon: "Really, Mom, I need this cut exactly . . . do you understand me?" But that's nothing compared to what Susie's mother then caught her doing: *reading*, out loud, from her favorite storybook. Little Susie had *taught herself* to read! Now what? her mother thought.

Steven is four years old and somewhat frail for his age. And he's in perpetual motion, apparently unable to sit still for more than thirty seconds at a time. Unable, that is, unless he's playing with his wooden blocks. Then his concentration impresses everyone. One evening after dinner, Steven slipped away to his room and wasn't heard from for a full hour. "Mom, Dad, come see what I built," he finally announced, bounding out of his room. In his room was a three-foot-tall structure, balanced in such a way that it seemingly defied the laws of gravity. "Don't touch *this* one," he said, pointing to a block on the lower-left side of the base. "If you do, the whole thing will topple." His parents just looked at each other in amazement.

Peter, not yet four, is the youngest boy in his preschool. It doesn't seem to matter, though. Unlike most boys his age, he *can* sit still and pay attention. And he seems to prefer playmates who are a bit older than he is. The "problem" with Peter, from his teacher's point of view, is that he is the class clown. Oh, he's creative, too — like the time a classmate was trying to hold a door open using an old sneaker as a doorstop; Peter suggested stuffing the shoe between the hinged edge of the door and the jamb. It's just that his sense of humor gets the best of him all the time and he cracks jokes about everything. His parents are concerned that Peter's behavior won't be tolerated when he hits the public school system.

Jill is a natural born leader if ever there was one. Though only three years old, she exhibits social skills way beyond her years. Just the other day, for example, Jill and two playmates were about to start playing a board game when a quarrel erupted among her friends over who would get a particular token to move around the board. Jill quickly stepped in, designating who would get it this time, and who next time. Problem solved. But what concerns her mother and father is that Jill *always* dominates in her relationships with peers. She's great at orchestrating their activities ("You be the lion, I'll be the scary monster"), but more than once a playmate has gone home exhausted and a little deflated. Jill's parents are afraid she'll end up a lonely, unhappy child.

And then there's Bruce — by nearly every standard an *average* child. The battery of prekindergarten tests he completed and the psychologist's statement say so: "average ability, average creativity, developmentally on schedule." That's not fair, his dad felt when he heard the results. They don't know Bruce the way I do. He was referring to certain characteristics of his son that academic-readiness tests just don't measure — like the way Bruce persists at a puzzle, problem, or task until he gets it right. Bruce's father knows this is atypical for the "average" kindergarten child, and is concerned that the school may overlook possible hidden talents in his son. He wonders what he can do to help bring them out.

Susie, Steven, Peter, Jill, and Bruce — yes, even Bruce — are gifted children. Sometimes such children are easy to spot; their abilities far surpass those of their age-mates. But other times identification is difficult. A child's giftedness can be cloaked behind behaviors that are inaccurately assessed (as in seeing Peter merely as a cutup or Jill as a little tyrant) or otherwise discredited for lack of knowledge on the part of teachers and parents.

How *do* you identify gifted children? What does "gifted" mean, anyway? How reliable are tests to identify these children? What should *you* look for in your young child at home to tell if he or she has special talents that should be recognized, nurtured, and developed?

It wasn't long ago that being "gifted" only meant having a high intelligence quotient (IQ). This notion is associated with the psychologist Lewis Terman, who developed the first broadly used tests of comparative intelligence and studied gifted children and genius over a period of nearly sixty years. In fact, use of a high IQ (usually 130 and above) as a chief means of identifying the gifted is still prevalent despite a broadened definition, ushered in by the federal government, which includes academics, creativity, the arts, and leadership along with strong intellectual ability (IQ) as categories of giftedness.

While there is much controversy about the definition of "gifted" and how to determine which youngsters can be so categorized, studies have shown that parents — not teachers — most often identify gifted children first and most effectively. If these findings are valid, it is important that parents be aware of relevant facts, fictions, and current debates concerning identifying giftedness.

DEFINING AND IDENTIFYING GIFTEDNESS

A 1972 report to the United States Congress — *Education of the Gifted and Talented,* by Sidney P. Marland, commissioner of education — established the federal definition of giftedness, which was to influence the field from then on. It said:

> Gifted and Talented Children are those identified by professionally qualified persons and who, by virtue of outstanding abilities, are capable of high performance. These are children who require differentiated educational programs and/or services beyond those normally provided by regular school programs in order to realize their contributions to self and society.
>
> These are children with demonstrated and/or potential high performance in the following areas:

— *General intellectual ability*
— *Specific academic aptitude*
— *Creative or productive thinking*
— *Leadership ability*
— *Ability in visual or performing arts*

This broadened definition distinguishes between "gifted" and "talented," a distinction that plagues the field's most noble efforts to integrate the two under one definition. Sometimes the two terms are used interchangeably. The implicit distinction is that "gifted" refers to intellectual abilities and "talented" to artistic abilities. But in most cases, "talent" — encompassing the fine and performing arts — is at best relegated to second-class status and at worst not even considered in the same league as "giftedness," as if the two were mutually exclusive.

The federal definition also recognizes that gifted children require special educational attention and includes potential as well as actual performance as a criterion. When framing the 1978 Gifted and Talented Children's Education Act, Congress used the definition in requiring schools to identify and provide activities for children with "demonstrated" or "potential" capabilities in the five areas Marland specified.

Identification Processes

An alternative to the federal definition of giftedness, the "three-ring conception," was developed in 1977 by Joseph Renzulli of the University of Connecticut (see figure). Renzulli's system, using three interlocking criteria (creativity, above-average ability, and task commitment), cuts across all curriculum and talent areas. It deemphasizes IQ and states that all three characteristics must come together in a child's area of interest. Renzulli's work with children has shown that a child's intense interest and motivation in an area indicate possible giftedness. His model for identifying the gifted has been adopted by hundreds of school districts around the country and can be interpreted to fulfill the federal requirements.

Even Terman's own samples and studies do not validate the idea that IQ is *sufficient* to identify the gifted. A 1982 assessment of the same subjects first identified by Terman as gifted in 1921 indicates that those identified as gifted based on IQ fell into two

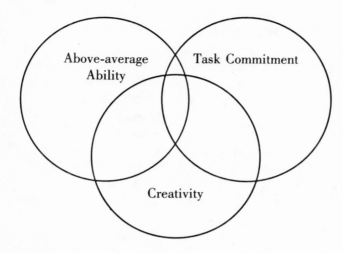

groups: an "A" group, whose members made exceptional achievements and outstanding contributions to their fields, and a "C" group, whose members did not. The former — among them Isaac Asimov, for example — are generally recognized by society as gifted, while the latter are not.

A system such as Renzulli's "triad model" encompasses a broad definition of giftedness and provides a more effective method of identification at the same time. Studies of eminent children and adults regarded as gifted show that they have the three traits of the triad in common. This would include Terman's "A" group. The "C" group apparently lacked — or did not demonstrate — creativity, task commitment, or both. Renzulli's model and the most recent data from the studies of Terman's successors illustrate how measurements of ability can differ from applied performance. Task commitment — high motivation, perseverance, and just plain hard work — is apparently an extremely powerful factor in giftedness. Most experts think that using a variety of formal and informal methods of identification is most effective.

The Debate about Testing

Standardized testing of ability and achievement has been around since the beginning of the century, and despite continued criticism of the inherent limitations and shortcomings of norm-based test instruments, some form of standardized testing seems destined to remain a widely used tool in evaluating children and identifying their comparative levels of capability and development.

Those who emphasize using alternatives to test scores — checklists and rating scales, for example — contend that standardized testing is not sufficient to identify the gifted and that such a use is based on a narrow definition of giftedness. They point out that highly creative thinkers — which in the estimation of some experts best describes gifted individuals — are often stifled by the need to focus on the single "best" answer to a standardized test question. Consequently, many gifted children do not score high on such tests and therefore go unidentified. Another disadvantage to the tests is their tendency to reinforce a conformity of thinking to the detriment of originality.

One of the most flagrant deficiencies in standardized testing is neglect of the thinking *process* children use in reaching their answers. The importance attached to converging on a test maker's predetermined "correct" answer can thwart a child's creativity and authentic discovery. Doing well requires being able to make your thinking conform to psychometrically determined "systems of relevance."

Here is an example: In a test question shown on *Sesame Street*, children were presented with a group of four objects and were asked to choose the item that did not belong. The set consisted of a yellow rain-hat, an orange baseball cap, a red mitten with a white stripe, and a white hard hat. Subsequently it was explained that the correct answer was the mitten, because it was the only object that was not a hat.

In this example we witness an impoverishment of possible embryonic systems of relevance in the child's world. The hat grouping is not the only valid three-object class among the four objects. The same "correct" result (mitten) could be arrived at by recognizing that only one of the objects has two colors. Thus the *same* result can be derived from two schemes of relevance, or from both simultaneously. *Different* results are possible and valid as well. For example, the child of a construction worker might detect an organizational scheme of "mine or Dad's" and answer that the hard hat does not belong. Or the items might be classified into hard and soft. Interest structures and cognitive operations are never completely disentangled, even by adults.

A Clinic for Gifted Preschoolers

The Gifted Child Clinic, a part of the Rutgers University Medical School Department of Pediatrics, was established to identify gifted children at very young ages. Funded in part with grants from the Gifted Children Advocacy Association (the philanthropic division of *Gifted Children Monthly*), the clinic provides the following services:

- It identifies gifted children from birth through elementary-school age through standardized tests, informal assessments, and behavioral observations.
- It serves as an educational center for pediatricians and day-care professionals — offering lectures, special seminars, and continuing-education courses on issues related to the identification and development of gifted children.
- It serves as a model program for other clinics throughout the nation.

For a free brochure describing the program in more detail, send a self-addressed, stamped #10 envelope to Dr. Michael Lewis, Director, Gifted Child Clinic, Department of Pediatrics, UMDNJ-Rutgers Medical School, Medical Education Building CN19, New Brunswick, NJ 08903.

IDENTIFICATION BY PARENTS AT HOME

One study on identification of the gifted, conducted by Virginia Ehrlich when she was with the Astor Program in New York, found that there are at least forty-six broad traits commonly cited in the literature as being associated with intellectual giftedness at all ages. Parents of children up to age seven usually cite from one to fifteen of these traits, with the average being four or five. The brighter the child, the more traits they mention.

For the young child aged three-and-a-half to five-and-a-half, those traits that turned out to be significantly associated with intellectual giftedness were

- having a large vocabulary,
- complex-thinking ability,
- unusual capacity for symbolic thought (mathematical skills),

- insight (capacity to see relationships),
- early physical and social development, and
- sensitivity.

The ability to read was mentioned more frequently than any other trait, but this information was valuable in discriminating between children of high versus low IQs only when the parent was able to cite a specific level of reading ability (for example, "She's seven and reading at the fourth-grade level").

Except for the seven traits cited above, there is no clear pattern of characteristics that can be used as a measure. A parent may observe only a few traits and yet conclude, justly, that the child is gifted. Much, much more research will be required before we can rely exclusively on any checklist for positive identification.

Following are some other general and subjective characteristics that parents can use in estimating whether their child is gifted:

Verbal facility   Facility in writing
Good memory   Ability to learn easily
Flexibility of thought   Abstract reasoning
Complexity of thinking   Planning and organizational
Energy   ability
Creativity, imagination   Originality
Curiosity   Sense of wonder
Range of information   Broad range of interests
Aesthetic interests or talents   Attention to detail
Outstanding performance   Scholastic achievement
Leadership   Attention and concentration
Persistence   Self-criticism
Responsiveness   Strength of character
Candidness   Dependability
Social responsibility   Cooperation
Enthusiasm   Sense of humor
Ability in spatial relationships Emotional stability
Good health   Self-sufficiency and self-
Favorable comparison with   confidence
   siblings, others   Preference for older playmates

Judgments about their gifted children are inevitably affected by the parents' own level of education, community demographics, and intrafamily experiences. Bright, well-educated parents sometimes expect their children to exhibit bright behavior, so they consider it "normal." In families with several bright children, expectations for the younger children are high and thus their behavior may not be recognized as being superior. In areas where unusually well-trained personnel congregate, a child's superior performance may not be recognized simply because it does not differ markedly from the local norm. On the other hand, in the general population, many parents do not recognize intellectual giftedness simply because the circumstances do not permit a display of such abilities.

What parents need most is confidence in their own skill in evaluating their children. Regardless of all the objective criteria psychologists, educators, and others may wish to cite, parents seem to have an intuitive sense about their own children. They know, frequently without being able to explain how they know, that a child has unusual ability. During interviews this is often stated as "I don't know why, but I just know this child is different!"

While the characteristics cited above pertain to children of all ages, there are some more specific indicators of giftedness that are especially suitable for identifying infants, toddlers, and preschoolers.

To Glance or to Stare? That Is the Question

How quickly does your infant lose interest in familiar objects? How quickly and for how long does he or she attend to something new? Answers to these questions may be a window into your child's intelligence.

According to Marc H. Bornstein of New York University and Marian D. Sigman at UCLA, there is continuity in mental development from infancy to early childhood, and a child's verbal IQ can be moderately predicted on the basis of how he or she *attends* to visual and auditory stimuli in the nursery.

As reported in an issue of *Child Development*, the researchers take issue with the long-standing belief that little, if any, continuity in mental development exists between infancy and toddlerhood. This view is based on the notion that classic developmental milestones — sitting, walking, talking — don't always correlate with degree of intelligence.

But gazing at objects apparently does. According to the researchers, "Relatively greater amounts of looking at novel stimuli, or reciprocally lesser amounts of looking at familiar stimuli, are generally interpreted as more efficient information processing." In addition, attention behavior has been found to predict childhood "cognitive competence" more accurately than traditional infant developmental tests do.

NATURE AND NURTURE   Some infants seem to *prefer* novel stimuli, which has prompted the researchers to explore the extent to which attention patterns in infancy are genetic versus the extent to which they are environmentally conditioned. "Parents doubtlessly transmit some talents genetically to their offspring," Bornstein and Sigman state, "but parents also act with their offspring in ways that . . . influence their infants' performance. Infants, too, for their part may provoke their parents to act in specific ways with them."

The implications for caretaking appear to be two-fold: first, you should pay attention to how your infant attends to objects. Does he or she prefer new objects and stimuli over familiar ones? Provide rich variety. Second, by providing this kind of stimulation, you may be helping your infant internalize a preference for novelty and complexity, thereby enhancing the development of his or her information-processing abilities.

The researchers call for further study on this point, however, so as to be able to specify precisely the kinds of early caretaking that would contribute to this newly discovered continuity in mental development.

A Test for Baby's Intelligence

A book entitled *Test Your Baby's I.Q.* offers an easy and interesting way to find out how advanced your child is for his or her age. Simple self-scoring "quizzes" — checklists, actually — help you measure your baby's developmental rate (advanced, on schedule, or lagging) from birth to age four, in order to discover early strengths and weaknesses and set your child on the right track to success. The title is misleading in that no IQ score is assigned — which is good, as IQ is too volatile at this age.

The author, Marcia Rosen, in consultation with pediatrician Henry Harris, designed the checklists based on early-learning research in language skills, social skills, and motor skills. A brief chapter at the back is devoted to "How to Improve your Child's Performance."

Another way to assess how developmentally advanced your child is (relative to other children his or her age) is to consult almost any developmental scale that charts the stages of gross-motor, fine-motor, and cognitive abilities. These are available in most books on caring for an infant (see Select Bibliography). Check the months that infants and preschoolers "normally" display a certain behavior, and determine where your child stands in relation. If your child is performing a given task at least 25 percent earlier than usual, he or she is developmentally advanced in that area. For example, the normal age for speaking in short sentences is twenty-four months. A child who is advanced in this behavior will do so at eighteen months or earlier.

Big Potential Comes in Small Packages

Merle B. Karnes, professor of special education at the University of Illinois and a nationally recognized expert in early childhood education for the gifted, has described a cluster of traits that will help you spot high potential in your child. These traits were drawn from the general population of gifted children — not all of them will be found in any one individual.

- *General Advanced Development:* Even in infancy, gifted children tend to attain milestones at a younger age than others. For example, they smile, crawl, and walk sooner than other children.
- *Early Language Skills:* Gifted babies and toddlers demonstrate an advanced understanding of language. They respond to directions and listen to conversations at a noticeably younger age. Likewise, they often begin to talk earlier than other children. By eighteen months, some gifted toddlers talk in full sentences.
- *Unusual Attention Span:* While other one-year-olds flip quickly through picture books as an adult labels pictured items, gifted children often listen attentively to a story or study the pictures carefully.
- *Keen Observation Skills:* Gifted toddlers will often surprise parents by noticing details, such as tiny specks in a flower.

- *Unusual Curiosity:* Gifted youngsters stop to examine things for longer periods of time and more often. Once gifted children are able to talk, their curiosity becomes very apparent.
- *Exceptional Memory:* Gifted toddlers need to review information far less often than other young children in order to master it. With little practice gifted children are able to remember the names of shapes, colors, and people easily.
- *Interest in Reading:* While some gifted children teach themselves to read as early as two years old, most simply show a keen interest in books and printed words.
- *Impatience with Their Own Limits:* Gifted toddlers can become very frustrated when they attempt tasks that are within their mental abilities but beyond their physical capacities. Typically, a gifted child will cross out his or her own drawing of a tree and ask an adult to draw one as he or she describes it.
- *Understanding of Complex Concepts:* Gifted toddlers usually show advanced understanding of number concepts, such as the values of numerals, or the ability to add and subtract in their heads. They can perceive advanced cause-and-effect relationships — "If I put my glass of milk in the freezer, it might crack."
- *Normal or Advanced Performance Despite Handicaps:* Toddlers who perform at or above age level in spite of physical handicaps, speech problems, or visual or hearing impairments have overcome many learning barriers in order to perform at that level.

A Dozen Ways They'll Tell You, "I'm Gifted"

The following checklist of behaviors was developed by Rita Haynes Blocksom, an educational consultant from St. Marys, Ohio. Keep in mind, once again, that most preschoolers — even the gifted ones — will probably *not* display all of these characteristics. But if your child displays several, he or she has exceptional abilities that should be encouraged and developed further.

1. Can your child interpret stories in his or her own words?
2. Can he or she predict appropriate outcomes for unfamiliar stories or new and original outcomes for familiar ones?

3. Does your child create rhymes that communicate his or her own thoughts or feelings?
4. Does your child exhibit curiosity by frequently asking "Why?" or by other types of behavior?
5. Does your child perform independently when given a task, often without awaiting directions?
6. Does your child readily adapt to new situations or procedures? Is he or she flexible and undisturbed by changes in routine?
7. Does your child initiate new activities, new tasks, or new ways of doing things?
8. Does your child seek to dominate or control an activity, even to the extent of appearing critical of the efforts of others or being impatient with them?
9. Does your child explore new ideas or invent new ways of saying things?
10. Does your child offer suggestions for solving problems that come up in the home or preschool, or provide alternatives to parent- or teacher-made solutions?
11. Is your child a keen observer, who often sees more than others? Does he or she add details or provide further pertinent information when presented with an opportunity to do so?
12. Does your child look for and find similarities and differences in people, events, places, and things?

For the Record

For your own reference, as well as to provide "documentation" for preschool teachers and, later, your child's elementary school, keep a diary or journal of your child's behaviors, comments, and reactions to different situations. Save "works of art" in a scrapbook.

In addition to checklists and developmental scales, other observational methods are useful in identifying gifted toddlers and preschoolers. Take note of the items listed below and record them in a "baby book."

• Noteworthy facts about your child's growth and development, including all major milestones

- Anecdotal information that captures something unusual your child did or said for his or her age
- Humorous events that reflect exceptional abilities almost to the point of disbelief, implying unusual behavior for a very young child

Parents know their children best and can provide critical information in assessing their development. The records you are keeping today will assist school officials in identifying your youngster as gifted when he or she reaches school age.

Looker, Listener, or Mover?

Although not directly related per se to identifying gifted children, understanding your child's predominant learning style can help you enhance those areas of cognitive ability that are already strong and can bolster those areas that may involve secondary ways of perceiving and learning.

Moreover, differences in learning style between parent and child (or between teacher and child) can cause the gifted child's abilities to go unidentified. Parents who process information differently from their children may tend to project their own learning biases onto their kids. For example, if you're a visual learner who absorbs information best by seeing something or reading about it (a "looker"), but your child is an auditory learner who prefers sound to sight (a "listener"), you may tend to perceive only your child's "weakness" (a lack of interest in books, say) relative to your own tendencies, rather than his or her strengths (such as an avid interest in music).

Until recently, learning-style assessment has been pretty much restricted to older children — those of elementary-school age and up. But a new handbook by Lauren Carlile Bradway, *Quick Check of Children's Learning Styles,* affords parents and teachers an easy way to determine learning styles in children from birth through age eight. The handbook explains what learning style is, includes an activities section for each kind of learner, and comes with a supply of checklists for easy scoring of observations.

For more information write Beeby-Champ Publishing, Inc., P.O. Box 1714, Stillwater, OK 74076.

The Role of "Significant Others" — It's a Family Affair

IF THERE is one myth surrounding the development of gifted toddlers that has been particularly difficult to dispel, it's the notion that they can "make it on their own." This is truly a myth — it just isn't so. Far too often, insufficient parenting or teaching techniques contribute to unhappiness, behavioral problems, underachievement, and sometimes even suicide among these children once they grow older. The cream doesn't always rise to the top; it sometimes sours and curdles.

Most children are born into traditional families, a network of significant others — primary and secondary caregivers with whom they establish relationships and bondings. (Chapter 8 provides a detailed discussion of gender-based parent-child bonding.) Important for all children, this infrastructure is especially critical for the gifted ones. The foundation laid during the early childhood years — more precisely, the kinds of nurturing roles assumed by the child's significant others — will influence to a large extent the scope and limits of his or her giftedness.

This chapter discusses the family's collective role in helping a bright child to develop well. The first section, "Your Child's First Mentor Is *You*," is an essay by June Scobee, assistant professor in gifted education at the University of Houston–Clear Lake, and chairman of the Challenger Center for Space Science Education, a tribute to the ideals of the seven crew members who perished on the space shuttle *Challenger*. (Scobee's husband, Dick, was commander of the *Challenger*, which exploded in January 1986.)

Subsequent sections separately cover maternal and paternal

roles. The former discussion includes a comparison of mothering in the United States and Japan that illuminates how the mother-child bond in Japan relates to that country's push for high student academic achievement. Also discussed in this chapter are the role of grandparents, single-parenting of gifted children, and sibling relationships and rivalry.

YOUR CHILD'S FIRST MENTOR IS *YOU*
An Essay by June Scobee

I believe the children are our future,
Teach them well and let them lead the way,
Show them all the beauty they possess inside;
Give them a sense of pride —
To make it easier, let the children's laughter
Remind us how we used to be . . .
                            — Linda Creed

Parents can claim no greater challenge or reward than serving as their child's first mentor. In this role you have the power to help your child begin the insightful journey toward self-identity and self-fulfillment.

The concept of having a mentor is not new. The word "mentor" originated from Homer's epic *The Odyssey*. When Ulysses left for his long adventure, he chose his older friend and adviser, Mentor, to serve as a guide and counselor for his son. Thus, someone older and wiser serving in a supportive or instructional role has come to be called a mentor. Such relationships have existed throughout history. Among the more prominent examples are the ancient Greek philosophers Socrates and Plato, the pioneering nineteenth-century psychologists Freud and Jung, and even the futuristic likes of Yoda and Luke Skywalker!

Studies on mentor relationships indicate the importance of a "significant other" in a child's life. In fact, E. Paul Torrance, the acclaimed father of creative education for gifted children, has learned — from his twenty-two-year longitudinal study of 212 young adults — that having had a mentor is a better predictor of adult creative success than either IQ or creativity scores.

Formal mentorship programs usually are established to offer high-school students an opportunity to pair up with community members who are willing to share their expertise in a particular field that matches or complements the students' interests. Generally, these mentors serve as faithful counselors or prudent advisers, while students take on the role of apprentice.

But mentorships can exist at any period of life. Children need not wait for the high-school program to benefit from such a relationship. They have *you* — their very first mentor. Serving in this role involves essentially three tasks: you need to nurture your child's aspirations, cultivate a creative environment, and provide opportunities for your child to explore the future. By doing so, you will help lay a foundation for personal development upon which your child's talents and abilities can grow and flourish.

Nurture Aspirations

First and foremost, you must respect your child's aspirations and talk together about his or her dreams of future accomplishments. Don't try to sculpt the child into your image. With the right kind of encouragement, children will learn to imagine themselves making contributions in a future role of their own choosing. As a result, their self-confidence increases and goals are more easily attained. Without your encouragement and reassurance, your child's self-identity and self-expression could be stifled, and dreams left unfulfilled.

In an article in *The Creative Child and Adult Quarterly*, Torrance wrote that considerable evidence exists to show that our image of the future is a powerful motivating force determining what we are motivated to learn and achieve. Consequently, respect for your child's need to aspire, along with the time to dream together or at least talk about aspirations, can help build a positive image of the future that, in turn, can help make a child's dreams come true.

Cultivate a Creative Environment

Creativity, though it can be taught, is not a simple skill like tying your shoes, but rather a complex mix of factors — involving both feeling and thinking — that blend together in a special way to influence the whole life of a person. Fostering creative problem solving, creative insight, and creative expression can make all the difference to your child's healthy, happy, and productive development.

You can increase the likelihood and incidence of creativity in your child by providing a special nurturing environment in your home. In a classic study on the subject by J. W. Getzels and P. W. Jackson, several factors were identified that discriminate between the creative and noncreative family environments. In the creative family environment, the tendency is to stress *internal* characteristics such as "a sense of values, interest in something, and openness." Noncreative environments stress "external characteristics such as good family, good manners, and being studious." Here are some specific suggestions for cultivating a creative home environment:

- *Provide a supportive atmosphere*. Respect your child's ideas and opinions, even the seemingly outlandish ones; encourage questioning and open-ended discussions.
- *Allow opportunities for "brainstorming" and creative problem solving*. That is, ask kids to come up with as many ideas as they can for possible solutions to a given problem. After many ideas are explored, they should evaluate them and select the best to implement. Encourage your child to use creative thinking when solving real problems (for instance, how to avoid an unpleasant task or improve peer relationships).
- *Refrain from judging the worth of all activities and products*. Provide a nonjudgmental attitude, allowing your child opportunities to make decisions based on reasoning and choice of consequences.
- *Recognize and value your child's nonacademic interests and strengths, not just intellectual ability*. You'll create a safe and comfortable psychological space for self-discovery.
- *Encourage your child to discover and pursue with intensity and dedication something he or she loves doing*. Explain that he or she need not waste energy trying to be good at everything.

Guide Their Vision

As your children's first mentor, your most meaningful legacy will be the results of helping them "see" possibilities — for themselves, our world, and their future. The knowledge and wisdom that you hand down — the really important information, that is — will have less to do with substantive facts and more to do with the stuff that dreams are made of. In some ways you'll be helping your children keep laughter and fantasy alive — a soothing poultice for the world's harshness, and essential ingredients in making a personal statement.

It's not surprising that with history's most famous mentorships, student ultimately surpasses teacher. And this is as it should be. Such examples highlight for all of us just what kind of impact we can have on our children: "Teach them well and let them lead the way . . ."

CHECK YOUR PARENTING STYLE

Parents of gifted children, unlike their kids, may not be especially distinctive when compared to other parents of similar backgrounds and economic status. In fact, researchers at the University of Illinois Institute for Child Behavior and Development found many more commonalities than differences between parents of the gifted and parents of children with normal or above-normal intelligence.

However, there were some significant differences in their *styles of parenting* — differences that experts can begin to look at as a basis for developing ways to train all parents to work with their young gifted children. The researchers, Merle B. Karnes, Allan Schwedel, and Deborah Steinberg — writing in an issue of *Roeper Review* — note that there is strong evidence indicating that parents can learn to change their behavior toward their children, and that "these changes are positively related to their young child's development."

The researchers compared two groups of middle- to upper-middle-class parents — the parents of ten gifted preschoolers and the parents of ten normal or above-normal preschoolers, as measured by IQ. Both groups of parents had similar incomes and a similar distribution of occupations among the fathers. Fifty percent of the mothers of the gifted children worked full-time, compared to only 10 percent of the other mothers. Each parent was interviewed individually. The study sought to determine whether there were meaningful differences in "attitudes, values, and behaviors" between the two groups of parents vis-à-vis their parenting styles.

Results of the Study

• As to school-related activities, the parents of the gifted tended to spend more time reading to their children than parents of the nongifted, and mothers of the gifted were more likely to encourage language development (through rhymes, nonsense songs, and other "creative verbal activity"), love, and freedom in their child. Only fathers of the nongifted children indicated that they had little influence on their child's learning, interests, and development.

• All the parents reported that they took their child to child-oriented activities; parents of the gifted, however, were much more likely to use resources not designed for a specific age group — such as art museums, nature walks, and natural-history museums. All parents reported only light TV viewing at home (the median was 1.5 hours a day). However, parents of the gifted were more likely to prohibit watching violent programs; parents of the nongifted were more likely to turn off sex-oriented programs.

• In the affective areas, mothers in both groups tended to talk to their children about feelings and emotions. Both parents of the gifted additionally used praise and "doing something special" for the child as a way of enhancing the child's self-concept.

• Parents had high aspirations for their children, with those of the gifted leaning toward professional or scientific careers and those of the nongifted more likely to cite altruistic or creative careers.

• Parents of the gifted were much more interested in being involved in their child's schooling. For example, 90 percent of mothers of the gifted wanted to be involved in teacher selection, compared to only 40 percent of the mothers of the nongifted.

• Intellectual capabilities were viewed as an area of strength by all of the parents of the gifted, but by only 35 percent of those of the nongifted; parents of the nongifted were more pleased with the social abilities and psychomotor abilities of their children than were the parents of the gifted.

• Nearly half of the parents of the gifted wished their children were more independent of them. Few parents cited discipline as a worrisome problem; however, a significantly larger percentage of the parents of nongifted children said they spanked their children as a disciplinary technique compared to parents of the gifted.

MOTHERS

A question of increasing concern is whether it is essential for mothers to stay home with their young children. Mothers who do decide to stay home, believing that it's better for their toddlers' development, now have some research to back up their instinct. Frances F. Schachter, clinical psychologist at Queens College and Coney Island City Hospital, maintains that the mother's presence at home encourages the development of the child's intellect, particularly if the family is a middle-class one.

Children with superior intellects have always been well represented in middle-class families, but often this abundance has been attributed to more resources within the home, to greater communication among the children and adults, or to wider experiences as family members, such as travel. Schachter, however, says that it may be the result of more attention given by mothers to very young children, from birth to age three.

In her study, as reported in *Today's Child,* seventy preschoolers matched for age, sex, and background all attended the same "toddler center" in New York City part-time each week. The thirty-two middle-class working mothers in the study were "particularly intelligent and well educated, and their offspring could have been expected to score higher on intelligence tests than the children whose middle-class, *non*-working mothers had less education." However, the children whose mothers had full-time jobs scored significantly lower on IQ tests than those whose middle-class, less-educated mothers stayed home during the first three years.

Furthermore, Schachter says, it is only in the middle class that this phenomenon occurs. Other research shows the opposite effect with children from lower-class backgrounds whose mothers work. These children tend to do better on IQ tests than children from lower-class families where the mothers stay home.

Although the children of working mothers tended to be more self-sufficient, in other ways the study showed little difference between the children of working and nonworking middle-class mothers. They had similar language development and no obvious differences in emotional development.

Schachter claims that the important ingredient of middle-class mothering may be the specialty of the "tuning in" to young children, which substitute caregivers may not supply. Mothers with a choice, she advises, should consider not working during a child's very early years or working only part-time during that period: "Independence is fine, but too much too soon can produce a phony poise . . . that can cover up real gaps in development."

Small Incidents Shape Baby's Psyche

Commonplace events play a major role in a toddler's development. That's the conclusion of Daniel Stern, a psychiatrist at Cornell Medical School, according to a report in the *New York Times*. Stern says that it is the small, everyday interactions with parents that have more influence on shaping a child's personality than large-scale, dramatic happenings. His ideas run counter to some of the most time-honored Freudian theories in behavioral science, such as the assumption that adult problems derive from some catastrophic "big moment" in childhood.

Stern videotaped mothers and their infants over a two-year period and found a pattern he described as "a long continuum of important moments." For example, the natural development of an infant's nervous system gives the child a series of feelings about autonomy — from deciding to avert his or her eyes at the age of four months, to walking away at about twelve months, to saying no at about eighteen months. How parents respond to this continuum can have a great impact. For instance, a parent who *insists* on making eye contact with a four-month-old infant, says Stern, could foster fear and dependency in a child.

REACT, BUT DON'T IMITATE   Stern found that the ways mothers let infants know they are attuned to their feelings are especially important. If a baby squeals with delight, for example, a mother might give the baby a gentle shake — a touch that conveys a feeling of excitement in another way. Merely *imitating* what the baby does tells a baby that its mother knows what her child did, but not how he or she felt. One mother observed by Stern continually undermatched her baby's level of excitement, and the baby gradually became passive. Working mothers, in particular, need to make time for their babies — cuddling with them, talking, reading, pointing out and naming objects. Such interactions should be enthusiastic, but not forced.

Stern believes, however, that patterns set early in life are not irrevocable. People throughout their lives constantly reshape their relationships, he says, and other researchers have concurred. No data yet confirms that a "nonattuned" mother impairs her child permanently.

Mothering East/West: What's the Difference?

Researchers for years have been trying to discover the secret of superior performance by Japanese children in the math and science areas. Can a longer school day and more homework alone explain why they consistently outscore their U.S. counterparts?

No, say Stanford University's Robert Hess and the University of Tokyo's Hiroshi Azuma. The two researchers collaborated on a twelve-year study of families and school-age children in both countries. They found deeply ingrained cultural differences, of course, but also some highly illuminating contrasts in parenting — particularly mothering.

"The emotional ties between mother and child in Japan are so close," Hess says, "that they don't think of the child as an 'other.' They don't think of winning or losing a battle with the child, or whether or not the child is pushed around. When you think of this child as part of yourself, how can there be conflict?" Such bonding is so strong, according to an article in *Smithsonian*, that many Japanese wives apparently sleep in a room with their children rather than their husbands.

A Japanese child is taught early that he or she must do well in school or suffer ridicule — ridicule that extends to the child's mother. So devoted are mothers to the educational success of their children that a new cultural institution has sprung up: the *kyoiku mama* (education mother). This role represents a completely self-sacrificing existence for Japanese mothers, one that involves full responsibility for their child's schooling.

Baby-sitters and play groups are out; hours and hours of *juku* (cram schools to help prepare for one entrance examination after another) and "mother's class" to help with drills at home are in. Careers for Japanese women are out, but many take part-time jobs to pay for *juku*. There is increasing interest in how Americans are accelerating their children in academic preschools, though apparently Japanese mothers are unaware of the effects of "hothousing" (early academic saturation) on young children (chapter 6 discusses these effects).

What are the other significant differences between mothering in Japan and in the United States?

HOW MOTHERS CONTROL THEIR CHILDREN   Hess and Azuma wanted to determine which of four possible approaches each mother would take when presented with certain hypothetical situations that required parental intervention. If the child drew on a wall with crayons or created a disturbance in a supermarket, would the mother appeal to her own authority, to external rules, to the child's feelings, or to the consequences of the child's act?

Hess found that more than half of the mothers in the United States would have used an authoritative approach — through coaxing, demanding, threatening, or offering rewards — to change the child's behavior. Japanese mothers, on the other hand, would have appealed to the child's feelings or the consequences of his or her actions — how others would view the child or how what was done would affect the feelings of the family.

In the crayoned-wall incident, one U.S. mother said she would respond with: "You know better than that. You've been taught that you don't use crayons any place but on paper. If you can't use crayons properly, we will put them away. When you think you can use them in their right place, let me know and I'll take them out. But right now they are going back on the shelf and then we're going to clean the wall." One Japanese mother replied that she would have told her child, "The wall is crying."

ON SELF-CONTROL AND BEING A "GOOD" CHILD   The researchers generally found that Japanese mothers expected compliance, politeness, and emotional maturity at an earlier age. U.S. mothers, on the other hand, expected verbal assertiveness and social skills with peers at an earlier age. Indeed, U.S. parents even measure children's maturity by how well they adapt to their peers, according to Hess's research. In Japan, the emphasis was on orienting the child toward proper behavior with *adults*. The close bonding between Japanese mothers and their children is one of the subtle ways children learn to internalize adult norms and expectations — lessons that pay off eventually in the classroom.

The Japanese attitudes are reflected in how these mothers define a "good" child. "In Japan, a child is thought to be good if he is obedient, mild, gentle, and self-controlled," Hess says. "In the United States, the good child is assertive, socially competent with peers, and courteous."

TEACHING STYLES   When children failed to understand an instruction in a sorting task, U.S. mothers often "recycled" the instruction, sometimes verbatim, pressing a child for a verbal response to see if he or she had mastered the concept of the exercise. Japanese mothers often elaborated on the instruction and did not expect a verbal response from the child.

The Japanese consistently emphasized *procedural* aspects of the task, while their U.S. counterparts emphasized *conceptual* grasp of the sorting principles. According to Hess, "these differences also suggest that Japanese mothers expect the child to infer the correct principle or concept of the task by repeating the correct behavior."

These traditions have an impact on classroom learning, the researchers say. Japanese children, for example, took more time with problem-solving tasks — and were more accurate. Azuma described the Japanese approach as "slow and sticky" while the American one is "quick and snappy." When a child failed, Japanese mothers were confident the problem could be solved with persistence and hard work. American mothers tended to blame the school, which is usually nonproductive. U.S. mothers might consider emulating their Eastern counterparts when it comes to overcoming difficulties their child is having learning something.

FATHERS

How do fathers contribute to their children's intellectual growth? Can fathers actually make a difference in the cognitive development of a gifted child? Can they be the catalyst that sparks their sons' or daughters' giftedness? Recent studies suggest that the answer to both questions is yes.

While it is obvious that both mothers and fathers influence their children's intellectual growth, it is becoming clearer that they do so in different ways and that they influence boys' and girls' intelligence differently as well.

In his book *Fathers*, Ross D. Parke reports that as early as infancy male babies are affected by the presence or absence of their fathers. Those whose fathers do not live with them tend to score lower on cognitive-development tests than male babies who have frequent contact with their fathers. The main predictors of male children's cognitive development appear to be the father's prowess as a playmate and his expectation of independence for the child.

With female infants, on the other hand, neither the father's absence nor the extent of his involvement, if present, seems to affect the child's early cognitive progress. A father's influence on his daughter's intellectual growth apparently comes a bit later in her development.

By late infancy and early toddlerhood, the pattern of parental influence on their children's intelligence becomes well defined, Parke says. "Both mothers and fathers influence girls through verbal interaction and warmth and boys through physical interaction." However, which specific cognitive skills are affected by each parent is still unknown.

Parke reports that with school-age children, fathers' presence and availability affect both boys' and girls' academic performance. Citing findings from "father absence" studies, Parke writes that "the sons of highly available" fathers attain superior academic performance and reach their full intellectual potential compared to boys from fatherless families.

Girls' cognitive development also seems to be adversely affected by the absence of fathers. Girls from intact nuclear families tend to have higher IQs, better achievement-test scores, and higher grade-point averages than those from fatherless families.

Much speculation surrounds the how and why of paternal influence on children's cognitive development. Some researchers point to the father as a model of perseverance, achievement, and motivation — a perhaps outdated but still prevalent perception. Children pick up their fathers' behavior patterns and values and assimilate them as their own. Others explain that the lower levels of cognitive ability of children from single-parent households are due to lesser amounts of attention and interaction than are found in two-parent families.

And what about nontraditional two-parent families? Parke cites a study, conducted by Norma Radin, that focused on American families of preschool children whose fathers were the *primary* caregivers. A significant conclusion drawn from this research showed that boys and girls raised primarily by their fathers scored higher in verbal ability than children raised in traditional family settings. Where fathers were the primary caregivers, both boys and girls showed a higher belief in their own ability to control and determine their fate than did children who were raised in traditional families. Girls, in particular, seemed to fare well from the influence of the child-rearing fathers. This appeared to be related to the fathers' awareness of "sexist influences" in society and their concern for their daughters' future success.

Adding to the complexity of parental influence on children's cognitive development is the issue of socioeconomic status. A study reported in *Child Development* suggests that a father's salary may have more influence on his children's IQ scores and educational achievement than his physical presence. A research team from Indiana, Purdue, and Cornell universities found that kids who were fatherless as a result of divorce performed nearly as well intellectually and academically as those with fathers, as long as the household was socially and economically stable.

Despite somewhat conflicting research findings — the jury is still out — it is apparent that in many cases the father, by virtue of his presence and availability, is a significant environmental influence on his son's and daughter's intelligence. And this can mean the difference between "average" and "gifted." It's not that fathers are more important than mothers (or vice versa, for that matter), but it is now acknowledged that having a father in the traditional role of breadwinner exclusively is not sufficient for a child's optimal cognitive development. A father should play and interact verbally with his son or daughter, nurture the child toward independence, and help him or her plan ahead for the future.

GRANDPARENTS

Grandparents have played significant roles in the lives of eminent personalities, and usually in positive ways. Adlai E. Stevenson, twice Democratic nominee for president of the United States in the 1950s, had a grandfather who used to "coax the children into the library with milk and cookies, then read to them there while they enjoyed their refreshments," according to Victor and Mildred Goertzel's book *Cradles of Eminence*. The grandfather read to them from *Hamlet,* and stimulated Stevenson's interest in history so much that the boy had read "all thirteen volumes of Markham's *The Real American Romance* before he was thirteen."

Margaret Mead devotes a whole chapter of her autobiography, *Blackberry Winter,* to the topic "On Being a Granddaughter." Meade says: "My paternal grandmother . . . was the most decisive influence on my life."

As psychologist Erik Erikson stated in a *Psychology Today* interview: "Old people can be generative. . . . They can be good grandparents, and not only to their own grandchildren. I'm convinced that old people and children need one another and that there's an affinity between old age and childhood that, in fact, rounds out the life cycle."

According to Virginia Ehrlich, of New York State's Advocates for Gifted and Talented Education, there are several specific positive roles that grandparents can serve in gifted children's lives: as listeners, as storytellers and sources of information, as mentors, as identifiers of giftedness, as reinforcers of social values and standards, as guides to social living, and as sources of love, comfort, and security.

Grandparents as Listeners

Gifted children love to talk, to share their ideas and discoveries, and they frequently prefer older children or adults as an audience. For the very young, the talking (frequently more of a monologue) can just be the endless chatter of the child expressing wonder at natural phenomena. For the older child, it may be a description of a current school project or a special hobby or achievement.

Grandparents make ideal listeners. They can provide an appreciative, attentive audience who are genuinely enchanted with the achievements or observations of their young progeny. By their affectionate attentions, grandparents will tend to encourage hobbies and special interests. Freed of the many responsibilities of parents, grandparents often indulge the child and cater to the interest or hobby, not only by purchasing suitable items, but also by sharing treasured collections or seeking out special information to share with the child.

Grandparents as Storytellers

Grandparents are celebrated storytellers and, most often, their stories are true, rendered a bit romantic and exciting because they happened in that mysterious "long-ago-and-faraway" place. For example, N. Scott Momaday, Pulitzer Prize winner for his novel *House Made of Dawn,* recalls in his book *The Way to Rainy Mountain* the tales his grandmother of the Kiowa Indian tribe told him: "Although my grandmother lived out her long life in the shadow of Rainy Mountain, the immense landscape of the continental interior lay like memory in her blood. She could tell of the Crows, whom she had never seen, and of the Black Hills, where she had never been."

It is evident that a major role of grandparents for gifted children, as for all children, lies in their capacity for providing interesting and unusual information. Since gifted children have an insatiable thirst for knowledge, this is a particularly significant role, which is usually enjoyable to both adult and child. It is often the grandparents, more than any other persons, including the parents, who can provide lessons in genealogy, history, geography, customs, standards, time, and distance. They provide the link between the past and the present, and are perhaps the best interpreters of the significance of time in our lives.

Many children have learned about foreign lands, customs, language, and historical developments through their grandparents. The grandparents like to reminisce, and they appreciate their receptive audience. The children listen, thinking they are hearing a marvelous story, meanwhile learning many lessons of life. For gifted children, who have retentive memories and a strong capacity to see relationships, these stories form a foundation for future reference.

Grandparents as Mentors

Parents of gifted children should take advantage of the specialized knowledge and skills the grandparents may have. For example, a boy of seven in a class for the exceptionally gifted became intrigued by trigonometric problems. A patient grandfather undertook to teach him, and the boy showed impressive knowledge of the subject for his age. Immigrant grandparents in this country frequently converse with each other in a foreign language and use it with the child as well. A gifted child has no difficulty with the transition from one language to another. Such bilingualism should be encouraged, especially when the child is gifted.

Grandparents happily share the special knowledge they have with these very receptive young pupils and will pursue special interests with them. Realistically, parents frequently are so pressed with other responsibilities that they, too, welcome the time that grandparents make available to the child.

Grandparents as Identifiers of Giftedness

Although no study is available on this subject, the biographical literature and experience with gifted children indicate that grandparents can be significant sources of information. It is likely, because of the constructive roles they play, that they have access to insights about the child that may escape even parental observation. Achievement-oriented parents, for instance, set high expectations for very young children and often take for granted behavior that is far above normal for most children. Grandparents may have a broader base for reference and thus judge the child's abilities more objectively.

Grandparents as Reinforcers of Values and Standards

Inasmuch as the grandparents have relinquished their supervisory roles over their own sons and daughters, there are distinctions in roles between parents and grandparents. In all situations, these distinctions in roles must be respected.

Grandparents have the obligation to reinforce constructive values established by parents and to maintain a careful regard for the ultimate authority of the parents. Gifted children are quick to sense discrepancies in attitude. These can confuse the child and undermine the parent-child relationship. Casting a child in a mold, by saying "You are just like your father" or "You are just like your mother" when he or she misbehaves, deprives the child of individuality, creates a sense of inevitability that can be harmful, and diminishes the status of the parents. Because gifted children have such retentive memories, they can suffer from such unfavorable comparisons even more than the average child would.

Differences between parents and grandparents should be discussed privately. Certainly, grandparents need to keep in mind changing patterns of behavior as generations change and to focus only on significant differences in values. Parents, on the other hand, can find guidance in grandparents' tendencies to be less restrictive and more tolerant of infractions. The grandparent knows from experience that "looking the other way" or moving to prevent misbehavior can frequently be more productive than observing and punishing every minor fall from grace. The grandparents are not as likely as the parents to set a higher standard of behavior for a gifted child than for other children.

Grandparents as Guides to Social Living

Grandparents provide lessons in social living in ways that the child can appreciate and understand. They may have slightly different customs from the parents — the clothes they wear, their values, what they eat — or particular needs that must be respected. The child accepts these differences in their proper context and thus is introduced to the world of cultural diversity.

The child with loving and involved grandparents comes to understand something of human frailty, of beginnings and endings, of life and death. A warm bond between a child and grandparent may be the cause for grief at separation, but it also creates a basis of understanding and acceptance of the patterns of life. Gifted children, with their insightful view of the world, have much to gain from such experience. Parents should encourage them to develop such understanding and compassion, so that they can transfer these traits to their later roles of responsibility and leadership.

Grandparents as Sources of Love, Comfort, and Security

No child can have too many sources of love and care. The wider the circle, the happier the child. Grandparents should, quite naturally, be an integral part of this network. Because gifted kids seem to understand events more readily, because they seem to be able to take care of themselves with greater ease, they are frequently denied the satisfaction of these emotional needs. Parents frequently respond to these children on the basis of their intellectual capacities rather than in terms of their emotional and developmental needs. On the other hand, grandparents may marvel with frank admiration at a major achievement, but seem to retain a capacity to superimpose a demonstration of affection that may be shunned yet secretly wanted and relished by the child.

The presence, or even the memory, of an understanding, loving grandparent can serve as an emotional bulwark against the slings and arrows of an unfriendly world. Wise parents include grandparents in their arsenal of security and protection for their children.

SINGLE PARENTS

How are single parents meeting the needs of their gifted children? Do gifted children have more or less difficulty adjusting to divorce? It is hard to find answers to these questions, but they are becoming increasingly important as nearly one out of every five school-age children lives with a single parent.

Studies have traditionally shown that intellectually gifted children are more likely to come from two-parent homes and that there is a high correlation between performance and family income. Lewis Terman, creator of the Stanford-Binet Intelligence Scale, found that boys whose performance began to drop off in high school were more than twice as likely to come from divorced homes. And Parke reports in *Fathers* how studies show that cognitive development of both girls and boys is adversely affected by the absence of fathers.

But highly creative children often have to overcome some kind of problem in childhood, either with parents, siblings, or themselves, according to Max Fogel, formerly director of Mensa's Education and Research Foundation. "As long as children aren't psychologically crushed by problems in the home," says Fogel, "divorce may actually enhance their creativity by heightening the need to find their own way and by giving them more responsibility than is usually allowed in American homes." Though very little guidance or counseling is being offered to single parents of gifted children, single parents who are successfully coping with their gifted children's needs seem to share some common characteristics: a positive attitude and a "we'll-make-this-work" collaboration with their children.

"Gifted children are more perceptive and intuitive," says one mother, "so a parent should be honest about his or her feelings and the financial situation without burdening them with the problems. I told my children that we really didn't have a lot of money to work with, but that didn't mean we were going to be held down; we'd find ways to do things."

"I let my children see I'm not perfect," says a mother of two young children. This type of honesty is especially important for gifted children in single-parent homes, says Susanne Richert of the Educational Information and Resource Center in Sewell, New Jersey. "They seem to have an obsession with perfection and tend to be highly ethical. They will challenge parents on a moral level, which can be especially difficult without the support of another adult." Single parents also tend to look to their gifted children to satisfy their own sense of self-esteem, which places an extra burden on the children, she says. But "by showing our gifted children we're not perfect, we allow them to let up a bit on themselves."

Many divorced mothers studied found that building their own self-esteem and becoming assertive were more painful than the economic hardships they experienced, particularly in the early years of their divorce, but that the process was quite valuable for themselves and their gifted children. Not only did these parents come to rely less on their children for their own sense of worth, but their children came to see in their mothers a special strength and capacity for rising above adversity. Support groups ranged from Al-Anon and Parents Without Partners to some mothers who formed a "parachute group" inspired by Richard Bolles's best-selling book *What Color Is Your Parachute?* "We worked our way through the book, looking at our gifts and skills," says Mary L. "Then we created a summer camp for our children, producing and filming a puppet show."

Studies of single fathers raising children show they experience guilt and a sense of loss and often seek psychotherapy or counseling during the first two years after divorce. Although single-parenting placed limitations on their earnings, working hours, and work relations because of time constraints, none reported a significant loss of income in assuming his new role.

Most comfortable with the effect of divorce on their gifted children are parents who have arranged joint custody (sharing important decisions about their child's upbringing) or shared custody (sharing physical care). They feel it diminishes their children's greatest fears — that they will be abandoned and that they may be responsible for the breakup — and gives them the support of two parents on a regular basis. "Our children know we are both interested in their development," says one father.

Joint custody also provides two listeners to children's problems and two points of view, which are particularly important for the gifted child who tends to ask the hard-to-answer questions at an earlier age. One father, a filmmaker, sees his daughter benefiting from multiple points of view in what he calls "an opening up" of the family. "She is meeting many more people than before, because there are more people in my life now and she attends my film openings — and also spends Saturdays with her mother."

Meeting the young child's needs for intellectual and creative stimulation seems to be the easiest task for the single parent. A single mother says: "We go to the library and read together often. I phone county agencies to find good, inexpensive activities and I look for day care that provides a learning experience." (For more on day care, see chapter 6.)

But meeting the needs of the preschooler who has a short attention span or who may be "hyperactive," as many gifted children are, is extremely difficult when there is no one with whom to "time-share." One mother says: "My three-year-old son was terribly curious and got into a lot of trouble. I tried to allow for his creativity, but I never knew how much space to give him and how much firmness. Finally, I found a psychiatrist who showed me how to be firmer in placing limits. My son and I both liked each other better when I had more control."

Richert counsels single parents to find other parents who have similarly demanding children and "trade time with them." This gives the parent a rest and the child a peer to engage his or her interest. Friends, neighbors, and relatives may also share some of the burden at this time and act as role models. One mother with two children became a Quaker after her divorce and finds that her Friends Meeting provides her with an extended family. "I can borrow a grandparent whenever I need one, and my children have developed a lot of adult friendships."

A number of mothers found family therapy helped their gifted children adjust to the new family structure. Gifted boys were angrier at their fathers for "leaving" them than their gifted sisters were, and they sometimes became underachievers, "dropping out" intellectually or developing behavioral problems.

One mother turned to the Big Brother organization for a surrogate father for her son. "His 'Big Brother' took him camping and fishing," she said, "but didn't just work with my son in isolation. We were all invited to picnics with his family, and our families are still close friends."

Although single-parenting of the gifted child places extra burdens on the parent, several mothers said their children would never have developed their giftedness if the predivorce tension in the household had not been removed. And they attribute their children's maturity and sense of responsibility to the need for them to contribute actively to the family's emotional survival.

Some single parents, feeling that their children need as much attention as possible, spend all their free time with them. Other single mothers and fathers say they need to date and have some time with other adults in order to restore their emotional energy.

In a study of sixty California families five years after divorce, a psychiatrist, Judith Wallerstein, and a psychologist, Joan Kelly, found the children who had made the best adjustment were living with a psychologically healthy parent — the same factor that produces good adjustment to life in the two-parent home.

SIBLING RIVALRY

Sibling rivalry — the competition among offspring — has existed as long as families have. As far back as Genesis, Joseph was despised by his brothers for finding special favor with his father; and without sibling rivalry, there would have been little premise upon which to base the story of Cinderella. Indeed, some degree of sibling rivalry in childhood appears inevitable.

In its many and varied forms, sibling rivalry is a function of sex, age, and birth order. It occurs in most families where education and achievement are priorities. It is generally acknowledged, for example, that firstborns tend to be high achievers who take initiative and assume responsibility. And yet, some studies have found that unequal levels of accomplishment are not sufficient to cause sibling rivalry. It takes something else. It takes parents emphasizing that "more is better."

Parental values and favoritism, whether overt or covert, figure as key factors in precipitating often intense and destructive competition among children. Perhaps, as parents with well-intentioned, high expectations for our children, we tend to reward most lavishly the accomplishments of whoever does "the best," and maybe our children themselves being to compare, placing themselves in a race for our attention, love, and recognition.

For the gifted toddler — and especially for the youngster who is one of several siblings with above-average abilities — the competition can be especially keen.

Although many gifted children "talk a good game" about understanding individual capabilities, their outward behaviors may display little of this comprehension. So, they may pout, or be insulting or resentful, or repress their feelings and anxieties. Their goal, though, remains the same: a reaching-out for parental acceptance "the way it used to be," before the reality of equally able siblings intruded upon their world.

As parents, our roles become those of mediator and interpreter for our children's overt rivalries and resultant internal conflicts.

"We're OK, You're OK"

"We're OK, you're OK" might well be the message family members give each other when one sibling is labeled "gifted" and others are not.

A University of Iowa study sought to determine the long-term effects of labeling a gifted youngster on the rest of the family, particularly on nongifted siblings. Researchers Nicholas Colangelo and Penny Brower studied sixty-seven families of junior-high-school students who had been identified as gifted at least five years earlier. "While the five year criterion is arbitrary," the two report in *Gifted Child Quarterly*, "we feel confident that any effects that were only 'immediate' would have been extinguished. . . ." Initial effects might include jealousy, insecurity, or uneasiness.

The results confirmed the transitory nature of these effects. Just as you would expect siblings to adjust to a brother or sister recognized for accomplishments in sports, music, art, or social leadership, for example, so too do they adjust to the gifted label. "Brothers and sisters perceived themselves as significantly happier about their gifted siblings' participation in [a gifted program]," Colangelo and Brower report, "than the gifted youngsters perceived their siblings to be [about it]."

Likewise, parents reported overall positive feelings about having had one child identified as gifted and taught in a special program.

According to this study, if anyone remains uneasy about the effects of the gifted label on family members, it's the gifted child. While the immediate effects on others seem to wear off, they seem to remain in the mind of the gifted youngster.

Colangelo and Brower conclude: "Family therapists, school counselors and school psychologists should anticipate immediate difficulties for siblings, and to some extent parents, when a youngster is identified as gifted. But, it seems that in the long-term it is the gifted youngster who needs some attention regarding the label."

Some Do's and Don't's

What follow are some major do's, don't's, and clarifications of ways to reinforce siblings' efforts and performances, while minimizing the negative competition that often accompanies such strivings. The guidelines were provided by James R. Delisle of Kent State University in Ohio.

DON'T COMPARE For parents of gifted children, the comparison of one child with another is the most flagrant misuse of parental persuasion — and the least effective. When younger Julie is reminded of Craig's accomplishments, or elder Craig gets chided for "losing ground" to little Julie, any resultant change in their behaviors will involve either resentment (of parents, self, or siblings) or loss of family status, both to the detriment of self-esteem.

Instead, separate goals should be encouraged and comparisons made only in relation to each child's own previous efforts. The goals, as well as the "acceptable" levels of effort and accomplishment, should be set by children with parental guidance, but without parental pressure.

DON'T DISMISS OR SUPPRESS RESENTMENT The real world is seldom equal or fair, and competition in our society is the name of the game. But it doesn't have to be debilitating, even among siblings. As some studies indicate, sibling rivalry can even be fun and motivating. But when quarrels, disappointments, and resentments invariably arise, they should be discussed and worked through. More often than not, however, siblings rarely talk about their rivalry per se. So, it's up to parents to initiate the dialogue.

Research has shown that sheltering your children from such encounters can cause more problems in the long run.

If an emotion exists — positive or negative, strong or subtle — then it will surely have an effect on outward behaviors. As a parent, you can share with your children avenues of expression for voicing their feelings, and you should encourage them to do so. (Parent: "Craig, you look upset [angry, depressed, whatever]. Do you want to talk about it?" Craig: "When you tell me Julie's gonna catch up to me in piano, you make me feel like I'm lazy — is that what you mean?") Telling children to disguise their hostilities and resentments, or to dismiss them as passing moods, encourages dishonesty and is not the path of true family harmony.

DO BE HONEST AND ACCEPTING   As much as most parents would like to believe that each of their children is "omnitalented," the fact is that different people — including gifted children — have abilities and talents in different areas. Talk openly about this reality with your children so they can begin to develop appropriate self-expectations. You can do this by examining your *strengths* and those of your spouse, your own siblings, other family members, or friends. The emphasis should be twofold: (1) a person doesn't have to be, and shouldn't expect to be, great in everything; and (2) recognize, feel good about, and develop those strengths you do have.

Help your children do the same among themselves, with the goal being greater understanding, caring, and respect for one another.

You may also discuss with your children those strengths you wish you had, but don't have. ("Oh, how I wish I were better at getting my point across at business meetings . . .") Be a role model of self-acceptance of your own areas of limitation — in scholastics, sports, business, homemaking — whatever they may be. ("I realize I'm not as good at making oral presentations as I'd like to be, but I do the best that I can . . .") Help your children do the same. Certainly it is an admirable goal to strive to strengthen areas of weakness as well, but not to the point that major concentration and emphasis are on shortcomings.

Above all else, honesty and acceptance are the greatest consideration you can afford your children in discussing their abilities.

DO ENCOURAGE DIFFERENT AREAS OF INTEREST   Ofttimes, children develop interests and goals that parallel our own. This is fine, and to be expected and encouraged. However, for the child who pursues computer programming when you can't even type, or auto mechanics though you can't distinguish a carburetor from a cylinder, an occasional boost must be supplied here as well. Remember, too, that later-borns may deliberately avoid direct competition with an older sibling who excels in a certain area and may compensate by channeling their abilities in other areas. You want this to be something healthy and productive and not the destructive attention seeking of the "first-worst" distinction (the first one to "fail" preschool, to throw stones through a window, to paint the living-room carpet, and so on). So, don't throw up your hands with the defeatist rejoinder "OK, but you're on your own!" This leaves your child further isolated from the attention he or she seeks and needs. Some gifted children tend to experience more than their share of isolation as it is.

Instead, bolster their enthusiasm with the encouragement to pursue their different interests. React in the same positive way to this child's activity as you do the hobby or craft that is right up your own alley. ("Sally, I don't know the first thing about gardening [model rocketry, whatever], but I think it's great that you're so excited about this. We can learn some things together.") In this way, you will soften the often damaging intensity of competition among highly able siblings, help divert their strengths and energies into alternative areas, and lessen the likelihood of one child developing a sense of failure or inferiority for not measuring up to the other's standards of performance in a specific area.

As Emotional Growth Goes, So Goes Intellectual Growth

IT WASN'T too long ago that educators and psychologists alike believed that intellectual development and emotional development were relatively independent of each other. Growth in these areas seemed to be parallel but not congruent.

Today this view has largely given way to a more holistic approach in viewing early childhood development. Of course, the emotional and intellectual dimensions of a person can still comprise separate areas of study, but as far as the developing child is concerned, they are interwoven in the formation and crystallization of his or her psyche.

Likewise, in the most enlightened circles, the emotional side of cognition no longer takes a back seat to the intellectual. The notion that emotions are inferior to the intellect is at the roots of Western thinking, extending all the way back to the Greek philosopher Plato. Today we realize that a person's emotional fabric can influence, if not determine, his or her intellect, attitudes, happiness, and productivity as a human being.

You can now recognize the indicators of giftedness in your child and better understand the family's role of responsibility in nurturing his or her abilities. This chapter is about a gifted child's fundamental emotional needs and what you should do to nurture them.

THEY'RE CHILDREN FIRST . . .

They're children first and gifted second. Although this premise is subject to debate within the field of gifted education (some educators believe that giftedness is so fundamentally differentiating that it is primary to the child's identity), it will help you keep the relationship with your child in perspective and check the tendency to see only your child's abilities or accomplishments and not the little person behind them. ("It's *You* I Like," the essay by Fred Rogers in chapter 7, underscores this premise.)

A second premise to keep in mind is that a gifted child's perception and experience of his or her social and emotional needs are often more intense than those of other children, which in part accounts for a relatively high incidence of emotional turmoil in gifted children. Third, you and your child will discover all too soon that giftedness itself is often an obstacle to satisfying the child's social and emotional needs.

But despite some essential differences in the psychological and intellectual makeup of gifted children (discussed in next section), these kids have the same social and emotional needs as other children: to be loved, to be accepted, to fit in, to feel worthwhile, to have a purpose, to have an identity of their own. This interplay of differentness and sameness is fraught with conflicts and can be especially trying for the gifted child.

Dimensions of Giftedness

A child's emotional growth and intellectual growth may not be commensurate — and this is especially true with gifted children. Emotional maturity often lags behind intellectual precocity. This is one important reason why being smarter or brighter doesn't necessarily carry with it security, stability, happiness, or success. In addition, certain psychological and intellectual characteristics of gifted children can lead to emotional problems.

EXTRA PERCEPTION Even very young gifted children respond intensely to environmental stimuli, shades of meaning, body language, and tone of a parent's voice; they can perceive and feel complexity and ambivalence within relationships but cannot understand these things.

HIGH CREATIVITY Seeing and doing things differently is a common trait of gifted children. For example, they may manipulate objects in unusual ways (play with a toy in a way other than its intended purpose, or color a barn green instead of red). Acknowledging and accepting such things validates their being; trying to change their thinking to conform to convention ("This truck is for playing in the dirt, not the water") violates their being.

SUPERSENSITIVITY   Relative to their age-mates, gifted children may show early concerns about ethical or social issues (for example, sadness for the needy in the community or even worry about global hunger), and vulnerability to certain social dynamics, such as a troubled or broken home. They may overreact, not yet having developed an experience-based understanding of the complexity of reality or adequate coping skills, yet desiring that harmony and fairness prevail.

HIGH STANDARDS   There is some evidence that gifted children may be driven internally to strive for perfection in whatever they're doing. (Consider the young child who sits amidst a pile of crumpled-up art papers, perpetually starting over rather than erasing an unwanted mark.) Their perception of an ideal, though impossible, goal that they want to attain — and their failure to do so — can lead to feelings of inferiority and inadequacy and to low self-esteem. (Chapter 7 says more about this.)

REFLECTIVE CONSCIOUSNESS   This is the awareness, even among some four- and five-year-olds, of just how differentiating superior abilities can be. It is the child's initial recognition of his or her giftedness, his or her differentness from most other children, that can leave the child confused and insecure — particularly if significant others or peers are reacting negatively to the gifted child's views or behaviors.

All of the above factors — singly or in combination — can lead a gifted child to sense at a visceral level that being different is a mixed blessing of isolation, rejection, and stress as well as creativity and perception that his or her age-mates don't have.

HELP THEM LOVE THEMSELVES

In Greek mythology, the story goes that a youth named Narcissus pined away for love of his own reflection in a pool. Hence, narcissism carries the connotation of being egocentric. But in the myth, Narcissus didn't realize it was his own reflection. He unknowingly longed for something he already had. Unaware of his inherent fulfillment, he became self-alienated to the point of destruction. To ensure a gifted child's healthy emotional development, we must guide the child toward self-acceptance.

According to Judy Galbraith, author and publisher of *The Gifted Kids' Survival Guide*, among the "six great gripes of gifted kids" is "No one explains what being gifted is all about — it's kept a big secret." But it shouldn't be, states Dorothy Sisk, professor of exceptional-child education at the University of South Florida at Tampa. Below, she answers the question "What are the best ways to explain giftedness to young children to make them feel more comfortable about it?"

WHO AM I?
An Essay by Dorothy Sisk

Here's a situation concerning a parent of a very bright five-year-old, Kenny, who was not doing well at school. The teacher reported that he was asking silly questions, talking incessantly, and demonstrating bossy behavior with the rest of the kindergarten group. These behaviors were not new to the parents, for Kenny was demonstrating similar aggressive, active behavior at home and in the neighborhood. And as a result, many children his age and older were reluctant to play with him; consequently, Kenny was becoming a lonely and unhappy child.

Kenny's mother said that when the five-year-old next door wanted to talk about his pet puppy, Kenny wanted to discourse on galaxies and how many stars there were in them. In fact, just that morning he had blurted out that there were 150,000 stars in . . . and his eight-year-old brother had stomped from the breakfast room muttering, "Not again."

Kenny's mother, a remarkably sympathetic and wise woman, took her young son on her lap and said, "Kenny, have you noticed that the other children often don't want to talk about what you want to talk about and they really don't like you telling them what to do?" The child nodded and sadly said, "Yes." Then with a deep sigh, she continued, "Kenny, you know about the early explorers who sailed far beyond their own lands and discovered new lands?" "Yes," Kenny eagerly nodded, as he loved it when his mother told him interesting stories. "Well," she continued, when they returned with tales about people with brown skin, who wore fine silk of many colors and ate rare and strange food, the people did not like hearing this and did not believe it. In fact, they stayed away from the explorers."

Kenny's eyes opened wide. "Well," his mother went on, "you are like those early explorers, but where they explored new lands, you explore new ideas in your mind and you go places other children cannot go. Sometimes other children are like the people who didn't believe or understand and that is why they pull away."

Kenny sat quietly looking at his mother, and she thought, I've gone too far over his head and he doesn't understand. Then Kenny nodded and slid off his mother's lap, giving her one of his wide grins, and said, "I wish you had told me that last year; I thought there was something wrong with me."

Kenny's mother said that she quietly wept for her own son's deep understanding and also for the heavy burden that all young gifted children bear — that of being different. All gifted children are different, and they will perceive this differentness to the degree that they do not have age-mates at school and at home who are also gifted.

Helping Children Understand Their Giftedness

First, unless the child is suffering from his giftedness and consequent interactions with others, don't have a heart-to-heart discussion on the *problems* of being gifted. However, if such problems do emerge, an analogy similar to what Kenny's mother used should prove helpful. Still another way to explain giftedness to young children is through "bibliotherapy" — using literature as a stimulus to enhance communication among family members, increase awareness, facilitate exploration of personal feelings, and encourage sound social-emotional development.

There are three steps to bibliotherapy: *identification, catharsis,* and *insight*. Then there is *action* or changed behavior on the part of the child.

For a young child to understand differentness, a delightful book entitled *Flutterby*, by Stephen Cosgrove (Price, Stern and Sloan, 1980), might be helpful. In this book, Flutterby, who is a wonderful, flying white horse with a unicorn horn, doesn't know who he is. In exploring an ageless theme, the author has Flutterby thinking he might be an ant, because he likes to work; but disaster befalls him when he tries to help roll a cookie down an ant hole. Flutterby's travels take him to many places, with as many misadventures, until finally he realizes that he is satisfied and happy to be who he is.

That simple message can be the insight that young gifted children gather. They need to hear, accept, and adopt the notion that "I am different and I prize that differentness. I am who I am."

Identification comes about when the child can say, "Gee, I'm like that unicorn and I feel that way too." *Catharsis* takes place when the child feels sad when Flutterby is misunderstood and even stung by a bee! *Insight* comes when he or she grasps the notion that it is truly all right to be different and can prize it. *Action* results when the gifted child evidences less concern about being gifted and pursues his or her unique interests, needs, and abilities.

Parents can do much to encourage this understanding through gentle, unobtrusive questions such as "Do you think Flutterby likes himself now?" or "How else could Flutterby have found out who he was?" or "Have you ever felt like Flutterby?" The atmosphere should be relaxed and casual. Gifted children can feel when they are being probed. Remember that they are very sensitive to "con acts" and will sense your anxiety if timing is not just right. Easy does it!

Don't Deny It!

The importance of gifted children accepting their giftedness and developing it cannot be denied. Being gifted is being different — not better than other children or more precious to parents or society. Yet, many times when gifted children are misunderstood or confused about other people's actions, they misread and malign their own personal dignity and worth.

Too often, we try to pretend that a child is not gifted and we attempt to shield that gifted child from recognizing his giftedness or differentness. Leo Buscaglia, in a book entitled *Personhood: The Art of Being Fully Human*, says that "the most damaging course of action is attempting to keep children from experience or protect them from pain, for it is at this time that children learn that life is a magic thing . . . if not a rose garden. The parents' role is primarily to stand by with a goodly supply of bandaids."

DISCOVERING PURPOSE

Gifted toddlers and preschoolers don't ask themselves the "existential question" (Who am I?) explicitly. But as they become aware of their differentness, and as they experience the implications and consequences of their giftedness on others, they may begin to sense a dimension of "plight" to their situation. Like Kenny, they may begin to feel a kind of burden associated with being different. They may feel: "This isn't fair. Why me?"

This kind of child seeks personal meaning early, trying to make sense out of something he or she didn't ask for — to be different from most other children. On the whole, you want your child's experience of him- or herself to be positive. This is one reason why gifted programs for school-age children are so critical — they provide avenues for challenging and applying a gifted child's intellect and creativity in some area(s) of personal choice, thereby assisting the youngster in becoming who he or she is. This is the true meaning of self-fulfillment.

For the preschool child, the principal mode of discovering purpose is through *self-directed* "learning" — that is, through informal, self-initiated activities wherein the child follows his or her own impulses, exploring here and there at will. In other words, play! Adult interference with this process — say, by not allowing such freedom and by imposing formal learning activities too early — can cause the child to develop a strong sense of guilt at the expense of personal initiative. (For more on this subject, see chapter 5.) Guilt — for wanting to go one's own way and for not conforming — is a debilitating monster that can eat away at a child's self-concept and emotional stability.

DEALING WITH FEELINGS

Key to helping gifted children move toward self-acceptance is acknowledging and discussing their feelings — the negative as well as positive. As we've seen with Kenny, gifted kids need opportunities at home and school to discuss the nature of giftedness, what it means, its pros and cons; its burdens, responsibilities, joys, and frustrations. This can take the form of an explicit discussion or some product or expression: story, poem, piece of art, song, journal entry, and so on.

Sometimes children don't find it easy to open up. Maybe your child is shy or withdrawn or a loner or simply frightened to expose his or her vulnerabilities. Sometimes kids don't know what they're feeling. According to J. Kent Hollingsworth, a school psychologist in Bogota, New Jersey, the basis of all healthy development is emotional support, so you have to work on communicating. But how?

Hollingsworth says that children learn to trust the world as a result of the trustworthiness demonstrated by their parents, starting when the child is born. Parents who are physically and emotionally available to their children establish a foundation upon which trust is built. It is important that you listen to your child in a concerned, supportive, and nonjudgmental way.

We may hear what others are saying without truly listening. Hearing is passive; listening is active. A good listener seeks to clarify by asking the speaker questions such as "This is what I'm hearing — is that what you mean?" A good listener does not interrupt, moralize, give advice, or negate the other's feelings. Compare, for example, the following exchanges:

CHILD: I hate Jimmy!
PARENT: What a terrible thing to say! You don't hate your brother.

CHILD: I hate Jimmy!
PARENT: Sounds like you're pretty mad at your brother. Did something happen?

The first example cuts off communication and makes the angry child feel put down and misunderstood. The second opens up communication, promoting a dialogue, expression of feelings, and ultimately a resolution of the problem (or at least a defusing of the situation).

Here's an example that compares two responses to a child's frustration over being different:

CHILD: I wish I weren't smart!
PARENT: You don't mean that! Being smart is a good thing.

CHILD: I wish I weren't smart!
PARENT: You do? Did something happen in preschool today?

Again, the first example denies the child's feelings and reality. The second one acknowledges the child and tries to get to the incident that's behind the statement.

Other Factors in a Supportive Home Environment

EXERCISE EFFECTIVE DISCIPLINE   Gifted children need fair and consistent discipline in order to develop a sense of security, self-discipline, and mastery over their impulses — thus developing positive feelings about themselves as competent and worthy individuals. (Discipline is discussed in detail later in this chapter.)

GIVE RESPECT   Children will learn to respect themselves (and others) if they are taught that they are worthy of respect. You can demonstrate respect for children by accepting them for who they are. This means accepting your child at his or her developmental level and not giving implicit or explicit messages that he or she must behave like an older child to be worthy. It means giving them age-appropriate responsibilities — chores they can handle and limited decision making (as discussed below).

HELP CHILDREN COPE WITH STRESS   Parents often forget how stressful childhood can be. The notion that childhood is the "best time of life," full of carefree, happy days, is a romanticized distortion. Not only do children experience stress, they are less able than adults to cope with it. Moving to a new town, parental discord, parental expectations, loss of a pet or loved one, poor grades, difficulty making friends, too rigid or formal a preschool — these are among the many stressful circumstances faced by children.

Parents can help by encouraging children to express their feelings, and by introducing ways to relax and cope with stress. Playing noncompetitive games, hiking, reading, fishing, painting, listening to music, and so forth are all adaptive ways of unwinding — even for the "little ones" whose lives are becoming more harried and complex. (See chapter 4 for more on stress.)

FRIENDSHIPS AND RELATIONSHIPS

Nothing helps validate a child's sense of self-worth and cultivate social skills like an appropriate playmate. "Appropriate" means a child of similar abilities and interests to those of your own child. (Of course, the bottom line is that the kids hit it off.) The time shared together should involve genuine give-and-take, in which each can discover something about himself or herself and about the other child. Neither child should dominate in the relationship or get his or her way all the time.

The reason it's important that "like play with like" is that healthy friendships — even at the preschool level — imply that each person, to the extent possible within the relationship, is able to respect, appreciate, and mirror the other's strengths. In other words, something positive happens for both children when they're together. Educators have observed situations in which one child's energy level was so much higher than the other's (a common trait in gifted children) that he or she completely dominated, overwhelmed, and exhausted the other child — who then refused to play with the gifted youngster.

It's not easy, if possible at all, for a three- or four-year-old child to understand, appreciate, or change the social dynamics of a relationship. You may try to help by orchestrating an interaction now and then, but you can't be there all the time (nor should you be), and you cannot keep the lid on a gifted child for the sake of "socialization" without risking emotional and psychological trauma. It is a lonely and emotionally unhappy child who feels, on the one hand, isolated or rejected by other children, or, on the other, squelched by his or her parents, who are trying to help overcome the child's isolation.

Your role is to help your child get together with other children who are appropriate so that they can appreciate and reinforce one another, not in spite of their differentness, but because of it.

Personality "Plus"

Without a doubt, some gifted toddlers are delightful and some are obnoxious — the same assortment of personalities found on any playground. Yet, psychologists have observed that one cluster of personality traits in particular tends to alienate nongifted age-mates: belittling sarcasm, abrasiveness, or snobbishness.

You should observe how your toddler interacts with others. Listen to how your son or daughter talks with peers. Not every child will exhibit all the following behaviors; but does he or she

- argue incessantly?
- imply that what others say is unimportant or irrelevent?
- always have to prove his or her point?
- insist on describing every detail of an event, report, story, show, or whatever?
- dominate every discussion?
- appear bored if someone else is in the limelight?

Gifted children may also display a second cluster of personality traits and act shy, awkward, detached, single-minded, and fiercely independent — to the extent that nongifted peers are unsuccessful in their attempts to establish friendships.

Ask yourself, does my child

- prefer to be alone?
- discourage incidental, unimportant comments from others, and scorn chitchat or silliness?
- appear nervous around others?
- seem totally absorbed in his or her interests?
- refuse to show interest in others' pursuits?
- express intolerance?
- appear lazy or laid-back so he or she won't have to get involved with others?

Smoothing the Rough Edges

Whether the first or second cluster of personality traits, or some combination, best describes your toddler, here are some strategies to help your child polish his or her interactions with peers.

• *Confront your child with the offensive behavior you've heard or seen.* Don't let it go unnoticed. Explain that you are concerned because this kind of behavior is damaging to friendships and isolating to your child. ("Jamie, if you don't let Susie get a word in when you're playing she's not going to want to be with you again.")

• *Express dismay when your child cracks a joke or plays a prank at someone else's expense.* Point out that such behavior can hurt and alienate others, preventing close relationships from developing. ("Sam, you like to have fun, but you're not to treat others as playthings. How would you feel if . . .")

• *Be prepared for defensive retorts such as "I want to do it my way" or "I was only trying to show Susie something."* Acknowledge that your child has a right to his or her point of view, but also that the manner in which he or she expresses it is important as well. Explain that making others feel rejected or inferior rarely wins many converts.

Teach your child that there are appropriate and inappropriate times for pursuing personal interests and discussions. Likewise, teach your child to share knowledge concisely and understandably so as not to offend or overwhelm others. ("Linda, Billy's here to play, not to watch you mount your whole stamp collection. You can show him one or two of your favorites, then find something to do that you both like.")

• *Teach your child the value of listening.* Explain that listening enhances relationships by showing respect for another's point of view, although you may not agree with it.

• *Try to ascertain why a shy child avoids interactions.* If you see evidence of extreme insecurity, fear of failure, inferiority, poor self-concept, or low self-esteem, you might want to consider professional counseling. (See also chapter 7 on perfectionism.) These same characteristics, by the way, also may be present in an outgoing but obnoxious youngster whose behavior is masking a poor self-image; that is, who is acting out in aggressive ways to make other children like him or her.

When They Poke Fun

It's not uncommon that a gifted child may become the special target of teasing, verbal abuse, or ridicule by his or her peers. Poking fun is one way that children and adults alike deal with things or people that are different. This can wear on the gifted child, particularly if he or she is hypersensitive and shows that the teasing is bothersome, and it can intensify feelings of vulnerability, isolation, and self-alienation. Very young children usually don't understand the source of abusive behavior, what is causing them to be singled out in this manner.

Once again, you need to listen, acknowledge, be supportive,

and discuss your child's feelings. Just like Kenny's mother, who sat him down for an intimate little chat, explain to your toddler that people who are different sometimes get teased — just for being different. Other reasons include jealousy, feeling threatened or put down, and maybe sometimes just for fun.

Help your child develop some coping strategies. Explain that this may include ignoring the ridicule, laughing at it, walking away, calmly telling the other child how such remarks make you feel, standing up with an "Oh yeah?" and shooting back a remark of your own, or other responses (short of physical violence) of your choosing that give you a sense of confidence that you're in control of the situation rather than a helpless victim. Role-play a couple of incidents or situations. Assuming your child raised the problem, have him or her describe what happened. Next, say, "OK, pretend I just teased you that way, what are some things you can say or do? Go ahead . . ."

EMOTIONAL GROWTH DEPENDS ON DISCIPLINE

It's one of those paradoxes: healthy emotional development — a positive self-image and freedom to create, take risks, and express yourself openly and honestly — is founded on structure and discipline, not permissiveness. Of course, this can be taken to extremes. Authoritarianism is as stifling as permissiveness is directionless.

What kind of discipline should you establish in your home that will nurture your child's emotional well-being? What kinds of household rules are appropriate in setting limits and expectations for your preschool child? How do you balance your desire to give your child plenty of room for experimentation and independence, yet maintain your authority as "rule keeper"?

The Role of Discipline

Discipline is an emotionally loaded issue that is often associated with authoritarianism, coercion, and punishment. Those of us who consider ourselves to be enlightened and fair-minded may well react negatively to the notion of imposing this kind of discipline on a child. It may be argued that the more important considerations when raising a gifted child include fostering divergent thinking, inquisitiveness, a thirst for knowledge, and an independent spirit. But discipline rightly conceived — as in the teaching and consistent application of rules, structures, values, and behaviors held to be important by the family — is necessary in cultivating these things. How can parents nurture *this* kind of discipline?

The primary factors in raising an emotionally healthy child are quite basic: the child must know that he or she is loved, and the child must know the rules that establish limits and expectations appropriate to his or her age. Discipline plays an important role in both of these areas.

All about Love

Of course we love our children! But too often we forget that children need demonstrations of our love — the more, the better, and as appropriate to the child's developmental age as possible.

Spending time with the child is one of the more fundamental expressions of a parent's love. Parents of infants should spend time holding, rocking, and talking to their children. As the child becomes a toddler, encouragement and descriptive praise gain importance. "I like the way you're sitting" or "I'm happy to see you playing so nicely with your brother" are much more useful to the child than simply saying "You're a good boy today," because it tells him *what* he's doing that earned the praise. (See chapter 5 for more on the right way to praise a child.)

As the child grows older, other demonstrations of parental love become appropriate. For example, giving children responsibility as early as possible shows them that they are competent in their parents' eyes. It is important that the responsibility be age-appropriate. A four- or five-year-old is perfectly capable of setting the table or deciding whether to wear his red shirt or blue shirt to school. That same child is *not* capable of deciding what constitutes a balanced diet or whether the family should visit Aunt Mildred on Saturday.

Giving a child child-size responsibilities helps develop a sense of competence and self-worth. Giving a child adult-size responsibilities leads to insecurity and inappropriate behavior. Children need to know that the world is an orderly place with a degree of predictability to it. They depend upon their parents for that orderliness. When parents do not fulfill their parental roles, the child's view of the world becomes chaotic and the child can become maladjusted.

Demonstrating respect for your child's ideas is another way of showing love. There should be times for family conversations, when children may express their thoughts, feelings, and opinions. The dinner table was the traditional setting for such conversations, and where circumstances permit, this is a tradition well worth preserving. The open forum or "brainstorming" atmosphere should prevail, and gifted children should feel free to express their own ideas on politics, religion, sex, or Baskin-Robbins's flavor of the month without fear of ridicule or censure. One way of doing this is to have conversations on selected topics. Take turns picking them, and give each person, including the youngest, a chance to express his or her feelings or thoughts about the topic. (Parent: "Well, that's interesting . . . what a different way of looking at it. That must have really pleased [bothered] you.")

Equally important, the child should be taught that most conversations (those that take place away from the dinner table) are *not* open forums and that it is a matter of courtesy not to intrude on others' conversations (even parents').

Limit Their Tongue, Structure Their Choices

Perhaps the most common discipline problems with gifted children are related to their reasoning skills and verbal facility. In his practice, dealing with gifted children, school psychologist Hollingsworth has seen many four- and five-year-olds lead their parents into lengthy debates over matters that were quite properly within the parents' sole province. Gifted children quickly recognize parents who are loath to use the intellectually stifling "Because I said so," and therefore almost any edict can be questioned, argued, and debated, with the resulting reinforcement of parental attention. It's best to cut off unproductive debates, stating that you have decided what is best in this circumstance — as mother or father — and will not discuss it any further right now.

An important parenting skill involves learning to limit and structure a child's choices. In choosing clothes for a preschooler to wear, for example, the parent should define the *range* of choices: the child may choose among styles, colors, and patterns, but the parent should preselect a group of shirts appropriate to the season and occasion. Similarly with bedtime — the child may be given the choice of bathing before or after a favorite program, what bedtime story is to be read, what kind of snack (within limits set by the parent), and so on. The child may even decide whether to sleep or stay awake. But no matter what, it's "in bed and lights out" at a specific time.

Sure, children will test the limits. They'll complain. They'll try your patience. That's their nature. But despite their protests, young children are more comfortable, and therefore happier, when their parents are the final authority.

The Value of Rules

Enforcing rules is what we usually mean when we talk about discipline. The best way to enforce a rule is through its consequences if the rule is broken. But you should view discipline as helping your child learn how to control his or her actions rather than as a blind act of punishment. The end goal is to teach your child how to cope within the bounds of family rules and those of the larger society, at the same time maintaining his or her individuality and special gifts and talents.

It is easier for children to accept and abide by rules if you state them clearly in language they understand, if you tell them what to expect when they break rules, if you are consistent, loving, fair, and firm, and if they know you will not argue or give in about expectations or consequences. (For example: "You may play with your toys in Daddy's study if you pick them up when you're finished. If you don't, you won't be able to play in there anymore.")

Dorothy Ohlhaver, a longtime teacher of young gifted children, says: "First decide if an issue is worth a confrontation. Then keep rules to a minimum, saying no as infrequently as possible." Just like no rules at all, too many rules break down the system, confuse both parent and child, and can inhibit the ability to solve problems creatively.

"Make sure the rules are not for your convenience but benefit the child," writes Susan Baum, assistant professor of graduate gifted education at the College of New Rochelle in New York. Suppressed but seething rebellion can result when you punish a child to satisfy your own frustration, helplessness, or anger — particularly if you use verbal abuse, shame, or guilt. That's unfair, and if you deal unfairly with young children, the stage is then set for teen rebellion when rules and validity of values will be certainly questioned.

WHAT MAKES A GOOD RULE?   Betty Roschlau, who has taught gifted children creative problem solving through art, believes children actually love rules, and she supports her stand with evidence that children make up rules if none exist. Listen to them during play: "This is the way we play: If anybody . . . , they're out of the game."

Children do not question the validity of having a rule so much as they do its fairness. They want to see rule breakers punished. Through discussion and example they come to understand that some rules are broken by accident, and that there can be extenuating circumstances under which people deserve a second chance. Exceptions to rules should be considered. They will learn that some rules are for children their age; some are different for the handicapped; and all rules depend on the situation and context.

The result will be more thoughtful and selective behavior on kids' part. Roschlau adds that "a rule should state the *desired* behavior, not the undesired." Examples: "Shut the door quietly," not "Don't slam the door." "Hold the glass with both hands," not "Don't spill your milk."

She reminds parents: "Be fair and let the punishment fit the crime. If consequences are too long in duration, the connection will be lost. A four-year-old child sent to his or her room for an hour will get bored, start playing, and forget why he's been isolated." A youngster who slams the door when asked not to may be asked to close it several times quietly so he "gets the idea," or may be delayed ten or fifteen minutes from joining his friends outside, or may be prohibited from watching a TV show that evening.

GIFTED: EXCEPTION TO THE RULE   The development of self-esteem is critical, and the often urgent, all-consuming drive for excellence must be carefully considered in disciplining gifted children. This drive for excellence can lead them to paint themselves into corners, pursuing interests just beyond their reach. Avoid sarcastic remarks or destructive criticism that imposes limits through shame, guilt, or inferior feelings. ("If you're so smart, why can't you keep your shoelaces tied?") Instead, allow kids to save face; give a warning or second chance for an infraction of a rule committed with a higher purpose in mind.

For perfectionists (discussed in chapter 7), even fewer rules are needed. These children rarely are completely satisfied with anything they do, and they set enough limits for themselves. You can help such children best by allowing them enough time to complete tasks, and by helping them set intermediate or more realistic goals. To some degree, you'll have to learn to live with their self-criticism and with their high expectations of themselves.

Another trait to consider when disciplining a gifted child is his or her ability to sop up information quickly. Children absorb bad habits with the good from watching parents and siblings. If models are harsh, teasing, or sarcastic, children will be the same. If a parent manipulates a spouse, a child quickly learns to twist others around his or her fingers. Instead, take advantage of the gifted toddler's quick mind and purposely model desired values, ethics, and behavior.

ENFORCING RULES   Once children understand cause and effect, the keys to discipline are isolation, reduction of privileges, and deprivation of freedom. When children are left to "think things over," they can control their own destiny by deciding when they are ready to rejoin the family. And when kids are left to think about what they have been doing, they begin to accept responsibility for their own behavior.

When time is involved, issue a warning: "You can play five more minutes, then we must leave." Don't extend and don't argue. Or, "You can read two more books, then lights out." Set habits that reinforce responsible behavior within a clearly defined structure.

Some gifted children need little or no limit-setting. They seem to be born with self-discipline and sunny dispositions. They're rarely bored into mischief and instinctively manage within family rules. Don't set up this kind of child as a paragon or a threat to siblings — as in "Why can't you keep your room neat like your sister?"

Siblings will accept fair exceptions to rules if you explain why the well-behaved child is allowed special privileges: "John is allowed a newspaper route because he does his chores, completes his homework, and goes to bed earlier so he can wake himself up early. When you can take responsibility for your actions, we'll consider letting you have a route." Give concrete reasons why special exceptions to rules are made.

OTHER POINTS TO REMEMBER   Wesley C. Becker, in his excellent book *Parents Are Teachers*, describes it as "Grandma's Rule" — and it's particularly applicable to very young children. Simply stated: "You do what I want you to do, before you get to do what you want to do." This means, for instance, making the bed before leaving the house, and peas before ice cream.

Hollingsworth offers some other commonsense principles:

- *A rule is a rule*. Just ask any four-year-old whether it's OK to change the rules of a game. They'll tell you — absolutely not. Similarly, it's usually best to be consistent and not give in when a toddler wants to change a rule. If you give in to your child's challenge, you've unintentionally taught him or her several things: Rules can be broken; if you push long and hard enough, you'll get your way; parents are not really in charge.
- *Choose your battles*. When you decide to draw the line, be sure it's fair and appropriate. It's appropriate to demand that a four-year-old stay out of the street, or that a thirteen-year-old be home at a reasonable hour. On the other hand, it's not appropriate to demand that a four-year-old stay out of puddles, or that a thirteen-year-old conform to your tastes in clothes or hair style.
- *There's a time and place for discussion*. Children should have *some* say about rules, and often they're tougher on themselves than their parents are. But negotiations and discussions should take place at a time when calm and reason can prevail, not in the middle of an argument or tantrum.
- *Let them act their age*. A gifted child with an adult vocabulary is still just a kid. Don't push your child to be a miniature adult. Expect some setbacks and anticipate that the desired behavior will come gradually. Even gifted preschoolers will throw tantrums because they're kids. Let them act it out in a safe environment; don't give in to a tantrum that's being used

as an attention-seeking device. Get discussion started again when calm prevails.

To sum up: Treat young gifted children with respect. Teach behavior by example. Be fair; discipline with kindness and compassion. Always hear your child's side, but don't give in to manipulation. Be consistent, reasonable, and sensible, and clearly explain your expectations so that the child has direction and can avoid your disapproval more easily. Allow experimentation within limits; don't stifle creativity with unnecessary rules; be flexible and willing to negotiate rules as your child grows older.

Healthy Minds in Healthy Bodies: Giving Talents a Chance to Show and Grow

OR CENTURIES philosophers have sought to understand the relationship between the mind and the body. Yet, despite the most scientific and technological advances, in many ways we are no further along in our understanding than what was reflected in the ancient Greek adage "A healthy body makes for a healthy mind."

Of course, our understanding of *that* is much expanded, as we have become much more cognizant of the breadth and impact of specific environmental factors that affect both our physical and intellectual development. No longer bound by a nineteenth-century view of genetic determinism, today we realize that environment and genes interact in a dynamic way: their *combination* determines the direction and scope of human growth.

Thus we are affected — right down to the individual cell level — by what we breathe, what we eat, and even whether or not we receive adequate mental stimulation to ward off boredom!

This chapter takes a look at how environment and nutrition affect toddlers' behavior, their capacity to develop cognitive abilities, and, ultimately, their school performance and giftedness.

The object is to recognize and thwart negative factors and cultivate positive ones *early*, so that your son or daughter has the advantage of surroundings from birth that will allow his or her full genetic potential to blossom fully.

YOUNG BRAINS CHARGED WITH ACTIVITY

Young children have "supercharged" brains, according to new evidence from neurological studies, but this tremendous energy begins to wane as youngsters enter early adolescence.

Several studies of children's brain activity, reported in the *New York Times,* coincide with a dominant theme that has been emerging in neurobiological findings over the past decade — that nervous systems "regress" as they mature. These studies show that between the ages of three and eleven children's brains use twice as much energy as those of adults, and that this activity subsides to the adult level by age fourteen.

Further, the number of synaptic connections in your child's brain — the treelike branches where brain cells meet up — is double that of adults initially, but falls to half the number in early adolescence. All of this brain energy also leads to prolonged deep-sleep patterns in young children, again twice as much as that of a fourteen-year-old.

Another field of research — why nerve cells die off — also ties in to the research on brain activity of children. Max Cowan of the Salk Institute in La Jolla, California, says cell survival seems to depend on "nourishment" or stimulation. "In this view," the *Times* article concludes, "the child's brain develops virtually all potentially useful neural interconnections by the age of two. But it is childhood experience that shapes the architecture of the brain, strengthening the neural circuits that are used and ultimately sacrificing those that are not used." Like a sculptor who chips away at a rough framework, nature seems to form the brain through experience, says Cowan.

ENVIRONMENT AFFECTS BRAIN CELL ACTIVITY

"We don't affect children at the behavioral level; we affect them at the cellular level," explains Barbara Clark, professor of special education at California State University, Los Angeles. She says that environment can change the biochemistry of brain cells and accelerate the rate and complexity of children's thinking.

Clark contends that a good environment can enrich brain cells by increasing their synaptic activity, the electrical charges between cells that are at the bottom of all cognitive performance.

Unlike the behavioral model exemplified in the Skinner box, in which rats are conditioned using electric shock, a gifted child's learning environment, Clark says, must cultivate joy and pleasure in learning, not responses on the basis of reward and punishment.

Citing research on how the many parts of the brain function interdependently, Clark states that the emotional center of the brain, through its biochemistry, can either "facilitate or shut down the higher levels of cognition" in the brain's two main hemispheres. Emotions such as anxiety, tension, and fear apparently diminish or prevent cellular synaptic activity. Thus it is critical that programs and activities for the gifted also include relaxation techniques to expunge those emotions that interfere with accelerated brain activity, Clark says.

Clark lists a number of activities that encourage brain-function integration and that are used for preschool to high-school students in her New Age School Project — an extension of Southern California's Center for Educational Excellence for Gifted and Highly Able Learners, which she directs. Among them are reduction of tension and anxiety through relaxation exercises for the purpose of mind-body unity; use of "fantasy trips" and other imagery in teaching subject matter; physical and verbal "touching" to show children they are valued; a curriculum of sufficient complexity to challenge and increase synaptic activity; and lessons stressing development of creativity and intuition. (See chapter 9 for more on the brain-environment connection.)

SHOULD YOU PICK UP A CRYING BABY?

If your infant is crying, should you go to the crib and pick it up? Emphatically yes says Lee Salk, clinical professor of psychology in psychiatry and clinical professor of pediatrics at the New York Hospital–Cornell Medical Center. Don't *ever* feel you are spoiling your baby if you pick it up. Many parents are told that if you pick up a baby and he or she stops crying, you will be encouraging the infant to cry in the future. That's nonsense!

One of the main reasons babies cry is *boredom*. Unfortunately, a baby can do little to provide stimulation, so its cry of distress or boredom means "Pick me up, hold me, cuddle me, show me things, and otherwise make my environment stimulating."

A crying baby who is not picked up will eventually cry itself to sleep to relieve tension and stress. If this pattern of unresponsiveness from others persists repeatedly, he or she is encouraged to give up easily. This is an acquired pattern that we call *learned helplessness*, and it can persist into childhood and even adult life. Studies have shown that depression in adult life is related to this kind of early pattern, Salk says.

STRESS: CAUSES AND CURES IN GIFTED KIDS (AND THEIR PARENTS)

Stress is energy. It can motivate us, help us concentrate, and keep us working toward goals. These are positive aspects of stress. But, as we all know, stress can be negative, too. The anxiety experienced before taking a major exam or going to the dentist are examples of negative stress, or *distress*. (Hereafter "stress" will refer to negative stress only.)

Most adults are familiar with the physical and emotional symptoms of stress: irritability, headaches, insomnia, ulcers, high blood pressure, heart disease, aggressiveness, depression, withdrawal, tension, substance abuse, rigid thinking, forgetfulness, loss of appetite, overeating, intense anxiety, and insecurity.

You may not realize, though, that gifted children are particularly susceptible to stress, which if not checked may result in any number of chronic maladies or "burnout." This is characterized by a state of mental and physical exhaustion from prolonged, unrelieved stress that can lead to withdrawal, hopelessness, and inactivity.

But the kids aren't the only ones to suffer, according to Kathryn Ferner, a certified psychologist, and Stan Heck, a social worker. Speaking at a conference of the Ohio Valley Association for Talented and Gifted, Ferner and Heck said that parents and teachers are also subject to stress in raising and teaching gifted children. "All give each other stress," Ferner stated. "It's cyclical." A lack of understanding and knowledge, fear, uncertainty about the appropriate parental role, and lack of support from others rank among the top causes of stress in parents of gifted children.

Teachers of gifted children often experience unrelenting pressure from students and parents to provide additional stimulation and enrichment, and there is sometimes a fine line between being challenged by a gifted student and being intimidated by him or her.

At High Risk for Burnout

The reasons gifted children are at high risk for stress and burn-out are multifaceted, ranging from excessive environmental demands to negative self-perception habits and coping patterns to undeveloped stress management skills. And — according to Ronald L. Rubenzer, founder of Thinking Dynamics, a stress management consulting firm in Greensboro, North Carolina — specific developmental factors also lead to stress in gifted children. Some of these are listed below.

PERFECTIONIST TENDENCIES   Leanings toward perfectionism may be learned, brain-based (part of an individual's psychological/neurological makeup), or both. Children who suffer from perfectionism are in a constant state of frustration because of the ever-present gap between how they feel they are actually performing and their sometimes unrealistic, sometimes self-imposed achievement goals. This can lead to perfectionistic "freeze-up," which is a type of internal stage fright or fear of failure associated with any new, perhaps threatening challenge. (Chapter 7 discusses perfectionism in detail.)

EXCESSIVE ACHIEVEMENT DEMANDS   Pressure caused by the ambitious demands of others is undoubtedly a great source of anxiety for gifted children. A general "achievement anxiety" can be generated in children by well-meaning adults who want their kids to do their best all the time. Rather than "achieving to live" a satisfying, productive life, gifted children overburdened in this manner may learn to "live to achieve." Achievement-anxious children are often plagued by such fears and implicit questions as "Can I maintain this level of achievement?" and "Will only more be expected of me once I achieve these goals?"

INTELLECTUAL/SOCIAL DEVELOPMENTAL GAP   A gifted child of four may well have the intellectual interests and abilities of an eight-year-old, but obviously will not have the physical/social development of an older child. The efforts of a bright youngster to socialize with older children will quite often be blocked by the older children's rejection of the "little kid." Thus the gifted pre-schooler feels "out of it" with his or her own age-mates as well as with older kids who pay no attention. Social isolation can cause stress.

HEIGHTENED SENSITIVITY TO ADULT PROBLEMS   Gifted kids tend to be "info-maniacs" about what is going on in their environment — everything from family problems to global issues — and this, too, can create stress. They often worry about problems that truly don't affect them, or over which they have no control.

How Stress Takes Its Toll

Almost without exception, stress decreases the academic performance of kids and their mastery of new skills — no matter what their intellectual capabilities. Too much stress at an early age can severely retard development.

But it's a child's creative thinking — an essential hallmark of giftedness — that seems to suffer most. E. Paul Torrance, a pioneer in the field of creativity, observed that by the fourth grade it is very difficult to reverse the early harmful effects of stress and anxiety on creative thinking. Children so afflicted are unable to relax. They begin to display so-called Type A personality characteristics: tension, extreme competitiveness, impatience, and the like. In addition to preventing a gifted child's creative juices from flowing, stress can lead to certain psychosomatic illnesses: headaches, stomachaches, and depression.

The ABCs of Stress Management

The most important element in dealing with stress, according to Ferner and Heck, is for all involved to "acknowledge and validate that the situation is stressful and to build on that mutual support."

The following checklist of excessive-stress warning signs will help you determine how "stressed out" your preschooler is. The more symptoms a child has, the more likely he or she is suffering from excessive stress. (Physical complaints should be investigated to identify or eliminate possible somatic causes.)

- A major change in attitude or temperament (irritability, lack of enthusiasm, depression, carelessness)
- Withdrawal, outbursts, or tantrums for little or no apparent reason
- Hyperactive behavior (fidgeting, nervous tics, jumping from task to task, trouble concentrating)
- Suspicious complaints of fatigue and vague illnesses — "convenient" sickness to avoid certain tasks or situations
- Insomnia or refusal to get out of bed
- Stomachaches or headaches
- An increase in allergic/asthmatic attacks

The Stress Management Triangle

Stress management can be accomplished through relaxation training that takes a "whole-child approach" — one that pays attention to attitude, behavior, and environment, as illustrated by the accompanying diagram.

ATTITUDE   Attitude forms one-third of the equilateral triangle and refers to that set of beliefs, values, and responses that go to make up a person's general outlook, composure, and comportment. Although a very young child may not be aware of such factors explicitly, you can guide him or her from negative to positive attitudes (for instance, from pessimism to optimism, from disbelief in self to belief in self), or to circumvent the negative ones altogether, by building an "internal locus of control" in your child.

"There is nothing more anxiety-producing than feeling you have no control over a situation or your actions," states Barbara Clark, author of *Growing Up Gifted* and *Optimizing Learning*. In her work with the New Age School, Clark has found that children as young as two years old have begun to experience stress and tension over expectations about their performance.

On the other hand, Clark says, *choice* is very empowering. When children are always told what to do, how to do it, and when to do it, they feel out of control; and they do not develop the ability to make good decisions. Parents and teachers can provide clear alternatives, information about the consequences of those alternatives, and a chance to practice choosing among them. In this way, gifted kids can come to feel in control of their abilities, their time,

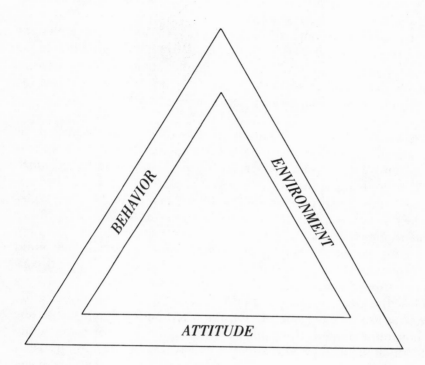

and their energy. They begin to believe in themselves and in their power to handle stressful situations.

An effective attitude-enhancing activity involves positive self-talk. Children who have habitually come to make negative assertions in the face of challenge or unknown outcomes ("I can't do this"; "This is stupid"; "I'm no good") need help seeing their strengths and practice saying "I *can* do this"; "This is *fun*"; "I'm pretty *good* at this!"; "I'll *try* it!"

The technique of mental rehearsal can be especially helpful with your children. Encourage your child to visualize each step and each detail of a coming anxiety-producing event. Remember, *what* event causes anxiety will vary from child to child. It might be going to preschool, attending a birthday party, or playing a competitive game or sport. Picture the place, people, and possible happenings. Have your child see himself or herself carrying out the task, dealing with any problems or obstacles that arise, and bringing it to a successful completion. Together, work out alternative ways of handling the event so he or she will have maximum flexibility when it does occur.

Research has found that when gifted children are given choices and control over themselves, they seek out challenging tasks and feel joy and satisfaction in their accomplishments. They view errors as feedback and as clues to improving their efforts. Learning for such children becomes an exciting adventure.

BEHAVIOR   Behavior forms another third of the stress management triangle. It involves learning relaxation responses to stress and tension. Your child's goal in stress management is to recognize the attitudes and behaviors connected with stressed and with relaxed states, and to learn that he or she can control stress levels. The tips below will help you with the behavior aspects of the stress management triangle.

• *Encourage "one-thing-at-a-time" thinking*. Teach your child to concentrate on one thought or action at a time. A useful concentration technique is to have him or her imagine (with eyes closed) a single digit, sculpted out of wood. Then have your child repeat this number silently for about a minute. When distracting thoughts emerge during this exercise, simply instruct your child to watch them "flow downstream like a leaf traveling down a river."

• *Practice muscle relaxation*. A key principle in stress management is that anxiety and deep muscle relaxation cannot coexist. By deeply relaxing tense muscles, anxiety states can be reduced.

Autogenic training involves alternately tensing then relaxing. Try this with your youngster. With guidance even a four-year-old can follow. First, from a standing position, make a fist with your right hand. As you squeeze your fist shut, push your arm away from your body. Continue pushing and squeezing until you feel discomfort in your arm, then quickly release all tension and allow your arm to hang beside your body.

Notice how your hand and arm feel. Be aware that you can relax them even more. Allow your hand and arm to relax more deeply. Notice how that feels. Allow your hand to feel very heavy, even a little warm; now notice the difference between your right hand and arm and the left side. (To avoid muscle imbalance, use the same procedure on the left hand and arm.)

Progressive, whole-body relaxation is another technique, in which you try to relax the whole body (without tensing) starting with the feet and progressing up to the jaws by major body sections: feet, ankles, legs, hips, stomach, chest, back, shoulders, neck, scalp, facial muscles, and jaws.

In guiding your youngster through relaxation exercises, it is helpful to "suggest" the desirable behavior. For example, "Relax your feet [ankles, legs, and so on]. Feel your muscles becoming loose, limp, heavy, and warm. Feel the warmth extend upward through your hips [stomach, chest, and so on]." Proceed slowly, pausing ten to fifteen seconds after each major body section. After about ten minutes of this, introduce a concentration exercise (like repeating a single digit), so children can reestablish their normal, focused consciousness.

• *Practice deep breathing.* There are many kinds of deep-breathing methods that also enhance relaxation and reduce tension. Instruct your child as follows: "Sit comfortably with both feet on the floor. Put your hands over your tummy as you breathe deeply. Let your tummy push out when you breathe in and pull in when you breathe out. Close your eyes and slowly breathe in, stomach out. Hold your breath to the count of four, and slowly breathe out. One. Two. Three. Four. [Be sure your child's chest cavity remains basically motionless, with only the abdomen moving in and out.] Imagine any worries or upset leaving your body through your arms and legs and your mouth as you breathe out. Breathe in through your nose and out through your mouth."

• *Remember good old-fashioned exercise!* Nothing helps release tension and anxiety better and promotes mental health at the same time. Don't push your toddler/preschooler into organized sports, however. That will just add to his or her stress. What's important is some kind of regular physical activity, particularly for youngsters who may be early, heavy readers or engaged in other highly cerebral pursuits much of the time. Simple calisthenics (jumping jacks, toe touching, and so on), bike riding, hopscotch, tag — the classic games of childhood — these are all good sources of exercise.

ENVIRONMENT   Environment, which forms the third leg of the stress management triangle, refers to those aspects of the child's life that make up the pervasive conditions, primarily at home, under which the child's biological, cognitive, and emotional growth are being nurtured. Here are some tips:

• *Encourage a stress-reducing diet.* Caffeine and excessive sugar intake induce tension. Therefore, encourage children to limit (if not eliminate) consumption of food with these substances. (See the section on nutrition later in this chapter.)

• *Allow the "space" for daydreaming.* And for relaxation, doing nothing, and even just being alone. Build leisure into your child's life and yours. Curb the need to be accomplishing something every minute. Cultivate respect for a slower pace. Encourage your child to pursue a hobby of his or her choosing. Make sure you take family vacations.

• *Respect your child's heightened sensitivities.* Helping gifted children both deal with and respond to their emotions and sensitivity to certain global, "adult" issues takes a special effort. Ferner and Heck insist that such things must be addressed on the *child's* level, so that the seemingly enormous and insurmountable burden is lifted. For example, if a child is especially sensitive to world hunger, help him or her find an outlet for such "caring" that is concrete — such as contributing some allowance money to an appropriate cause or delivering food baskets to the local needy.

• *Be a role model.* Probably the most important thing to remember in a stress management program is to model the relaxed behaviors you're trying to cultivate in your youngster. Stress is very contagious. Your nonverbal behaviors (rushing, always seeming pressed for time, being impatient) will affect your child more than your assuring "Relax, don't worry." Here's a clear case where actions speak louder than words.

For more on stress management, get a copy of *Stress Management in Gifted Education* (see "Additional Resources" at the end of this chapter).

ENVIRONMENT AND NUTRITION: TWO IMPORTANT VARIABLES

When performance or behavior is affected in perfectly intelligent children (sluggishness, hyperactivity, diminished memory, for example), that should be as much a red flag to parents as is a high fever: something is wrong and the search begins. Is it nutrition? Is it allergies? Is it stress? It it vision function? Is it a poor and unhealthy environment at school, with a teacher, with peers, or at home? Below you will find discussions of some leading issues having to do with your child's mental and physical health, nutrition, and safety.

Lead in Blood Lowers Kids' IQs

The toxic effects of high lead levels in children's blood are well documented, but chronic low levels may be even worse, according to a report in *Family Practice News*. One problem is that low levels can go undetected as well as untreated, causing severe long-term consequences that, once they emerge, appear to be irreversible.

This information was presented by Sandra Shaheen, of Children's Hospital Medical Center in Boston, at a symposium sponsored by the New England Consortium of Childhood Lead Poisoning Programs.

A study of children with chronic, low-level lead poisoning, Shaheen said, disclosed IQ scores 2 to 10 points lower than those of similar children without lead poisoning. This included children who were exposed prenatally. Other problems surfaced, too: deficits in verbal processing, poor reaction time in fine-motor tasks, delays in visual-motor integration, distractibility, and lack of concentration in school.

SPECIFIC EFFECTS ON DEVELOPMENTAL STATES   The age a child is exposed to lead also has a bearing on its toxic effects, Shaheen explained. Children exposed before age two scored lowest on tests of linguistic skills. Those between two and three years old had problems with perceptual and spatial tasks. After three years old, no specific problems were found, but Shaheen believes that some problems will surface eventually.

Sources of lead in the environment include paint, some art supplies, leaded gasoline, lead solder used with copper pipes, lead-lined water fountains in schools and other public places, and even dust in some older homes. Lead paint might be found in old buildings that have not been renovated. The U.S. Environmental Protection Agency has yet to ban leaded gasoline as it had contemplated doing years ago when then-EPA-director William D. Ruckelshaus stated emphatically that high levels of lead in automobile emissions lower IQ.

FREEWAYS: THE LEAD POISON CONNECTION   Mary Meeker, a clinical psychologist and cofounder of Structure of the Intellect (SOI) Systems in Vida, Oregon, urges further caution. Meeker says:

> Although this condition [lead poisoning] is rare, at the SOI Testing Center for Gifted we saw four cases among gifted children during the period of 1974–1980. They all exhibited increasing, unaccountable lethargy [in] all activities — even those they loved. In our total assessment battery, when we measured six different kinds of memory, their scores were much lower than previously tested.

When referred for medical analyses, each of these children was found to have high blood levels of lead. Not only did they exhibit poor memory function and lethargy, but the coloring of hair and skin in two of the children was fading. Immediate medical treatment was instituted. "The only commonality we could identify," Meeker says, "was that all of these children lived within sight of major freeways," where vehicular exhaust is the major source of lead air pollution.

BE AWARE: RISKS OF DELEADING   Further cautions must be taken by parents who have leaded paint removed from their homes, a process called "deleading." If done improperly, the procedure can actually make the situation worse by putting lead-paint particles into the air, causing irritability and vomiting in children, and increasing the level of lead in children's blood.

Researchers at Boston's Children's Hospital urge parents to keep their children out of the home during deleading and to be sure that residual dust is thoroughly removed before reoccupying their home. Writing in *The American Journal of Disease of Children,* the researchers point out that while deleading carries some risks, it is a necessary health measure.

You Are What You Eat

Robert Rodale, editor of *Prevention* magazine, has stated: "We know that children will grow in a home where nutrition is low in quality. But they will not become healthy, resilient, energetic individuals with well-functioning intelligence unless their diet is full of nutrients."

The Structure of the Intellect Institute, which tests hundreds of gifted children each year for intellectual functioning, takes these words very seriously. The institute has compiled the "SOI Diet for Learning" on the premise that physical and mental health are closely related.

If this sounds like the ancient Greek notion, it is — but with modern scientific evidence to back it up. "We have seen over and over again," the SOI Institute states, "negative results from chemical/packaged foods that suggest pollutants and allergies cause hyperactivity and learning problems in children. When children who cannot sit still long enough to learn or play without fighting are placed on diets *free* of additives, sugar, and preservatives, their learning abilities improve dramatically."

Children's allergic reactions to certain foods and pollutants can be subtle and can often go undetected. Persons trained to administer the SOI test battery look for symptoms of allergic reactions that can affect a student's attention, concentration, and eye-hand coordination. The villain foodstuffs are well known and include products containing sugar; caffeine; white bread; preservatives, additives, and dyes; salt; and fried foods.

Too Much Sugar May Put Kids to Sleep!

Is sugar harmful to the body or not? Does it cause hyperactivity and behavioral outbursts in children?

No, according to *NEA Today*, the official newspaper of the National Education Association. A substantial body of new research on nutrition apparently has determined that sugar by itself does not cause hyperactivity, nor does it trigger hyperactive episodes in children. In fact sugar, a carbohydrate, stimulates the brain to produce serotonin, a chemical that hinders aggression and promotes sleep.

The real nutritional culprit among school-age children seems to be iron deficiency, the paper reports. Researchers at Penn State's Nutrition Education Center found that 66 percent of the nation's students receive less than half of the recommended daily iron dosage. And this *does* affect learning: "The adverse impact of iron deficiency on academic performance has been amply documented. Studies show that iron deficiency decreases motivation, impedes concentration, and impairs judgment."

CURB SUGAR INTAKE   All this doesn't mean that "junk food junkies" are off the hook. Too much sugar, coupled with insufficient protein, can cause a child to become "bloated with carbohydrates carrying 'empty' calories." The result of this protein/carbohydrate imbalance is increased serotonin and decreased alertness.

So, what's the solution? The sage advice is as old as it is . . . er, palatable: Eat a *balanced* diet. Today this means complex carbohydrates with fiber, moderate amounts of protein, and as little fat as possible.

And for that nutritious snack that provides *steady* energy without the ups and downs of a sugar fix — try unsalted peanuts.

Below are some of the SOI Institute's guidelines for proper eating and nutrition, condensed from a variety of sources. Many are foods high in iron.

- *Seeds, nuts, and grains* — eaten raw and unsalted, sprouted, or lightly cooked
- *Vegetables* — fresh, eaten raw, steamed, or baked, with as much garlic and onion as you can stand (dark leafy green vegetables are high in iron)
- *Fruits* — fresh or dried, lightly steamed
- *Proteins* — fresh broiled fish, shellfish, poached eggs, yogurt, unprocessed cheese (vitamin and mineral supplements are also recommended)

To get more detailed information on the "SOI Diet for Learning," write to SOI Systems (see "Additional Resources" at the end of this chapter).

Select Foods for Power Thinking

Choosing the right lunch before your child's active afternoon can make a big difference in how he or she performs. According to an article by Linda Heller in *Success,* certain foods can fire up your mind.

Look over the two menus below. Which is more typical of the executive lunch or, with a few modifications, the school lunchroom? Which is the better lunch for power thinking throughout the afternoon?

Menu A
hamburger on white roll
french fries
ketchup
pickle slices
chocolate milk
pudding/cake/pie

Menu B
fresh vegetable salad
baked fish/chicken
rice or baked potato
fruit juice/milk
fresh fruit

You are right — and are attuned to our nutritionally conscious times — if you said menu A is the more typical lunch, but menu B is the one to have for meeting the afternoon's challenges.

According to Judith Wurtman, a research scientist at MIT and the author of *Managing Your Mind and Mood through Food*, it's the chemicals dopamine, norepinephrine, and serotonin that enable the brain cells to send messages. In general, Wurtman says, high-protein foods — such as chicken, veal, and fish — supply the materials to produce dopamine and norepinephrine ("alertness chemicals"), and carbohydrates provide the building blocks for serotonin (a "calming chemical"). Wurtman gives some tips on eating for power thinking:

- *Stay away from high-fat foods.* The hamburger on menu A is loaded with fat (which is difficult to digest), not to mention cholesterol. Avoid serving excess pork, processed lunch meats, organ meats, and hard cheese also.
- *Plan your timing.* Serve young children a small, low-fat meal two hours before a big afternoon activity. For example, have two ounces of lean, skinless chicken; a cup of clear soup, vegetables, or a salad with light dressing; half a cup of rice or a small baked potato. Young children's appetites usually aren't very big, so small portions are fine — it's the balance that's important.
- *Don't start with carbohydrates.* Rolls, pasta, and the like will make your child drowsy. If you serve one of those items *after* the low-fat protein, your child will feel less lethargic.
- *Include variety.* Shellfish, smoked salmon, and tofu are other good sources of low-fat protein. Avoid deep-fried foods; instead have meat or fish baked, broiled, roasted, lightly sautéed, or poached.
- *Include fresh vegetables and fruits.* Steamed or raw vegetables and raw fruits are high in fiber and fill kids up without a lot

of excess calories or empty carbohydrates. Avoid deep-fried vegetables and french fries. Try some herbed rice or a small, lightly seasoned baked potato.

But what about lunch when your youngster goes to school? You don't have much control over what's served in the school cafeteria, but bag lunches can provide good nutrition and variety. Granted, it's a tough chore, but try to keep the basic principles in mind. Avoid high-fat foods; go for the low-fat proteins and plenty of fresh fruits and vegetables, unsugared juices, and milk. And if your child is "brown-bagging," have him or her help you select some good lunch items at the grocery. Be daring! Try whole wheat and rye bread, pocket bread, dark rolls; don't forget sliced turkey, tuna fish, and lean beef as alternatives to peanut butter and jelly.

A WORD OF CAUTION   With young children (up to age five), we must be careful not to assume that what's good for adults is good for little ones.

Fima Lifshitz, a pediatrician at Cornell University Medical College, and coworkers report that some health-conscious parents are inadvertently starving their youngsters by imposing low-fat diets and feeding them skim milk and raw vegetables rather than high-energy foods they need.

Dietary fat — like that found in whole and breast milk, fatty cheeses, cooking oils, and sweets such as cookies — is essential for the development of a healthy brain and nervous system.

High intelligence is a function of many environmental variables, not the least of which is diet. Apparently the way to a person's brain — as well as heart — is through the stomach!

One further caveat regarding nutrition: Claims that certain diets can increase your child's IQ score a specific number of points are at this time unsubstantiated. Consult your child's pediatrician for individual dietary needs.

ATTENTION DEFICIT DISORDER (ADD): A SPECIAL PROBLEM

"Gifted children are not immune to hyperactivity, learning disabilities, and what's called 'Attention Deficit Disorder,' " says John

Roth, a pediatrician and clinical assistant at the University of Louisville who has seen many children with ADD in his private practice. Various studies show that children of all intellectual levels may be affected, with an overall incidence of 5 to 15 percent. Boys are affected more than girls: several studies cite prevalence in ratios of 3:1 to 6:1. Occasionally the disorder is missed as the gifted child is called "bored."

Moreover, the frustration caused by this syndrome may be accentuated in these children because they cannot harness their talents at will. Gifted children often are especially sensitive, and their self-esteem may suffer greatly.

What is ADD?

Previously called minimal brain dysfunction or hyperactive-child syndrome, ADD includes children with school learning difficulties characterized by disturbances in regulating attention and behavior. The symptoms of ADD occur early — especially in boys — and mask high abilities. Sometimes such children are labeled learning disabled when they enter school, and sometimes they are put on drugs before they are given a chance to "outgrow" the problem.

Current medical classification includes three subtypes: ADD *with* hyperactivity, characterized by inattention and impulsiveness; ADD *without* hyperactivity; and ADD-Residual, which describes adolescents or young adults who were hyperactive when younger, but no longer exhibit significant hyperactivity.

Theoretically, ADD involves problems in the transmission of messages in the brain via chemicals called neurotransmitters. This is believed to be the case based on the biochemistry of these substances and the beneficial effects of certain stimulant drugs — such as dextroamphetamine sulfate (Dexedrine) and methylphenidate (Ritalin) — in treating the disorder.

How Is ADD Diagnosed?

The major symptoms of ADD include inattention, impulsiveness, and hyperactivity. A careful history of the child's behavior provides clues to the diagnosis. Three key questions are

- If the child is already in school, how is he or she doing?
- How does the child get along with peers?
- How does the child get along with authority figures?

Answers to these questions will show whether the child is easily distracted, confuses details, does not complete work, is excitable, disruptive, talkative, loud, can't wait his turn, is always on the go, or is fidgety. Normal children ordinarily don't display these behaviors to the same degree. They are able to sit still, pay attention, and control their impulses.

These characteristics, coupled with results on psychological tests that reveal a discrepancy between chronological age and mental age and a higher verbal IQ than performance IQ, strongly suggest the diagnosis. In several studies, nearly 92 percent of hyperactive children have been found to have a specific learning disability.

It is important for the physician to rule out disabilities such as mental retardation, cerebral palsy and seizures, allergies, deafness, or chronic fluid in the ears, as well as psychiatric disorders such as autism and childhood schizophrenia. Such conditions may mimic all or part of the ADD syndrome.

How Is ADD Treated?

The most successful treatment of this disorder requires a multifaceted approach involving the family, the school, the pediatrician, the child psychologist, and occasionally a child psychiatrist.

THE FAMILY   First of all, the family must understand the disorder and realize that there is no easy cure. Supporting the child with praise, emphasizing positive aspects of his or her personality, and building self-esteem are crucial to success in treatment and to long-term educational and social progress.

THE SCHOOL   The school must provide an educational plan that provides a structured environment, eliminates distractions, and modifies the curriculum for the child. In addition, the teacher, understanding the child's condition, can legitimize the child's need for "hyper" activity by having him or her help pass supplies or collect papers, and by avoiding excessive disciplinary action in class. The teacher must provide gifted children who are affected by ADD with challenging activities in short time segments in order to avoid boredom and lack of concentration in these students. Good supervision is a key to success here.

THE PSYCHOLOGIST   The psychologist can suggest techniques of behavior modification for use at home and in school, and can assist in counseling the child and family as they deal with the emotional effects this condition produces. Children with ADD can produce conflict at home, and this can lead to parental discord, sibling rivalry, and a deepening of the child's low self-esteem.

THE PEDIATRICIAN   The physician can provide medical therapy for some of these children. Stimulant medications (amphetamines) have been shown to provide significant improvement in 70 to 80 percent of afflicted children. The most commonly used drugs are Ritalin, Dexedrine, and Cylert. Positive effects have been documented in behavioral, social, and perceptual performance, as well as in motor activity (including fine motor, such as handwriting), impulse control, and attention regulation.

With supportive therapy and medication, academic skills and cognitive performance can be improved. By breaking the circle of disruptive behavior, inattention, and secondary emotional trauma to the child, stimulants help create a less stressful atmosphere that makes the child more receptive to learning, more successful in the academic environment, and more self-accepting.

SAFETY TIP:
TEACH YOUR CHILD TO SURVIVE WHEN LOST

Nevada County, California, deputies found four-year-old Elijah Fordham conversing with a log. Rescuers looked for the boy after he had lost his way from Marin Sierra Boy Scout camp twenty-three hours earlier. Eli turned to his rescuers and said, "What took you so long?"

The preschooler had followed the advice from a presentation called "Hug-A-Tree" (HAT): instead of trying to find his way back, he stayed in one place.

Eli was lucky. Apparently, unbeknownst to anyone, he had been paying attention to the advice being offered his brother's Cub Scout pack. "I had no idea he was listening," said his mother, Patricia. "He was fidgety and in and out of the room."

Jimmy Beveridge was not so lucky. It took more than four hundred volunteers five days scouring Palomar Mountain in San Diego County before they found the nine-year-old youngster: he was dead — having walked out of one of his shoes and stripped off his jacket in the cold rain and fog.

Like the Mythical Phoenix

Jimmy Beveridge's death in 1981 was the impetus for the HAT program. "If Jimmy hadn't died, Hug-A-Tree wouldn't have been born," muses Ab Taylor, an expert tracker who found both Jimmy and Eli. Since Jimmy's death, HAT has grown considerably. A slide presentation on basic survival skills in the outdoors has been shown to more than 200,000 San Diego children in over 200 schools. Programs now exist in at least 30 states and in Canada, France, and Sweden.

According to Taylor, as many as 200 children are lost each year in California alone. (National statistics are unavailable.) He says many people don't know survival techniques because our society has evolved several generations beyond an era in which such techniques were essential. The HAT program, born as it was from a tragic event, is an attempt to educate children and the community on how to increase children's chances for survival in the wilderness.

And it's working. HAT boasts a good number of success stories, and as Taylor exults: "It's the greatest thing I've been associated with. The most gratifying thing is to look for a little lost kid, and after twenty hours find him or her alive."

"It Can't Happen to My Kid"

"No one ever expects his or her child to get lost," Taylor says, but that doesn't keep it from happening. The HAT slide show pictures a young boy who goes camping and gets lost while following a bird — the result of a child's natural curiosity and fascination with nature.

HAT tries to raise adult's and children's awareness of the circumstances that usually surround getting lost, as well as instill some commonsense precautions and steps to take if it does happen. For example, the most "obvious" thing young children try to do when they're lost in the wilderness — find their way back — is wrong and life-threatening. As Sheriff Lieutenant Walt Petrosky said in the *San Diego Union* at the time of Jimmy's search, "A person can cover a mile, two miles or even three in an hour. The searchers are going to be moving in the same direction. If you're moving, it turns into a very tough footrace."

Another ironic factor that increases the problems of a search is that children often will hide from their rescuers. Taylor believes the reason for this is that children are taught not to talk to strangers.

Survival Tips for Parents and Children

First and foremost, experts say parents should tell their children they will not be punished if they should ever get lost. Fear of punishment will only add to the child's mental confusion. Other tips:

- Have your children wear bright clothing on a camping trip or in other environments where they can get lost. They will be seen more easily.
- If lost, children should stand in an open space to make themselves "big" or visible to rescuers and helicopters. If they've taken shelter from heavy rain or snow, high winds, and so on, they should still listen and look for rescuers and return to the open space if they hear someone or when the weather breaks.
- Parents should report lost children *immediately*. Bad weather can wipe out tracks that can lead to the child. Don't worry about false alarms.
- *Before* venturing out, make a shoeprint of the shoes your child will be wearing. (A footprint can save a tracker eight hours.) Here's how: Place a towel flatly on the floor or ground and place a piece of tinfoil on top of the towel. Have your child step firmly on the tinfoil. Keep a record of these and the clothes your child is wearing.
- *Before* venturing out, make sure your child is carrying a whistle. A person's voice tires easily and can't be heard as far away as a whistle.

• *Before* venturing out, make sure your child is carrying a large plastic bag with a hole cut out of the bottom for his or her head. This can be worn to help keep the child dry and warm. (Caution: Don't give a young child a plastic bag without first cutting a hole in it and explaining that it should never be used as a mask.)

The HAT program teaches children that rescuers will be on the way, so they should stay put. "If they stay where they are, in one place," Taylor advises, "they have friends who will look for them and they will be found."

And the program teaches confidence. Says Taylor: "The best survival tool is your brain."

To get more information on starting HAT presentations in your area, write to HAT (see "Additional Resources" at the end of this chapter).

SAYING NO FOR SAFETY'S SAKE

Each year, in too many of America's preschools and public schools, children are being asked to perform custodial tasks that end in serious or fatal injury to unsuspecting youngsters. TVs have toppled from audiovisual carts onto children; others have been crushed by cafeteria tables. Under the guise of "teaching students how to be responsible," assigning inappropriate tasks is the rule, not the exception. Unfortunately, only when privilege turns to tragedy do we step back and examine such folly — and by then, it is too late.

The Gifted Child: Vulnerable to Danger

School safety is (or should be) a concern of *all* parents, students, and teachers. But gifted children should be the focus of special attention in this regard. For many reasons, they may be more susceptible than most to potential school hazards.

Consider this: Who gets to be the teacher's helpers? Usually, it is the model students, the trusted ones, upon whom teachers rely. Unfortunately, parents and teachers can forget that these kids are just kids. That's why it is vital for adults to be aware of the dangers inherent in having children engage in duties that require the physical dexterity that develops only with age.

Examining the "Enriched" Environment

What are some common examples of possible safety hazards in the preschool classroom?

- *Televisions and videotape recorders and the stands on which they rest.* Even a TV that is bolted to its cart can be unsafe; in at least two separate instances, children died when the entire TV cart toppled over.
- *Electrical connections for computer terminals, especially in older schools with dated wiring.* As one audiovisual specialist said, a major problem is the removal by students of the safety or ground wire from the three-pronged plugs on his AV equipment.

Even tried-and-true materials designed to make classrooms more intriguing and enticing must be examined for possible hazards. For example, an aluminum-hooded aquarium, donated by a well-meaning parent, might prove lethal if equipped with a frayed cord or placed too near a source of electrical voltage.

And what about stoves or other cooking equipment — how accessible are these appliances to the hands of inquisitive little children who might be wary of such devices in a kitchen but not a classroom?

And don't forget about field trips: Does any adult accompanying the children on a nature hike have the knowledge to handle first-aid emergency more severe than a cut finger?

The Classroom: A Haven for Knowledge and Safety

There are many ways parents can help their children as well as their youngsters' teachers to become more safety-conscious. Here are some ways to begin:

- *Do not allow your child to move audiovisual equipment — period.* Tell your child that he or she has the *right* to say no and should say no if a teacher makes such a request.
- *Write a note to your preschool's supervisor or teacher indicating that your child is not to perform custodial tasks.* Moving cafeteria tables, heavy gym equipment, or pianos may be done under the guise of "teaching responsibility," but, in fact, the underlying reason is virtually always one of expediency or convenience.

• *Determine who is the main safety officer in your child's school.* Ask if teachers are aware of — and whether they implement — existing safety regulations. What form of sanctions or other consequences await school personnel who violate this code? Also, what provisions are made so that substitute teachers and parent volunteers understand and implement the safety code?

• *Sponsor a puppet production on school safety with the combined efforts of students, teachers, and parents.* Make sure it is shown to primary-aged children as well as preschoolers. Perhaps the gifted-education teacher can serve as the coordinator of this show.

ADDITIONAL RESOURCES

American Health Magazine: Fitness of Body and Mind. American Health Partners, 80 Fifth Ave., New York, NY 10011.

Attention Deficit Disorder (ADD). Digest 1987, no. 445. ERIC Clearinghouse on Handicapped and Gifted Children, Council for Exceptional Children, 1920 Association Dr., Reston, VA 22091.

Child Health Alert: A Monthly Survey of Current Developments Affecting Child Health. P.O. Box 338, Newton Highlands, MA 02161.

Feed Your Kids Bright, by Francine Prince and Harold Prince, Ph.D. Simon and Schuster, 1987.

Feed Your Kids Right, by Dr. Lendon Smith. Dell, 1982.

HAT presentations. Jacquie Heet, National Office, Hug-A-Tree, 6465 Lance Way, San Diego, CA 92127.

Managing Your Mind and Mood Through Food, by Judith Wurtman. Rawson Associates, 1986.

The Psychology of Cancer, by August de la Pena. Praeger, 1983.

Relaxation: A Comprehensive Manual for Adults, Children and Children with Special Needs, by J. Cautela and J. Groden. Research Press, 1978.

SOI Diet for Learning. SOI Systems, 45755 Goodpasture Rd., Vida, OR 97488.

Stress Management in Gifted Education, by Kim Stevens Smith. Document ED 253 037. ERIC Reports, 1984. ERIC Document

Reproduction Service, 3900 Wheeler Ave., Alexandria VA 22304-5110.

This is an annotated bibliography put out by the Educational Resources Information Center to examine the nature and effects of stress on gifted children. A separate chapter summarizes recommendations and suggestions for dealing with stress.

The Superbaby Scourge:
Walking the Tightrope between
Pushing and Encouraging

ALTHOUGH early childhood education is really still in its infancy, there have been sporadic growth spurts over the last few decades. Freud's "sensual" child, requiring nurturing of the emotional dimension, a view popularized by Benjamin Spock in the mid-1940s, took root in the suburbs a decade later. There, as reflected in TV's portrayal of middle-class family life, Mom stayed home for the good of the kids.

The social revolution of the 1960s, coupled with President Lyndon Johnson's dream of the "Great Society," gave birth to the Head Start program, which was the first large-scale study to validate the effects of a stimulating environment on children's IQs. It was really this concept applied to all children — not just disadvantaged kids — that saw "superbaby" born in the 1970s. This chapter takes a look at this latest trend from the point of view of the parent-child relationship. (Chapter 6 discusses it from the institutional side — day care and preschool.)

For several years now, the superbaby phenomenon has grown and spread throughout the United States. Thousands upon thousands of high-achievement-oriented parents are seeing to it that their children crawl and toddle in designer diapers, fine-tune their gross motor coordination at gyms for tots, appreciate classical music (and even play it!) at the age of two, and attend a top nursery school with a view toward a top college.

For all its sensationalized aspects, this phenomenon does reflect a general acknowledgement of the advances in knowledge of early childhood development, and it does reinstate the value of the intellect in our society. But it's a phenomenon that has gone awry. Also reflected is insecurity and a lack of confidence in our educational system, along with a fear of children being ill-prepared for an uncertain future, and a feeling that parents must take things into their own hands by buying every possible advantage and edge for the child during the formative years.

Many parents are doing more than just encouraging their children to explore diverse avenues of experience and introducing them to a host of options through which they can discover themselves. They're pushing their kids every which way, for mostly the wrong reasons. Early childhood educators are concerned that such parents may produce results opposite from what they intend. Their children may turn off to learning and become underachievers.

READY AT DIFFERENT AGES

Educators, rather consistently, have opposed accelerating childhood. Typical of the reasoning from the school viewpoint is an article in *Principal* by Don Friesen, principal of an elementary school in Fairview, Oklahoma. "The desire of parents to have their children read early is a good example of parental pressure to have children grow up too fast generally," he writes. "This pressure reflects parental need, not the child's need or inclination." Friesen cites considerable research to support his view that children are ready to learn at different ages and that there are emotional costs to pushing children to learn too early.

Even for children who seem more than ready to take on intellectual activities, most researchers advise a go-slow attitude on the part of parents. Several experts were quoted on this in the *New York Times*. "Children learn for the same reason that birds fly," said Edward Zigler, professor of psychology at Yale University. "They're programmed to learn, and they do it beautifully. You can't stop children from learning — and you certainly don't have to push them to."

Echoing Zigler's comments was Jerome Kagan, professor of psychology at Harvard University. Just because the new research shows children's extraordinary ability to learn, "it just doesn't follow at all that we need to cram more things into a child," he said. He acknowledged that some children thrive under pressure, but if the pressure is disturbing a child and making him or her anxious, parents should ease up and delay the "classic rat race."

CHILDREN AT RISK FOR NO GOOD REASON!

We are unnecessarily taking risks with our children. That's the crux of the "miseducation" of preschoolers and schoolchildren alike, according to David Elkind, Tufts University professor and author of *The Hurried Child: Growing Up Too Fast Too Soon* and *The Miseducation of Children: Preschoolers at Risk*. Elkind spoke at a conference cosponsored by the Gifted Child Society, the Gifted Children Advocacy Association (the philanthropic division of *Gifted Children Monthly*), and the Upper Saddle River (New Jersey) Board of Education.

"Early exposure to academic programs and formal learning is just not working," according to Elkind. Rather than accelerating children's intellectual growth, he said, pushing children too much, too soon, is causing wide-scale psychological damage and stress. The accumulated effects of this on society are seen in the rising statistics on childhood depression, aggressive behavior, eating disorders, substance abuse, teen pregnancy, and suicide, Elkind noted.

Where Are the Markers?

The markers that delineate childhood are gone. The way we are "hurrying" children, Elkind said, is by removing those traditional benchmarks of growth and development by which children "know their place and what's appropriate and inappropriate. . . . While we're aware of many more stages of adulthood, we're taking them away in childhood. This is what's leading to stress."

Some of the markers Elkind referred to involve clothing, school activities, and sports. Take clothing, for example. Elkind contended that dressing kids in designer duds from kiddie boutiques builds an arrogant yet burdensome "sense of entitlement" in children. "By adolescence they come to expect these things and other material benefits without working for them," Elkind said, implying that this sense of entitlement destroys motivation and incentive.

School activities once reserved for older kids — such as reading, traditionally taught in first grade — are being pushed on preschoolers and toddlers, sometimes with great difficulty and enormous stress on the child. Elkind cited Jean Piaget's "concrete-operations" stage of child development, which occurs between ages four and six, as ideally suited to learning the basic concepts required for reading. Forcing a child to read before he or she is developmentally ready "is stressful and ignores children's limitations and strengths," Elkind said.

His problem with sports activities for children is that they are too organized and too risky, physically, for the very young child whose musculature and bone structure have not yet developed fully. In addition, Elkind believes that organized sports introduce children to competition at an inappropriate age and take time away from spontaneous play. He says that spontaneous play — in which children make and break their own rules — best facilitates the evolution of mutual and self-respect.

The "Adultified" Child

Elkind claims that our society is, on the one hand, ignoring the powerful impact the media has in creating images that children internalize and, on the other, destroying the traditional markers between childhood and adulthood. He said that children "are portrayed in adult roles increasingly, and young kids do believe what they see."

In many ways, Elkind subscribes to the "less-is-more" school of thought. He advised that the appropriate parental role is to support, to encourage, to follow the child's lead — but never to push. "What's important is a rich intellectual environment," Elkind said, "a family that reads together, asks questions. This kind of intellectual broth is more critical than teaching a child particular skills." He said that sending children to special programs is OK, as long as the programs are age-appropriate and don't involve high pressure to achieve.

(In the following section, Elkind shares more of his ideas and focuses on the needs of the young gifted child.)

SELF-DIRECTED LEARNING IS BEST
An Essay by David Elkind

There is a story told about Mozart: An aspiring young composer came to Mozart and asked him for some advice about how to write a symphony. Mozart suggested to the young man that perhaps he might begin with a less ambitious project. To this the aspiring composer replied, "But *you* wrote your first symphony when you were nine years old." To which Mozart replied, "True enough, but I did not have to ask how!"

Mozart's response is perhaps as good a test as any of exceptional talent and precocity. Truly talented or gifted children usually do not ask how to write, or how to draw, or how to sing, or how to compose; they just do it. No one taught Steven Spielberg how to make films; he just began making them on his own when he was a child. Barbra Streisand put on musical plays for her family and friends even before she had reached her teens.

These anecdotes are supported by more systematic research. In two recent studies of gifted and talented people who have attained eminence, the majority showed evidence of their gifts in early childhood. As young children, the nascent musicians gravitated to the piano and simply picked out tunes, the budding mathematicians were fascinated by numbers, the young scientists were endlessly curious.

The parents of these youngsters were mainly concerned that their children did not pursue their special interests to the exclusion of other activities. While they encouraged and supported their children's inclinations, they also made sure their children played with other children, performed routine household chores, and participated in family activities.

Driven from Within

Exceptional talents and abilities seem to carry with them their own drive for realization — what I call the "structural imperative" — and there is really no need for external pressure to get children to find and pursue their "vein." What the parents of children with exceptional talent have to be concerned about is not pushing but its opposite, *restraining*. Such children have to be encouraged to acquire the basic set of social and academic skills and not devote all of their time and energy to the realization of their special talents or gifts to the exclusion of everything else.

All children manifest the structural imperative at those periods in development when major new systems of mental ability are emerging. Jean Piaget has provided ample evidence of these major stages of intellectual development. Recent brain research gives evidence that there are "spurts" of brain growth at just the age periods Piaget says are devoted to the construction of new systems of mental ability.

One of these periods [mentioned earlier] is the early childhood era from four to six years when children attain what Piaget calls *concrete operations* that enable them to engage in syllogistic reasoning and to quantify their experience. During this period the structural imperative is operative for all normal children. At this time children seek out the kind of stimuli that will nourish and give expression to their emerging abilities. For example, young children are very partial to tales like "The Three Little Pigs" and "Goldilocks and the Three Bears" because, at least in part, such stories are replete with quantitative terms and comparisons that provide nourishment for their emerging quantitative skills.

Be a Matchmaker, Not an Instructor

When you guide your young child by the structural imperative, there is no need to "teach" him or her how to acquire quantitative thinking, reasoning, and so on. Children will construct these abilities on their own if they are surrounded by the appropriate stimuli.

At the same time, just as a child with a structural imperative for music will be deprived if there are no musical instruments or music in the home, the child developing concrete operations will be deprived if there are no materials for classifying, ordering, matching, and counting in his or her environment.

Providing your child with developmentally and individually appropriate materials, however, is often not enough. In this regard you serve as a kind of *matchmaker* who not only finds materials to match your child's emerging abilities, but who also introduces him or her to the materials and suggests their special properties. If it is a good match, you can leave the child to proceed on his or her own with only occasional suggestions or guidance. When you try to be an *instructor*, to set specific tasks to be accomplished by specific points in time, you function more as an intrusive in-law rather than a matchmaker.

There are risks involved in being overly intrusive when young children are following their structural imperative. Psychologist Erik Erikson says children are resolving the psychosocial "crisis" of initiative versus guilt during the same time period in which Piaget says they are acquiring concrete operations. If children are matched up with appropriate materials and are allowed to follow the dictates of the structural imperative, they acquire a healthy sense of initiative — the ability to undertake a project and bring it to completion entirely on their own.

In contrast, if you are overly intrusive and give your child too many directions and limits as to the use of materials, the child's sense of initiative is blunted. Instead, you may enhance his or her sense of guilt — the feeling that there is something wrong with initiating explorations and taking responsibility. While a certain amount of guilt is a necessary counterpoint to a too-strong sense of initiative, the risk is that the child's sense of guilt will overwhelm the sense of initiative.

What sorts of experiences and materials might be best for a young child of exceptional talent or intellectual gifts? The "secret" in this regard is suggested by the "secret" of successful aging. As a wise older person told me once, "the formula for successful aging is not to stop doing anything you are doing but just to do it a little less."

With gifted and talented youngsters, I think the opposite is a good maxim: We should do a little more — not in a pure quantitative sense necessarily, but as a lateral expansion of what's good for all young children. We read to them a little more, discuss matters more, go to museums more, give them more complex books than we might do with children closer to the norm. In this way we recognize the child's speciality, but also his or her commonalities with all children.

Recognize and Ease Stress

Children are no strangers to stress. Just like adults, they can encounter excessive demands for adaptation to difficult situations. In most cases, these demands are mediated by parents. For example, when parents do not get along and are constantly quarreling, this is stressful for children. Such quarreling is a threat to the child's sense of security and requires adaptation.

Children who are in overly academic out-of-home settings on a regular basis also become stressed. High-pressure academic programs tend to increase rather than buffer (as healthy early education programs do) the stress of separation from parents. When parents enroll young children in too many programs of instruction, this can be stressful. Young children who are competing in beauty contests, in tennis, or in soccer may become stressed, because they often do not have sufficient reserves of self-esteem to deal with not winning. In addition, many television programs can create stress in children directly by presenting them with images of adult cruelty and violence.

Although the stresses of early childhood are comparable for both boys and girls, there is some evidence of sex differences in the way young children respond to stress. Boys are more likely than girls to act out their stress by fighting, aggressive play, and overt rebellion against adults. Boys are more likely than girls to show the effects of stress immediately, whereas for girls the effects may not be observed until the child reaches adolescence.

Because girls are more likely to deal with stress internally, the impact may be disguised or may appear as "sleeper" effects at later points in development. For example, young women who show eating disorders in adolescence are routinely found to have been "good" girls who were obedient and excessively concerned with pleasing their parents as children.

The early childhood period is an important one for all children, because it is the time during which youngsters attain their long-term attitudes toward learning, schooling, and themselves. For gifted and talented children, as for children closer to the academic norm, the most important thing you can do is to recognize that much of the learning at this age is self-directed, and that you help children most by serving as a matchmaker between them and significant materials and experiences.

TEMPERING OVERBEARING PERSONALITY TRAITS

Sometimes parents can be just too much to bear for gifted children! That's the view of Carolyn McGuffog, instructor in pediatrics and chief clinician at the Gifted Child Clinic, Rutgers (New Jersey) Medical School.

Writing in an issue of *Pediatric Annals*, McGuffog describes four parental personality types — parenting *styles*, really — that can cause or exacerbate problems in gifted youngsters. Take a look at them and, wherever possible, try to temper any overbearing tendencies that you may have with a more moderate approach. You and your child will be much happier for it.

1. *The Overly Critical Parent:* Such a parent imposes highly unrealistic expectations on the gifted child, says McGuffog, and consequently, the child may feel he or she can never live up to those expectations. She says such parents must learn to focus on the many positive aspects of their child's behavior.

2. *The Overly Dominating Parent:* Some gifted children come to feel that "they do not own their own giftedness," McGuffog states. Through assertiveness or manipulation, these parents dominate the child, and the child's decisions are based on the parents' needs and desires. "The child may feel that the parent loves only his or her special gifts, and not the child. As such, the fear of failure is tremendous, as it becomes equated with a loss of love." This is a difficult problem, she continues, because "it is likely the child is fulfilling unresolved psychological needs harbored by the parent." These parents must be made aware of the unfair burdens they are placing on their gifted child, McGuffog says.

3. *The Overly Conscientious Parent:* Parents should take their role seriously, McGuffog acknowledges, but an overly driven parent "very often fills every minute of the child's day with structured learning activities," thus denying the child "healthy, age-appropriate opportunities." She says parents need to see the value of unstructured time and self-initiated play with peers.

4. *The Overly Directive/Permissive Parent:* A parent who is overly invested in "teaching, challenging and testing the child" may forget to be "responsive, contingent, and to follow the child's lead." Although overly directive in play and verbal interactions, these parents are extremely lax — even uncomfortable — about setting limits and imposing discipline, usually with the excuse that they don't want to inhibit creativity. McGuffog advises such parents that a balance is best for the child, with the child leading in play, for example, and the parent pointing the way on what is acceptable and unacceptable behavior.

APPROPRIATE PRAISE: THE CORNERSTONE OF ENCOURAGEMENT

Have you ever been in this uncomfortable situation? One of your children, beaming with delight, shoves his drawing in front of you and proudly states, "Look what I made!" You look at his conflicting array of lines, scribbles, and colors that clash, wondering what it is. You keep staring and can't think of anything to say. If you ask what it is, you may hurt your child's feelings. Furthermore, you may convey the message that art must always be representative of reality.

Adults, particularly parents and teachers, critically influence a child's artistic and creative development. We do this directly by what we say about what they draw, write, or create. Though the kinds of comments and praise we adults give can make the difference between encouraging a child's creative impulses or nipping them in the bud, few of us give serious consideration to how we praise our children's artwork. A seemingly innocent comment may carry hidden messages that inhibit creative development.

Whether considering a child's early artwork or any other skill, activity, or behavior, a common mistake when applying praise is an error of focus: we praise the child instead of the act.

Witness the distinction in these two examples:

- "What a smart girl! Look at that report card!"
- "A report card with five A's and two B's shows real effort!"

In the first instance, evaluation of the child's work as reflected in her grades is secondary in emphasis to bestowing flattery upon the child. While this seems to be appropriate reinforcement, a child can come to associate her "smartness" and her "goodness" with her school performance. Consequently, if the next report card (or test, or footrace, or whatever) falls short of this present effort, "I am bad" can be the self-judgment.

The second statement lauds the act primarily, not its performer, which is the appropriate focus for a well-deserved tribute.

In Praise of Praise

Praising your child appropriately means offering the right kind of positive reinforcement, the kind that encourages growth, exploration, and discovery in your youngster, and joy in the process. The following ABCs of praise were developed by Stephen Jordan, a licensed psychologist from Winter Park, Florida.

- *Praise the process as well as the product.* A typical incident might involve a preschooler showing Mom a picture he or she has drawn. If the mother merely says how much she likes it, then hangs it up, ignored are the child's efforts, feelings, and thoughts that went into the picture. On the other hand, if you let a child know that you care about such things, he or she will glow with enthusiasm. (For example: "Tell me, Randy, how did you get this pretty color? By mixing two different colors together? Which ones?") Emphasis on *how* something is done can take pressure off a child overly concerned about *what* is done.
- *Emphasize the child's pleasure.* When a child draws a picture or performs some task or skill, it can bring pleasure to both child and parents. But the child's pleasure should be primary, as it guides the child's effort and helps him or her bring the effort to completion. Don't emphasize your own pleasure; this conditions children to perform according to others' expectations. Instead, offer comments like "I can see how pleased you are," or "You must be proud of yourself." Of course, follow these comments by "I sure am proud of you, too."
- *Doing the job is the reward.* If you've ever noticed the delight in the eyes of a child who has just learned how to ride a bike or has mastered a difficult word, you know you don't need to reward the effort with candy or money. In fact, adding something extrinsic to the achievement can serve to distract the child from enjoying the intrinsic satisfaction in mastering something. Praise can be used to help your child pause and reflect, verbalize about what went into the good performance, and reexperience the pleasure of a job well done.
- *Be specific when you praise.* Generally thanking your child for cleaning up his or her room is different, and more diffuse, than saying thanks for picking up the pencils, the books, and the other things scattered about. Detailed, specific praise shows that you really notice your child's efforts. It makes kids feel they've earned the right to be proud. Instead of "You are such a fantastic drawer," say: "I know how much time you

put into that picture and I'm not surprised those lines came out so straight."

Some More Do's and Don't's

Getting back to that young artist of yours — and most pre-schoolers are — here are a few more suggestions to help you encourage his or her artistic and creative activity with appropriate praise. Remember, also, that these examples can be applied generally to any of your child's activities or accomplishments.

- DON'T criticize the work by asking "Where's the sun?" or "Where is her other ear?" You'll be told that the sun is not shining or that she's only got one ear. ("What's the matter, Dad, can't you see?")
- DON'T deny the child's version of reality by saying "I never saw a red cow before," or "When did you ever see one?"
- DON'T ask what it is. They probably don't know.
- DON'T compare it to the work of another child, except in a nonjudgmental way. ("Okay, you made red circles. Billy made blue ones. I'm glad you both used the colors you liked.")
- DON'T ignore the work of art, hoping the child won't notice and will go away. The child will notice and will go away devastated.
- DO make a statement that is helpful, supportive, positive, and — above all — appropriate. You're helpful to your children's creative development when your comments focus on their needs — for attention, encouragement, self-exploration, and pride in their work. You're supportive and positive when you accept the drawings as they did them and say something complimentary. You're appropriate when your comments relate to the actual work done. A feeble "That's nice" will not suffice.

Here are some examples of effective comments:

- "Wow! I like the reds you used here."
- "These are very fine circles."
- "I like the way you made this line go up."
- "I like the off-center perspective."
- "This is certainly very colorful" (if there are many clashing colors).

- "I see you made good use of black" (if there is only one color).
- "I like the way you see things, draw, express yourself."
- "You must feel proud of this work."

Notice that no comment includes a negative. None implies that there is a right or wrong way to draw. The remarks are specific and appropriate. They do not label. If labels are to be applied, let the child do it. You should support the child's perceptions and taste as valid interpretations of reality and should encourage further creative expression.

In the accompanying drawing, for example, the child has combined "sea elements" and "sky elements" into one happy family. You might say: "I like the way you drew the sun and sky and fish and birds all living happily together." Not: "Why do you have the sun in the water? Why did you put a fish in the sky?"

Is all this really so important? Emphatically and unequivocally, yes! Adults should *not* try to mold a child's creativity; they should merely encourage its expression as the child desires. Consider how many inhibitors or blocks typical comments create for the child. To imply that items must be certain colors and have labels

by Jaimi Alvino

is to establish unnecessary rules. Such rules inhibit creative thinking! Furthermore, they teach the child that his or her perceptions must be similar to those of everyone else. In the end the child will draw simply to please others. All of this works against creative expression.

Displaying Work

There are two things to keep in mind about displaying family artwork. First, parents should set an example by displaying some of their own handiwork — whatever the medium. If you don't, two negative messages are transmitted to your child: "I'm not proud of anything I've done" and "It's immature for adults to take pride in their work — only kids do it."

Second, don't hang the child's work only on the refrigerator door. By engaging in this practice, you give your child the message that his or her work is second-rate. It goes in the kitchen. The quality work hangs on the wall of the family room or living room.

Adults exert a powerful influence on a child's creative development. We play a major role in determining whether our children will value and develop creative impulses or abandon and suppress this uniquely human aspect of intelligence.

ENCOURAGING LANGUAGE PROFICIENCY

Talking to your baby right from birth may be one of the most important contributions you can make toward his or her intellectual development. Two research studies confirm that parents are on the right track for raising an intellectually brighter child if they actively engage their child in early and deliberate communication.

J. V. Carew — as reported in *Young Children* by early childhood specialist Joseph Stevens, Jr., of Georgia State University — has found that verbal interaction is critical to mental development. Carew studied groups of preschool children reared at home and similar groups enrolled in day care and discovered for both groups that a high percentage of adult-led language activities was a good predictor of later high IQ scores in these children.

Just routine talk isn't good enough, though. The researchers say that adults must "put out" to stimulate the minds of infants and toddlers. This includes such focused involvement as labeling and describing things, comparing and contrasting objects, classifying things according to kind and function, and questioning.

For optimal intellectual growth (again reflected by IQ), the child needs to dominate these "dialogues" starting around eighteen months of age, the study found. No longer merely the "active observer," the child should be allowed to take the lead, while the parent continues to provide rich and substantive talk at the child's cue. The child may initiate labeling and describing things: "This is green." A parent might respond: "Yes, it *is* green. And what *shape* is it?" In short, what you put in is what you get out.

A Second Language

Many parents who are interested in stimulating the early acquisition of language skills in their children — and who may be proficient in a second language — wonder whether they should encourage their children toward bilingualism. Should you expose your child to a second language before he or she has mastered the first one? Does the experience of a varied language environment when young make it easier to learn and retain other languages later in life?

The following suggestions by Kathryn A. Knox, who teaches English as a second language at Colorado State University, will help to answer any concerns you may have about this kind of cultural and intellectual diversity in a young child's life. Remember, however, that it is important to stay within the context of encouraging, not pushing.

Current research supports the beneficial influence of simultaneous language acquisition for exceptional children. Children who learn another tongue demonstrate superior abilities in abstract skills, greater mental flexibility in approaching written words on a page, early awareness of the arbitrary character of symbolic systems, and an ability to manipulate language early.

Two-year-old Caroline, for example, had been consistently surrounded by French and English from birth. Early on, she used both languages while playing and showed awareness of both by using expressions in French *and* English for clarification. She would often choose the word from French or English that she thought was the easiest to pronounce ("fish" versus "*poisson*," and "spoon" versus "*cuiller*," for example).

Another child, Hildegard, was exposed to German and English by her mother and father from birth. Though at age three she mixed German and English pronunciation and vocabulary, by the time she was six, she was completely bilingual and was able to use the two languages separately with different people and in different situations.

When and how long a child is exposed to a second language and the consistent use of it by parents and peers are definite determining factors in how well a gifted child learns the language and whether or not he or she continues to use or remember it. Once a young child has acquired two working language systems, he or she usually evidences pride and shows increased interest in the mechanics of language in general. Specific questions that arise include the following:

• *How young should my child be exposed to a second language?* Whenever you feel comfortable with it! If a parent is bilingual, it may be the most natural thing to begin speaking in two languages from birth. One hypothesis concerning language development is that children don't learn two separate languages. They learn "language" as if all information given them in two or more languages were part of one language. As their intelligence and experience with the world widens, regardless of age, they learn to distinguish finer and finer contrasts of language and how to separate languages.

A child learning two or more languages simultaneously generally goes through two stages. The first stage is one of mixed speech, during which the child speaks both languages and mixes pronunciation, vocabulary, and any grammar rules he or she has learned. In the second stage, the child distinguishes between the two languages and uses them separately. (Gifted children generally approach this stage faster.) Parents sometimes become concerned during the first stage and discontinue second-language exposure, not realizing that the child is involved in a process of sorting language information and will soon learn to use the languages separately.

• *Should a child who is language-sensitive be taught reading in two languages simultaneously?* Speaking and reading are two different skills. Reading involves making "guesses" about information, remembering and putting together information, scanning, using pictures and world knowledge, and using decoding strategies (like sounding out words). General studies of second-language

reading involving young children show that children who don't
have good second-language reading strategies may "short-circuit"
the first-language reading skills they have already obtained. This
finding suggests that children shouldn't begin reading in a second
language until they achieve a level of competence in reading the
first language. According to some theorists, this means that even
children with exceptional reading ability shouldn't start second-
language reading until they reach the equivalent of the fourth-
grade level in their first-language reading skill.

• *Do children who have been exposed to more than one language
when young have an easier time learning additional languages
later in life?* No one knows for sure. We have all heard of people
who speak several languages fluently who had exposure to two or
more languages as a child. There is no definite evidence, however,
and there are too many variables between childhood and adulthood
to make any sweeping conclusions.

• *What are some things I can do if my own language background
is rather limited but I want to share what I know of a second
language with my child?* You can always employ a tutor, but one
of the best ways to introduce a child to the delights of language
is to show him or her how you enjoy and value language yourself.
Below are some language-development games for very young gifted
children who already have some oral language skills. The examples
are for French-English development, but they can be easily
adapted for other languages. These games will stimulate interest
in language concepts.

DIRECTIONS AND MEMORY   Have your child follow directions in
English ("Hop on your left foot," "Touch your right hand to your
head"), then give the same directions in French, using gestures.
If the child is able to understand both easily, mix the languages
and give directions in both. You can also play Simon Says in either
or both languages.

CLUES   In French, play "*Qui suis-je?*" ("Who am I?"). Give clues
with exaggerated gestures and facial expressions. (Example: "*Je
tombe du ciel goutte à goutte*" — "I fall from the sky, drop by
drop.")

NOUN-VERB DISCRIMINATION   Say a word in English or French

and have the child either point to it or do it. (Example: "Jump!" "*Neige!*" "Table!" "*Marchez!*") Have the child say words for you to act on.

STORY TIME   After your child has sufficient vocabulary and grammatical structures, have him or her draw three to five pictures about an experience (a day on the beach, for example, or an outing with a friend) and tell you about them in the second language as a short story.

CUBE AND MARBLES   Use a plastic cube and bright marbles to show distance words and prepositions in French. (Example: "near," "in," "under," "far" — "*proche*," "*dans*," "*sous*," "*loin de*.") After your child is familiar with this vocabulary, test him or her by saying an incorrect word to see if the child can catch you in a mistake. The words can also easily be expanded into sentences, using the same concept.

It is most important to give your young child exposure to language by making it fun as well as useful. Don't insist on absolutely perfect pronunciation in the beginning stages unless the child picks it up rapidly, but do model perfect pronunciation. Give your child opportunities to use the languages he or she is learning. Don't worry if your child mixes two languages in the beginning; he or she is only testing and sorting complex information and is not becoming confused. Most of all, have fun together!

ADDITIONAL RESOURCES

"Living Language" (records and tapes in French or Spanish). Presents for the Promising, P.O. Box 134, Sewell, NJ 08080 (609-582-2065).
    Write or call for more information.

Speak French to Your Baby, by Therese Slevin Pirz. Chou-Chou Press (P.O. Box 1525, Shoreham, NY 11786), 1981.

Speak Spanish to Your Baby, by Therese Slevin Pirz. Chou-Chou Press, 1985.

Day Care and Preschool: The Changing Face of American Childhood

MOST PEOPLE are familiar with the remark of mountain climber George Leigh Mallory, who, when asked why he wanted to climb Mount Everest, said, "Because it is there." Some individuals will take on any challenge simply because it is facing them.

A similar approach can be seen in a commonly held but debatable philosophy of science, including that governing learning theory in early childhood education. That philosophy is, if something *can* be done or tried, it *should* be. This mentality is at the root of most research — whether it seeks knowledge for its own sake or for more practical objectives.

The last chapter recalled the birth of "superbaby" in the 1970s — a concept born from the notion that young children may be capable of much more, cognitively speaking, than previous theory allowed. This enthusiasm at first overshadowed questions of appropriateness and long-term effects on children. It was the mountain-waiting-to-be-climbed presenting itself again: if children *can* learn more, earlier, they *should*.

But as the 1980s are mostly history, many educators — the most prominent among them, David Elkind of Tufts University — have come to describe the superbaby phenomenon and the advent of widespread formal academic instruction for toddlers and preschoolers as "the Age of Miseducation." The negative effects of pushing young children too much, too soon, are becoming increasingly evident. Many superbabies have become less than super children — with diminished emotional capacity, creativity, and initiative.

Still, the last decade has seen major demographic changes that necessitate finding nontraditional ways to provide early child care. With the tremendous influx of mothers into the work force, more out-of-home options are springing up and competing for a piece of the action. Nearly 40 percent of preschool-age children in America today are in some kind of preschool.

This chapter will help you sort through the issues involved in selecting appropriate day care or a preschool for your gifted child. Specific guidelines — what to look for and what to ask — are offered to help you find a setting that avoids the blight of "hot-housing" children (saturating them with academics), while reinforcing those values and attitudes you are trying to teach at home.

Following the sections on day care and preschool is a discussion of early admission to kindergarten and how to advocate for this option with your child's school district. Throughout this chapter runs an implicit theme: the best way to insure your child's optimal growth and development is always to remember that he or she is a *child* first and gifted second.

DAY CARE

You may not know whether your child is gifted at the age of five or six months, but if you have her or him enrolled in a day-care environment at that age, the outlook is not good for the child's optimal development, according to Burton L. White, director of the Center for Parent Education in Newton, Massachusetts.

White says that parents "cheat themselves and their children" by using day care as "storage facilities" during the early months of child development, and that the absence of an optimal rapport between the child and his or her environment can lead to personality problems and insecurity as the child grows older.

Why can't an optimal rapport be established in a day-care setting? "Because substitute care systems don't attend as much to the child as a parent would," White explains. "These early months are the foundations and precursors to optimal development. . . . It's not an easy adjustment for the child in such a setting."

White recommends that no substitute care take place for the first six months of the child's life. Afterward, a half a day at a time is permissible, he says. If it's impossible to stay home with the infant, then in-home substitute care — by a grandparent, other relative, or even a nanny, for example — is the next-best thing. Choose a person who has the capacity to tune in to the needs of the child by playing and talking to him or her profusely.

Some parents have formed "co-op" day-care settings in which parents alternately share day-care responsibilities for each other's children. In this way the children are more assured of being with warm, responsive adults. And in some communities parents make their homes available to a limited number of children, for whom they provide day care. Such a family day-care situation usually can offer more flexibility and individual warmth and support than an institutional day-care center.

Assuming that your child develops optimally for the first six months, there are other measures you should take, according to White, to prevent an early loss of potential. By the age of seven or eight months, for example, a gifted child may show signs of precociousness or advanced abilities with language. These skills should be encouraged and reinforced by constantly talking to the child, he says, "but some parents are silent and don't even talk to their children at this age, don't feed into the language system."

Parental silence can have devastating effects on the cognitive development of a child, gifted or not — effects that may or may not be made up later, White explains. "No one knows for certain."

Another critical period of development takes place at about one-and-a-half years of age, when "nine out of ten children begin to lose their potential and fall back intellectually," White claims. The fact that even gifted children may suffer losses in intellectual capacity results from a conflict between developmental needs and survival needs. White states that parental concerns for the child's safety dominate between seven and eighteen months, a situation that "causes many parents to inhibit their child's movement, creative exploration, and sense of curiosity."

Rather than inhibit early exploration and curiosity, White insists that "child-proofing" your home — putting dangerous or breakable objects out of the child's reach, blocking off stairways, and so on — is as important for optimal cognitive development as it is for safety.

WHAT TO LOOK FOR IN A DAY-CARE CENTER

The message is clear: Keep institutional day care to a minimum during the first two years of your child's life, especially during the first six months.

But when there is simply no other choice, what should you do? The following material summarizes guidelines from the Day Care and Child Development Council of America. They are published in *A Parent's Guide to the Education of Preschool Gifted Children*, edited by Roberta M. Felker. By asking pertinent questions, you can make informed decisions about the learning environment at the day-care center you are considering.

The learning environment is divided into four major categories: the physical setting, the interactional setting, the program, and the social-emotional climate.

The Physical Setting

USE OF SPACE   What place is there where a child can get off by him- or herself and have some privacy? How does the setting change for the children during the long day? What provisions are there for more intimate groupings at certain times (during meals, rest, storytelling, early morning, late afternoon, before lunch)?

MATERIALS   Are there materials for structured activities (such as puzzles, counting boards, pegs, beads, dominoes, form boards) as well as materials for unstructured activities (such as paint, clay, woodworking, dramatic play)? Is there a balance or does one kind predominate? Which?

Do most materials inspire children to thoughtful experimentation or do they merely lend themselves to perfunctory performance?

TIMING   Do certain events take place at specific times each day? Are schedules rigidly adhered to or is there some flexibility? (For instance, might the children have a snack a little later than usual because most of them are still deeply engaged in a project, or a little earlier because they are tired after a trip? Or might the children go outdoors earlier than normal because they are restless after several days of rain?)

Are children permitted to indicate whether there is too much time allowed for them to finish an activity or whether the time allotted is too brief? How do they do so?

The Interactional Setting

TEACHER-CHILD   Does the teacher show tolerance of childlike demands, of impatience, mood swings, self-assertion, negativism, impulsivity, exuberance, bragging, angry feelings, tears, testing behavior? How does he or she guide the children at such times toward adequate coping and acceptable behavior?

Does the teacher raise questions with children that communicate a real interest in learning? ("I wonder what will happen to the snow if we put it on the radiator?")

Are the teacher's questions open-ended, thought-inducing ones or are they close-ended with only one right answer?

Are limits explained or does the teacher merely "lay down the law"?

CHILD-CHILD   Are groups kept reasonably intimate so children can get to know and enjoy each other, or are they so large that children are overwhelmed by the crowd, the noise, and the commotion? Note the importance assigned to sociability: Are interactions fostered, are children shushed or in other ways discouraged from relating, or are they left to their own devices?

Do children tell each other about their experiences or demonstrate to each other a newly learned skill?

Is there opportunity to interact with children from a variety of backgrounds and thus to embrace different life-styles? Is interest in and respect for differences manifested by introducing different foods, stories, holiday celebrations, music, attire? Are children encouraged to explore both differences and commonalities?

TEACHER-TEACHER   Is there visual or verbal communication among staff members throughout the day? Do the adults act upon this communication?

Are staff patterns arranged so that each person has regular times away from the children during the day?

PARENT-TEACHER   Do teachers keep parents informed about the program? Is there evidence of written and oral communications to parents? Is the daily schedule posted? Is there evidence of information about pending field trips and visitors to the class? Are reasons for classroom procedures shared with parents?

How do teachers respond to parents' questions and comments? (Is there a back-and-forth sharing about the child and the program or does the teacher make pronouncements? Is the tone of the interaction respectful or authoritarian, concerned or detached, warm or abrupt, genuine or superficial?)

What is done to stimulate parents' interest in the program when they drop off and pick up their children?

The Program

CURRICULUM CONTENT   Which of the subjects, such as language arts, math, science, and music, are *ongoing* parts of the program? Which are limited to definite periods? Which are not included at all?

Which of the program components build self-knowledge, self-esteem, and self-confidence on the part of the children? Are mirrors used? Do the children make books entitled "Things I Have Learned to Do"? Are there photographs of the children, or height and weight measurements? Do the children care for pets, or for younger children? Do they dictate stories about themselves, perform short chores, move freely to music?

Take note of the modes and levels of symbolic play the children engage in. Note the variety of dramatic and creative expressions that are an ongoing part of the curriculum. What are some of the means by which the children represent their ideas, experiences, and concerns (for example, blocks, woodwork, painting, dance, symbolic play, dictation of stories and poems)?

TEACHING STRATEGIES   Which teaching strategies are most apparent in the setting? Note the match between (a) teaching strategies and competent functioning by the children and (b) teaching methods and developmental needs of a given group. In what way does the teacher's guidance assure the kinds of feelings and attitudes that permit the children's concentration on the learning at hand?

Are most activities initiated by children or by teachers? Is there a balance of both?

Are children allowed to complete what they are involved in or must they all stop at the same moment to do something else? What happens to those children who are "finished" while most of the others are still involved? How are children helped to move on when persevering in a task?

The Social-Emotional Climate

What evidence do children give of being aware of one another and of enjoying each other at least intermittently? Are natural-choice groupings encouraged or does the teacher frequently arrange for groups of children to play together?

Is there an easy mix of group play and solitary play? Is there opportunity for quiet reflection as well as for exuberance?

In what ways do teachers encourage children to help each other?

Throughout the long day, are there many changes of pace or does the program remain essentially the same?

PRESCHOOL AND THE TRANSITION

It is unfortunate that, in an era of computer technology and an explosion of general information, parents remain concerned but uncertain about the benefits or hindrances of preschool learning environments for a gifted child. Some parents may be concerned about the adverse effects of pushing a child; others may anticipate problems if the child already has mastered certain subject matter before entering school. But it is quite clear that learning experiences before entering school are more beneficial than hindering.

Early educational stimulation has been long considered important in this country as well as in others. Research by Benjamin Bloom has revealed that between birth and six years of age, children's IQs are about three-fourths crystallized. Thus the question of whether or not early schooling is necessary is seemingly moot. Instead, the discussion has centered around the pros and cons of the educational experiences that should occur for preschoolers. There are four basic philosophies about what kinds of experiences are most appropriate. (Specific preschool programs are discussed later in this chapter.)

First, many parents and psychologists believe that schooling outside the home should occur for just part of the day, and that its purpose should be for socialization only. For these people, the thought of "burdening" a preschooler with a structured school program is unconscionable. They feel that the child's preschooling must provide a very warm and loving environment filled with the rich experiences that come as part of a family and community. This type of environment is the most child-centered, and directions for activities originate with cues from the children themselves.

Second, there are those who advocate that a highly structured environment will help the child cope with his or her expectations of school. Many parents pursue this type of structure to extend their children's learning and "push" their children ahead. Parents of children with an unusual ability to perceive knowledge far beyond expectations for their age often desperately seek a structured plan to enhance or accelerate their children's knowledge. This type of experience is directed by the teacher, and the child has little control over what is taught. These programs lay great dependence upon extensive planning.

A third type of structure, which has received wide acceptance, is one that combines elements of both the types listed above. This approach combines direction by both teacher and child, and if it is well applied, takes away much of the argument against structured programs.

A fourth type of experience or learning situation consists of an extension of experiences that takes place in the home and family environment, just as the occasions arise, without any formal or planned program.

"HOTHOUSING" KIDS: A GROWING CONCERN

Before we look further at what a preschool should do, let's examine a national trend that it should *not* follow: "hothousing." Hothousing has become a fine art in Dallas and other major cities in the United States. Schools and programs for infants abound — as do the experts, and parents who start their children on a journey toward Harvard University before they are out of the crib. The affluence of the Dallas area in particular, as well as a strong streak of competitiveness that outdoes Texas's reputation as a whole, are contributing to what some see as a runaway panic over the stimulation of the very young.

"Hothousing" is the new term used by educators and psychologists to describe early academic saturation, reports Mary Candice Evans for *D Magazine*. She describes the early childhood programs now available to parents as well as their enthusiasm and rationale for using them. The end result, though, is becoming a recurrent theme: hothoused kids may pay too severe an emotional price for their presumed jump on life.

A Runaway Trend?

Evans claims that the child-development community in Dallas opposes what is happening, but the trend is continuing. Take "double-schooling," for example. Here's a situation in which parents are shipping their kids off to different half-day programs — filling their time with structured learning, then music lessons or sports practice before the child is allowed to go home and relax.

Experts in the Dallas area told Evans that parents are doing this because they hear about the pressure to get into the private school system and into the top competitive colleges. Further, the defenders of hothousing contend that adults need to realize the enormous learning potential of very young children.

However, Evans writes, "there is growing concern that the baby boomers have come to view their children as extensions of their own egos — as the ultimate status symbols. Authorities fear that parents are treating their children as products — new and improved products." Parents want to show off their children, but is Johnny a showpiece or a child? asks Evans. "The key, according to psychologists, is to have parents clarify their values. Are they doing this for their child or are they working out a hidden agenda through the child?"

Learning versus Development

Evans says that Dallas has its own extension of Glen Doman's Better Baby Institute, a Philadelphia-based enterprise considered the ultimate in hothousing techniques. And for parents who don't want to flip flashcards, the basis of the Better Baby program, Evans found schools in Dallas for babies from nine months to twenty-four months old that offer infant stimulation. There is a plethora of nursery schools and private kindergarten programs that promote learning rather than development, and even a commercial school that provides physical development for the very young.

According to Irving Sigel, a research scientist at Princeton's Educational Testing Service, "no one is saying it's wrong to teach your kids. But Doman advocates teaching by rote. See, learn, repeat. I want my kid to be a problem solver."

Evans reports that a director of one Dallas preschool, Ian Rule, thinks the hothousers ignore a key fact of child development: "The child can learn certain things only when his mind has matured sufficiently." In other words, very young children can be taught to memorize all kinds of things, but real learning and understanding may not have taken place in the process.

The Superbaby Syndrome Can Lead to Burnout

"Just about everyone agrees on the need for preschool education and for some emphasis on sports or music," Evans found. "But the problem with the double-schooling and card-flashing and loading up a child's agenda with lessons and enrichment programs surfaces when the child finally has a free hour. Often, he is lost and exhausted."

A teacher in a summer arts camp, who sees many of the children from these hothousing programs, told Evans that the children cannot make choices. "They do not know where to go unless I tell them," she said, in contrast to youngsters from nonpressure schools, who can make decisions by themselves about what they want to do.

Another drawback, psychologists explained to Evans, is that hothoused children are vulnerable to becoming future neurotics — "psychological cripples." Rule says: "The pressured child usually reacts by quitting. Giving up."

The dangers of hothousing are echoed by Jane Healy, a learning specialist at Hathaway Brown School in Shaker Heights, Ohio, and adjunct assistant professor at Cleveland State University. In an issue of *Independent School,* Healy advises parents to stop and reflect about what's going on. "Young children's independent exploration, problem solving, and just plain 'messing around' or staring at the sky are trendily reprogrammed into more 'stimulating' activities. Unfortunately, time for reflection and integration of mental growth is not always part of the package," she says.

Healy gives examples of obviously gifted young children pushed to such limits without time for emotional growth that they become "a social and emotional wreck." Such pressures on youngsters, she says, ignore children's need to develop "an internal locus of control," enabling them to develop responsibility for themselves and to enjoy the pleasures of earned successes.

"By replacing spontaneous play — messy, uncontrolled, and often painful as it is — with structured activities," Healy states, "adults promote not only passive fitness but also an external locus of control for mastering the environment, solving natural problems, and learning in its most fundamental sense. . . . We all need reminders that true learning is a process of trial and error that takes time, patience, and space — particularly for a child."

Evans concludes: "Critics of hothousing add a final irony to their condemnation of the push-push approach — almost all educators agree that by third grade, push and non-push students are at similar learning levels." But the difference emotionally may be significant, and a child's ultimate success and happiness may hang in the balance.

What Can Be Done?

Such problems are not simply going to disappear as more and more youngsters are being enrolled in preschool. "Encouraging as this public acceptance of preschool is," Samuel Sava, executive director of the National Association for Elementary School Principals notes, "it creates a demand for more trained specialists than we may have available. A fine preschool curriculum is not a watered-down version of third grade, and a competent pre-kindergarten teacher focuses on children's own interests to a much greater degree than a third-grade teacher, who quite properly emphasizes subject matter.

"Unless schools and teachers observe these distinctions," Sava cautions, "we risk losing the developmental potential of early childhood education in a misplaced effort to mass-produce little Einsteins."

Are early childhood education programs harmful to children? "No," insists David Elkind, president of the National Association for the Education of Young Children. "In fact they are extremely valuable if they are appropriate to the age and development of the child."

How can you know whether your child is being appropriately or inappropriately taught? Elkind gives a few examples: When your four-year-old goes to school, does he or she bring home dittoed worksheets or his or her own artwork? Is your child being taught lessons, or engaged in learning through projects such as making soup or building a puppet theater? Does he or she come home quiet and withdrawn, or joyful and talking a mile a minute about school?

"If you answered 'yes' to the first half of those questions, your child is probably being taught inappropriately," Elkind concludes.

EXAMINE PRESCHOOL ALTERNATIVES CAREFULLY

The fact that hothousing may actually stunt a young child's growth, particularly the emotional side and sense of initiative, coupled with a real lack of preschool programs designed to address the special strengths and vulnerabilities of gifted children, presents parents with a dilemma. What is appropriate preschool education for gifted kids?

Barbara Clark, professor of special education at California State University, Los Angeles, offers some guidelines in her book *Growing Up Gifted*. "Curriculum for all preschool children must be rich in variety and stimulating in process," Clark says. "For those who are developing faster and who show higher levels of intelligence, such variety and stimulation are even more important."

Clark encourages more experiences that allow for self-direction and exposure to abstract concepts, as well as more involvement with skills in reading, mathematics, science, research, art, music, writing, and understanding the world in which we live. Clark maintains that this can be accomplished by decentralizing instruction and by developing activity centers for academic and artistic pursuits that are rich in options. "Choice making can be developed and used by children as young as two and gives the child a sense of competency and achievement," she says.

This approach requires more complex planning and structuring by preschool staff, but Clark says it allows for the freedom and independence that "develops high levels of interaction for young children and ultimately produces higher levels of intelligence."

A responsive preschool environment allows the child to progress through the developmental stages with appropriate nurturing and support. Each stage should be viewed as an exciting opportunity for growth:

- The "terrible twos" are a time for testing limits and taking risks.
- The threes are when children begin building social skills.
- The fours are when they move from "me" to others.
- The fives are the stage during which they develop independence.

Choosing a Preschool

It's easy to become confused, but some guidelines offered by education writer Anne Lewis in an issue of *Parenting* can help you understand six styles of preschool programs. Be sure to observe a preschool firsthand before deciding on one that's right for your child.

OPEN CLASSROOM   Lots of hands-on materials to turn play into developmental learning; most suitable for kids who like independence and aren't quite ready for formal learning.

ACADEMIC   Specific instructional goals that focus on early reading, writing, and math; most suitable for children who seem eager for and adaptable to traditional learning techniques.

MONTESSORI   Children select their own materials and proceed at individual rate; teacher guidance only when necessary.

WALDORF   Emphasis on artistic and practical activities such as painting, storytelling, and crafts; best suited to children who enjoy art or seem to have an artistic bent.

CHURCH AFFILIATED   Structured and curriculum- and values-oriented; child must be able to work in a quiet, orderly fashion.

COOPERATIVE   Parents contribute time in the classroom and work as teacher aids; environment tends to be casual, not formal. (For more about this type, see "Preschools That Teach Parenting" below.)

Money: Preschools range widely in cost, from free public programs to as much as $5,500 a year for a half-day program in a prestigious school in the Washington, DC, area. According to Lewis, "tuition at most private schools will range from about $54 per month for a two-morning-a-week program to $540 per month for a five-day-a-week program that provides extended day care, lunch, and snacks."

The price range for religious-affiliated schools is generally less because they use church or synagogue facilities. Cooperative schools are also able to keep costs down by using parent volunteers.

Preschools That Teach Parenting

Cooperative preschools are unique among nursery schools in benefits to parents, teachers, and children. More than a play group, more than a private preschool, a parent-participation co-op is a place where parents not only assist the trained teachers in their child's class, but attend evening parenting meetings and donate regular time to such activities as serving on committees, repairing toys, cutting out name tags, typing, and maintaining grounds or buildings.

Most important, the ideal co-op nursery school is for *you* as well as your child. It is a continuing parenting class — really, a laboratory school for parents.

The cost of tuition for co-op schools is lowered in direct proportion to the amount of time and energy asked of the parents. In most cases, the school's monthly charge will be much less than private nursery schools.

The low ratio of children to adults in a co-op preschool means that the children enjoy a high degree of attention and freedom with adult supervision.

For gifted children, the biggest benefit might be the *lack* of emphasis on academic skills, which they will acquire on their own. This deemphasis of structured learning gives parents a refreshing alternative to preschool models born out of the superbaby syndrome. In general, the co-op preschools promote socialization as the primary and perhaps the only goal of a good preschool program.

The philosophy is that mastery of social skills is the foundation for mastery of academic skills.

More than a thousand co-op preschools are part of an organized network of schools called Parent Cooperative Preschools International. Those that belong to the organization are eligible for low-cost services from consultants, such as family counselors and speech therapists, as well as advice and support in organizing and running their schools. A newsletter sharing ideas and suggesting activities comes out three times a year.

For more information on the plan, write Parent Cooperative Preschools International, U.S. Office, P.O. Box 31335, Phoenix, AZ 85046.

EARLY ADMISSION TO KINDERGARTEN

"Perhaps the oldest and easiest approach to special education for a gifted child is acceleration," says J. Kent Hollingsworth, school psychologist for the Bogota, New Jersey, public schools as well as an active writer, lecturer, and consultant on gifted children. Below, he first explains, then advises about early admission programs.

Lewis Terman's monumental study of gifted children, originally published in 1925, included many children who had been "skipped" one, two, and even three years in school. Far from suffering from this "push," the children seem to have thrived on it. In Terman's view, the real danger lay in holding children back, in what he called the "lockstep" of traditional age-grade placement.

Over the years, several well-designed scientific studies have demonstrated that fear of grade-skipping is usually based on hearsay, horror-story anecdotes, or "gut feelings." Terman's thirty-year follow-up of his subjects and other long-term studies found that those who had been accelerated were better adjusted and more successful than those who had been held in lockstep.

Early Admission Is Common

Although most people might think of grade-skipping when acceleration is mentioned, the more common practice is early admission to kindergarten — say, when the child is four. Practicing school psychologists are well aware of the broad range of individual differences among children of the same chronological age, yet most schools expect all children in the first grade to learn to read sometime between September and December. Never mind the fact that some perfectly normal, healthy children are not developmentally ready to learn to read before they reach the age of seven, while others have taught themselves to read at age four (or three!).

Typically, it is found that when children are admitted to kindergarten early on the basis of psychological tests, they tend to participate in more activities, receive more awards, and more are admitted to good colleges, as compared to their normal-aged classmates. These children do well socially, too, because social and emotional development tends to be more consistent with mental age than with chronological age. The Council for Exceptional Children has stated that "research on acceleration through early admission to school is overwhelmingly favorable to early admission" for gifted children.

The advantages of early admission are clear: it allows the child to be grouped with others whose mental ages are closer to his or her own; it avoids the discontinuity of grade-skipping; and it ultimately allows the individual precious extra time for college and graduate study and entrance into a career.

Is Your Child a Good Candidate?

How do you know if your child is a good candidate for early admission? First, consider his or her intelligence. Does your child have a big vocabulary? Is he or she highly inquisitive? Does your child come out with answers to questions, solutions to problems, or bits of information that seem beyond his or her years? Does your child grasp basic calculations spontaneously, without previous instruction? Did your child teach him- or herself to read?

If you think your child is highly intelligent, you might consider having him or her take an IQ test. An individual IQ test, such as the Stanford-Binet or Wechsler, can be given to a four-year-old and will tell a great deal about a child's potential for schoolwork. In fact, children even younger can be tested, but the tests are less reliable when administered to younger children.

IQ tests should *only* be given by qualified psychologists. If your school is not able to have a psychologist test your child, you might try calling your state psychological association for the names of qualified people who are experienced in testing preschoolers.

A child who scores above the 98th percentile on an IQ test might be considered for acceleration. That level represents a score of about 130 or so on most IQ tests. About 1 person in 50 will score this high.

There are other considerations, of course:

• *How old are your child's friends?* Gifted children often choose to play with slightly older children, and this is another sign that favors early admission.

• *How big is your child?* A child who is physically big for his or her age will find it easier to fit in with older classmates than the "peanut" who may become the object of ridicule.

• *How are your child's fine motor skills?* This can be a cause of frustration and even lowered self-esteem if the child reaches first grade and is not developmentally ready to hold a pencil and write within the lines.

• *How about gross motor skills?* Children who can't run, throw, or catch as well as their classmates may find they are not as readily accepted by them. (On the other hand, the gifted child whose vocabulary and even sense of humor are on a higher plane than his or her classmates' also has a difficult time being accepted — there's always some sort of trade-off.)

• *How will your child react to being away from home at this age?* Some children aren't quite ready, emotionally, to be away for three or four hours every day. Leave yourself an escape clause. Stress to your child the fact that this is an "experiment," because he or she seems ready for kindergarten early. ("Although I have every reason to expect that it will go fine, we can always try again next year if there's a problem.") This allows the child to save face if it doesn't work out.

• *Is your child a boy or girl?* Beware particularly of pushing boys too much, too soon. They are on a slower developmental schedule than girls. Be convinced of your child's maturity.

ADVOCATING FOR EARLY ENROLLMENT

According to Patricia Mitchell of the National Association of State Boards of Education, when you are considering early enrollment, you should ask yourself these questions: What will my child get in the school program that I, a good preschool teacher, or both of us cannot provide? Will being with older children help my child? Will he or she enjoy being with older children? Will the placement with older children be a real improvement over the current placement — or will it still not provide what my child really needs? Am I certain my child is capable of handling the work?

If, after the most careful and objective examination, you still feel early enrollment is an important way to help your child, then you might follow Mitchell's steps:

1. *Find out if early enrollment is permitted in your school district.* State legislatures and state boards of education usually set admission requirements for schools. These rules often include a minimum age for enrollment in first grade and kindergarten, a date by which a child must meet the age requirements to be enrolled, and provisions about whether or not a local school board may make an exception to the age requirement.

    If your district may make exceptions, then you must find out how to arrange for an exception for your child. If state policies do not permit local exceptions, then your local district cannot legally admit your child before the age set in state policy. About two-thirds of the states do *not* permit local exceptions.

2. *To change your state's policy to permit early enrollment, seek additional information and support.* Changing a state policy is not easy. First approach your state association for gifted children and elicit its support. Then investigate which body (state legislature or state board of education) sets the age-of-enrollment or no-exceptions policy; and find out what key persons in that body think about changes to permit early enrollment. If attitudes are favorable for change (or if, at least, these persons are willing to consider it), then find a respected legislator or state board member to introduce the change. Back up this official in any way he or she suggests (visit other policymakers, make phone calls, write letters) to get the new policy accepted.

    Policy-making processes are quite complex, so be sure you read up on advocacy and invest your time in finding out who's important in your state's process and what they think about the early enrollment policy. Don't wear yourself out and waste your time trying to introduce a new or revised policy through a weak or ineffective policymaker to a policy body that is not interested in or supportive of the concept.

3. *If local exceptions for early enrollment are permitted in your district, seek additional information on local policies and procedures.* Find out what it takes to have your child enrolled in kindergarten or first grade before the "normal" age. Are specific scores on specific tests required? If so, how do you arrange for testing? Do you present your case to the superintendent, a staff member, or the local school board? What information and approaches did other parents use to present their cases successfully?

Use this period of initial investigation to find out more than just the formal policies and procedures that govern early enrollment. How people respond to your inquiries about policies will give you valuable information as to how they feel about early enrollment and who really decides on exceptions to age requirements. Use this information to prepare your case so that it will appeal to the key decision makers and win their support.

4. *If early enrollment is permitted by the state, but your district has a policy of "no exceptions" to the age requirement, seek additional information and support to change local policy.* Changing a local policy is similar to changing a state policy. It's not easy, and you'll probably need the support of others to be successful. If you have a local association for gifted children, seek its support. If there is no local association, find some parents, educators, other professionals who work with young children, or community leaders who will help you.

Next, investigate how, when, and why the local policy against early enrollment was made. This will give you an idea of how difficult it will be to change the policy. For example, if your school board recently made the policy, if it was suggested by the superintendent and approved by a clear majority of the board, and if most of those key people are still in the positions of authority, it will be difficult to change the policy.

If you decide it's possible to change the policy, find out

who the most influential people are in your district, what they think about early enrollment, and what it would take to get them to support a policy change. You can begin to determine this by attending school board meetings and observing the structure of such meetings — who is asked for advice among the board members, who is most outspoken, whose opinions are deferred to most often.

Again, this period of investigation is worth a substantial investment of time. You will find out not only who *makes* decisions in your district, but also who *influences* the decisions. By talking with both decision makers and decision influencers on an individual basis, you may find out their personal, as well as their public, stance on early enrollment. You'll know how to present your case to maximize your chance for success.

5. *If at first you don't succeed, keep trying.* The person who said "Where there's a will, there's a way" probably had not attempted to change a school policy. Remember that you are seeking recognition by the schools of your child's intellectual precocity and that the schools have a responsibility to help advanced learners. They may resist early enrollment for any number of reasons. For example, they may think that young children, regardless of intellectual ability, will be emotionally or socially hurt by "pushing" them ahead; or that by recognizing your child's advanced abilities through early enrollment, the school will also be obligated to provide a special instructional program, even though there may be no resources to provide such a program; or that if the school makes an exception in your case, even if well justified, then it will set a precedent and too many parents will seek early enrollment for their children.

You might answer these objections by providing evidence that emotional and social damage are not inevitable with early enrollment; by encouraging the school to initiate a gifted program with the resources already at the district's disposal (library, resource center, specialty teachers); or by assuring the school board that it is unlikely they will be inundated with early enrollment requests, and by pointing out that if they do get others, they will have a clear set of guidelines and procedures to follow.

If your attempts to get an exception made for your child, or to change a state or local policy to permit exceptions, are not successful, you can try again, find another way to meet the needs of your gifted child, or, as a last resort, move to another area. (Some parents have sent their children to private school, or hired a home tutor, or even started their own small school until age requirements were satisfied.)

ADDITIONAL RESOURCES

A Better Start: New Choices for Early Learning, ed. by Fred M. Hechinger. Walker, 1986.

A Parent's Guide to the Education of Preschool Gifted Children, ed. by Roberta M. Felker. National Association of State Boards of Education (444 N. Capitol St., N.W., Washington DC 20001), 1982.

Put the Brakes on Perfectionism
Before It Breaks Your Child

THIS CHAPTER is all about kids trying to be perfect, how and why they develop this need, and what you can do to ameliorate or prevent the specter of perfectionism from afflicting your child. Setting the stage is an essay by Fred Rogers of *Mister Rogers' Neighborhood;* he is also an advisory board member of *Gifted Children Monthly*.

IT'S *YOU* I LIKE
An Essay by Fred Rogers

My friend George keeps an old "Peanuts" greeting card pinned up beside his desk at work. On the card, Charlie Brown holds forth: "There's no heavier burden than a great potential." George tells me that he keeps it to remind him of the difficult time he had growing up labeled a "genius."

"Whenever I failed at something," George says, "my parents, teachers, friends, scout leaders — all of them — would say, 'We expect better of you than this.' "

For a while in his life, George did fail at just about everything.

"It seemed like I had lost the will to try. I didn't think much of myself. And each time I'd fail at a project, I'd imagine my teachers saying, 'We expected better.'

"That label really haunted me. If I could just be bright enough, I thought, I'd be good enough, and everyone who mattered to me would like me! On my first date with a girl, I'd even feel compelled to tell her my IQ, since that was the measure for me of being 'good enough.'

"I married the woman who gave me that Charlie Brown card. She got past my label to whatever it is that is me, and she liked that me, just for myself. What courage unconditional love can give us!"

When he grew up, George was able to go on to finish projects and to succeed at many things. He is a good father who gets a lot of pleasure from his son's accomplishments, and he says, "Something I do often is tell him I like him just for himself. I want him to see a clear distinction between the things he does and who he is."

"How Fortunate I Was"

It was my grandfather McFeely who gave me the idea for the statement I make to viewers at the end of every *Mister Rogers' Neighborhood* program: "You are special. There is no one in the whole world exactly like you, and people can like you just the way you are."

My grandfather was the kind of man who had such a positive view of life. He was one of the special adults I remember who had time for children. I was a fortunate little boy to have had many such adults in my childhood who gave me the feeling that children were important and childhood was an important time. Knowing that people care for you, no matter what you do or *how* you do, is something that helps children grow, just the way it helped my friend George to grow.

Labels like "gifted" and "talented" are probably unavoidable, but what we can avoid is seeing just the label instead of the person.

My friend told me about how his parents would introduce him: "And this is our George. He's a National Merit Scholar." He says he was just horribly embarrassed by that. "I wondered," he says now, "what was wrong with just saying 'and this is George,' and letting that be enough? What was wrong with letting 'George' be enough?"

Today, as an adult and as a parent, George understands something about parental pride — that it is appropriate and supportive to express pride in a child's accomplishments.

"My parents and other adults who expected a lot of me and set such high standards," George reflects, "certainly have affected how

I perform and my expectations of what I can do in a positive way. Now it has to be a careful balancing for me between the way I love my own son and the way I want him to be the best he can be. Now that I'm in the position of setting limits, I understand better what made adults who cared for me say some of the things they did to spur me on."

One of the *Mister Rogers' Neighborhood* songs called "It's You I Like" includes these words: "It's you I like, the way you are right now, the way down deep inside you — not the things that hide you, not your toys — they're just *beside* you."

Maybe we can best help our children and ourselves with labels like "gifted" by recognizing that a quality we attribute to the person is not the whole person. Along with our very reasonable hopes and expectations for our children, and for ourselves, there is a need for a kind of unquestioning love of the self that each of us deserves, the kind of love that shores us up and helps us just to be.

That's a real gift we can give to them!

ENTER ANOTHER DIMENSION . . .

If you can imagine the late Rod Serling — with *Twilight Zone* music in the background — addressing the issue of perfectionism and the way it possesses its "victims," he might have said something like this:

> It's a peculiar childhood disease afflicting mostly smart kids who tend to have high-achieving (sometimes pushy) parents. It creeps up on its victims from behind their backs, gets into the blood, and then sets its host upon a seemingly irreversible course of self-recrimination and doubt. It's the number-one killer of happiness and satisfaction — it's . . . the Perfectionist Syndrome (PS).

All dramatics aside, perfectionism is a common malady in gifted children and *can*, in fact, result in an unhappy and unproductive child. It can start in the preschool years in response to both internal and external expectations. By the time a child is in elementary school, the manic-depressive patterns of perfectionist behavior are clearly evident.

One eleven-year-old Michigan girl, cited in *Gifted Children Speak Out* by James R. Delisle of Kent State University, put it this way:

I think I push myself harder than my parents do. They have always accepted my getting good grades and when I get a bad grade I think I am more disappointed than my parents. When I set goals for myself they are quite high, and when I don't reach them I become downfallen, and sometimes I feel like there is no point in life and that I want to run away and who cares about school anyway. But I always get at it again and try even harder.

There's pathos in the story of this young girl. She drives herself into a frenzy and to the point of acute despair. You can't help wondering how much she can take and what self-destructive behavior she may be capable of.

A Look at the Demon

Perfectionism is a psychological, emotional, and behavioral disposition in which a person's sense of his or her worthiness is tied to perfect performance. Somewhere along the line, a child afflicted with PS has come to believe that love and approval are attainable only through perfection, itself an unattainable goal that foredooms its seeker to failure.

Perfectionist children behave in one of two ways: they either push themselves incessantly, like the girl above, or they refuse to work altogether and become underachievers. Indeed, obsessive-compulsive behavior and underachievement are two sides of the same coin. Both have the same source — inappropriate expectations, which will be discussed later.

Some of the symptoms of PS are listed below.

- High levels of anxiety
- Relentless self-criticism
- A tendency to magnify and generalize imperfections ("I'm no good at anything")
- Excessive criticism of others
- Fear of trying new things (fear of failure)
- Inability to share responsibility ("I'd rather do it myself")
- Feelings of inferiority or inadequacy
- Susceptibility to depression or feeling flat (especially after completion of a task)

Self-Concept and the Perfectionist

Perfectionists often don't like themselves very much. For one thing, their standards are so high that it's difficult to meet them. Being so self-critical, perfectionists are constantly putting themselves down — focusing on their shortcomings and not able to appreciate and enjoy their accomplishments.

"There is always an element of shame in perfectionistic thought," explains psychologist Tom Greenspon in the newsletter of the Michigan Association for the Academically Talented. "There is a sense that something is wrong, and that one must cover it up by outstanding performance. This implies a self-dislike, as well as a constant monitoring of oneself to make sure everything is being done to ensure success."

A perfectionist's identity, therefore, is too wrapped up in others' expectations and in performing for others. When parents of toddlers or preschoolers grant praise or approval just for outstanding performance at something (for example: "You tied your shoes perfectly — good boy!"), the child begins to associate his or her character with a completed task. Being successful means he or she is a good child; being unsuccessful means the child is bad. Such judgments, though not maliciously intended by the parent, are internalized by the child. (For a detailed discussion on giving appropriate praise, see chapter 5.)

Under such conditions, in which the praise-performance dynamic becomes habituated, a child is likely to develop a fragile sense of self — an underlying insecurity about his or her worthiness. In addition, the constant pressure to perform at maximum level is stressful and can lead to premature burnout or underachievement.

When a gifted young perfectionist risks taking a good look at him- or herself, he or she sees faults and imperfection, sometimes an "imposter" who's afraid of being found out as not as smart (good) as everybody thinks. There are two things going on here. First of all, when a task or learning comes easily to a child, praise for a job well done sometimes doesn't bring out a genuine satisfaction, but rather a diffuse uneasiness — as though one just got something for nothing. Second, this feeling of unworthiness can lead to guilt at the distorted self-perception of not measuring up in the eyes of significant others, and then in one's own eyes.

The crux of the matter is this: The drive for perfection is tied to a distorted self-concept in the first place — one built on performing according to others' expectations. The resultant low self-esteem precipitates an even more frenzied drive for perfection, and the child is caught in a vicious, debilitating cycle of guilt and shame.

It's All or Nothing

Gifted children can become "paralyzed perfectionists." Their addictive need to get things perfect all the time can cause them not to do or try new things for fear of "failure" in their eyes and yours. Even preschoolers — for whom little if any of the psychological reality is explicit — may start behaving seemingly as though it is better not to try at all than to try and fail. Of course, parents should attempt to instill just the opposite: "Better to try and fail than not to try at all."

What motivates your child to achieve may well dictate whether he or she accepts challenges and persists in the face of difficulty, or avoids them and crumbles at the first sign of trouble. This was the subject of an *American Psychologist* article by Carol S. Dweck of the University of Illinois, and it has a lot of relevance for you and your gifted child. Neither praise alone nor your child's level of intelligence can guarantee what Dweck calls an "adaptive motivational pattern."

Simply put, this is characterized by seeking challenge and persisting at it. In contrast is a "maladaptive" pattern in which a child avoids challenge and gives up easily. Children who tend to be motivated by *learning goals,* with their gradual mastery of material or skills, are well adapted motivationally. Children who tend to be motivated by *performance goals* — that is, who seek to gain favorable judgments of their competence or avoid negative ones — are maladapted, according to Dweck.

She says: "Recent research has shown that performance goals work against the pursuit of challenge by requiring that children's perceptions of their ability be high (and remain high) before the children will desire a challenging task."

Dweck says that performance goals promote defensive strategies in children that interfere with seeking challenge. Children motivated by learning goals are more willing to risk displaying ignorance in pursuit of skills or knowledge.

ABILITY VERSUS EFFORT   Children who are guided by performance goals tend to view intelligence as a fixed trait, and are more likely to interpret failure in terms of low ability, Dweck says. Success is attributed to luck, which can't be very satisfying, and "positive reinforcement" or praise can't convince the child otherwise. Children guided by learning goals tend to view intelligence as malleable, and attribute success and satisfaction to effort.

Because performance goals generally cause anxiety about ability, past successes don't help children develop confidence in future undertakings. Dweck says this is all the more true of children with high IQs, high achievement test scores, and high grades. "In short, being a high achiever and knowing one has done well in the past does not appear to translate directly into high confidence in current difficulties."

WHAT YOU CAN DO   Here are some ways to steer your child away from the paralysis that perfectionism can cause:

- Foster a learning-goal orientation by placing less emphasis on your child's performance per se and more on the effort necessary to progress gradually to a point of mastery at a given task. (Say with enthusiasm: "That's it. Keep working at it. You're improving.")
- Within a learning-goal orientation, build in challenge and even some "failure" to help your child accept imperfection and learn persistence. (Example: "OK, let's see you get a running start and jump to this line. Didn't quite make it. Pretty good jump, though. Give it another try.")
- Train your child to attribute failure to inadequate effort or strategy, not to low ability. (Say with encouragement: "Of course you can do it. You need to work a little harder at it, that's all. Try it a different way and see how you do.")

Relationships at Risk

Gifted toddlers en route to becoming perfectionists may also show signs of Type A personality and have difficulty forming close and gratifying relationships. Meyer Friedman, author of *Treating Type A Behavior and Your Heart*, says that Type A behavior frequently begins in young children because they do not receive enough unconditional love and affection. He lists these warning signs in children:

- Problems giving affection freely to parents, siblings, or others
- Incessant crying or throwing temper tantrums after losing a game or playing a sport
- Moodiness that won't let up
- Physical signs of restlessness, including knee juggling, tapping fingers, or interrupting conversations, particularly those of a parent

These behaviors can have adverse effects on relationships within a peer group. Other children will shy away from this kind of child; adults will tend to label the youngster "emotionally immature" or "highly self-centered." As the child approaches school age, and begins to project his or her perfectionistic standards on playmates, it could become increasingly difficult to maintain friendships. Other children may become alienated and refuse to take the brunt of the perfectionist's constant criticisms.

Remember, the perfectionist feels unworthy in the first place. The drive and frenzy of the Type A personality, the unattainable standards applied to self and others, these are walls — defense mechanisms — erected by the child to hide his or her vulnerabilities and emotions. Intimacy becomes impossible. Rejection by other children confirms the child's feelings of unworthiness, and round and round it goes.

"Oft Expectation Fails . . ."

"Oft expectation fails, and most oft there where most it promises," wrote Shakespeare.

Giftedness cuts both ways, and things have a way of turning sour if proper care is not taken. The pride new parents feel can turn to despair as their precocious infant — whom they regard as a "blessing" or at an "advantage" relative to other babies — begins to develop unforeseen problems. Most often the culprit is too-high expectations. While there may be some validity to the notion that *internal* high expectations are part of a gifted child's nature, most often trouble comes from environmental pressures.

So beware of being a source of such pressure. Having high standards, setting as one's goal the pursuit of excellence — these are appropriate and admirable ideals for gifted children as they grow and become aware of their identities and life's choices. But with toddlers and preschoolers, it's best to nurture a mastery-of-goal orientation, to deemphasize performance, and to temper overbearing expectations on your part. The suggestions below will help you do these things.

Curing PS

With proper care you can cure the Perfectionist Syndrome or prevent it from afflicting your child. Here's how:

- Give your child *unconditional* love. Try to keep separate your child's behavior (whether it warrants criticism or praise) from his or her sense of self.
- Forge strong emotional bonds. Respect your child's feelings — positive *and* negative — and communicate openly about feelings. Children need to know they're loved despite their mistakes, and despite inciting their parents' anger from time to time.
- Be conscious of implied criticisms that may take the form of a disapproving tone of voice, a frown, a raised eyebrow, and the like. Gifted kids are especially sensitive to body language, nuance, and intonation.
- As your youngster approaches school age, or as soon as he or she is capable of understanding the issues, talk about perfection as an unattainable ideal. As Judy Galbraith says in *The Gifted Kids' Survival Guide*: nobody is perfect or good at everything; it's perfectly OK to be imperfect (it's human!); doing things perfectly doesn't make someone a better person.
- Provide safe opportunities for your child to "fail" at things from time to time. A gradual but continuous commitment to trying new experiences — whether a new food, a new friend, a new place to visit, or a new skill — can go far in "inoculating" your child against the mental paralysis associated with fear of failure.

- Encourage your child to be a "persistent explorer," recommends Alice Chen, a teacher of gifted children in Rochester, New York. Help them see that trial and error is a legitimate means of discovering new things, that a mistake can be as illuminating a learning experience as an immediate success.
- In situations that require problem solving, help your child see that there are alternative ways of doing things, not always just one right way and the rest wrong ways.
- Be a good role model: let your child see you fail and bounce back; be able to laugh at yourself and at the foibles we all experience; show that you accept your own limitations and concentrate on your strengths.
- Implement a regular "stress reduction" program that includes exercise, time management, relaxation techniques, a good diet, and appropriate rest. (See chapter 4.)
- And remember this message:

IT'S YOU I LIKE

It's you I like,
It's not the things you wear,
It's not the way you do your hair —
But it's you I like,
The way you are right now,
The way down deep inside you —
Not the things that hide you,
Not your toys —
They're just beside you.
But it's you I like —
Every part of you,

Your skin, your eyes, your feelings

Whether old or new.
I hope that you'll remember
Even when you're feeling blue
That it's you I like,
It's you yourself,
It's you, it's you I like!

— Fred Rogers

Girls and Boys:
The Yin and Yang
of Giftedness

AVE YOU ever tried to put together a complex toy or puzzle, only to find at the end that you missed a part which should have been used at the beginning? Raising a gifted child is not unlike following a schema that requires a certain sequence of operations for all the pieces to fit and work smoothly.

However, unlike a toy or puzzle, it's not as easy with a human being to retrace your steps, undo the mistakes that were made, and start from scratch. That's why it's important to have the whole picture in front of you — where you're going, how to get there, what problems you might encounter along the way, and how to nip them in the bud.

Your goal or ideal is to raise your child in such a manner as to help produce what psychologist Abraham Maslow calls a "self-actualized" person — one who is happy, productive, and fulfilled relative to his or her abilities and interests.

Gifted children, though, by virtue of their special talents, are vulnerable to certain problems that emerge when their social, emotional, or intellectual needs are not fully met. Unfortunately, often by the time these problems become visible — whether during the elementary-school years, puberty, or adolescence — they are not as easy to solve as if the proper foundations had been laid in the first place, during the preschool years.

This chapter projects through adolescence the growth of gifted girls and boys, separately by gender, and profiles some "typical" difficulties that each encounters at home and school. Although your main interest now is your toddler or preschooler, you should look ahead to the outcome of your parenting and to the kind of person you'd like your child to become. Early experiences and conditioning are crucial to a child's growth as he or she progresses from one developmental stage to another.

Following an overview on developmental crises, and at the end of each major section — the one on girls, the other on boys — some additional strategies are suggested for getting off on the right foot with your gifted child.

CERTAIN CRISES YOU CAN BET ON!

They are as predictable as thunder following lightning, which is a fitting metaphor for understanding the developmental stages of most gifted children. It's a myth that healthy emotional development comes with the terrain; more often than not those early flashes of brilliance give way to rumbles and storms.

But according to Amy Clements Blackburn, head of the psychology and counseling department at Northeastern Oklahoma State University, and Deborah B. Erickson, a special-education supervisor for Greece (New York) Central School District, the storms can be anticipated. Writing in an issue of the *Journal of Counseling and Development*, the authors pinpoint five predictable developmental crises related to the academic and eventual occupational success of gifted students.

1. *Developmental Immaturity:* This trait tends to pertain mostly to boys at the outset of their schooling, because they are more likely than girls to have developmental lags — particularly with verbal tasks. A gifted boy's eagerness, curiosity, and creativity may appear locked in hyperactive overdrive as his neurological supersensitivity causes difficulty in screening out excessive stimuli. Such a youngster may be labeled difficult, immature, and even slow.

2. *Learned Underachievement:* Crisis number two affects both sexes and usually emerges around fourth or fifth grade, often as a reaction to inadequate curriculum, demands for conformity, or both. Reasons for underachievement range from underlying social problems, to negative and self-defeating attitudes, to perfectionism and its companion, fear of failure (see chapter 7).

3. *Adolescent Fear of Success:* This crisis affects mostly girls, as they are especially vulnerable to the confusing period of adolescence. Girls' social and physical development, markedly more intense than boys' as a rule, begins to take priority over their intellectual and academic interests. Conflicting social messages add to the problem. Cultural stereotypes and traditional values are stressed, forcing many girls to choose between achievement and femininity.

4. *Too Many Choices:* The fourth crisis is often a problem disguised as "a world of opportunity." In short, making personal and career choices can be overwhelming for gifted adolescents because of their multiple interests and abilities. Being a jack-of-all-trades, attempting to live up to one's potential, and balancing individual goals with others' expectations can lead to debilitating stress and can adversely affect self-esteem.

5. *Encountering Nonsuccess:* The fifth crisis may occur at any age: it's the first time the gifted youngster is challenged beyond his or her capacity for immediate success. Say Blackburn and Erickson: "Having had only the self-image of perfection, they are often devastated by not performing at the top. They may become 'paralyzed perfectionists,' unwilling to pursue any new experience unless success can be guaranteed."

Blackburn and Erickson say you can help ease the crises by assisting your child in working toward the following goals:

- A healthy and realistic self-esteem based on a clear understanding of strengths and weaknesses, accepting the latter, and learning from mistakes.
- A healthy sense of self-responsibility not contingent upon the actions of others; becoming internally motivated and capable of self-evaluation, free from competition and others' standards.
- Use of brainstorming and problem-solving skills to enhance divergent thinking and to help in setting personal goals.
- Assertiveness in communicating differences, concerns, choices, with others; use of creative methods to defuse frustration, stress, and burnout.
- A reflective sense of humor, allowing your child not to take things so seriously as to be debilitating and self-defeating.

SUGAR, SPICE, AND EVERYTHING NICE?

Although Lewis Terman could find only five girls for every seven boys in his famous study of gifted elementary-school children in 1922, girls are now being identified for elementary-school gifted programs in numbers that often outstrip those of boys. But the eventual success in life of these girls is going to depend on how well they are able to overcome the pressure of prejudice about sex-role behavior — the feeling that females should be, are, or tend to be passive, dependent, and self-sacrificing — that pervades our culture and inhibits girls' emotional and intellectual growth from the day they're born, in even the best of circumstances.

The point will be self-evident when you give yourself the following test: Name five male classical composers. Now name five female ones. Having trouble? Try artists or outstanding Pulitzer Prize winners or corporate executives. According to Carolyn Callahan, associate professor at the University of Virginia, while underachievement in school is usually considered a problem of boys, *lifetime* underachievement is a problem for many gifted girls.

Since the onset of the feminist movement, more and more subtleties of the inequities women face have become evident. And gifted girls and women are in double jeopardy. They have to overcome all the difficulties of being female as well as the stereotypes associated with the gifted. This section will give parents some insights into the problems of their gifted daughters and some ideas for helping them achieve to the best of their capabilities. It will deal with the influence of parents and society on gifted girls, the bias against these girls in the schools, and specific ways parents can help their gifted daughters early on.

The Role of Parental and Societal Influence

Parents influence their daughters' options right from the beginning with their choice of toys. Patricia Lund Casserly of the Educational Testing Service found that construction toys, especially Legos, had been as popular as dolls among the 161 gifted high-school girls she studied. Microscopes and chemistry sets were also part of their childhoods. As they grew up, the girls tended to become "tomboys" — assertive tree climbers and fort builders.

Carolyn Callahan, cited above, observes that boys are given toys that come apart; girls typically get toys to be played with as a whole, not to be taken apart to see how things work. This is the reason, she surmises, that as problem solvers girls tend to be more global — seeing the whole intuitively — and boys more analytical.

Add to these subtle environmental biases that begin in early childhood the cultural and social pressures of adolescence, and a gifted girl's problems are compounded. Girls actually fear success, Callahan claims, because it may make them appear to be unfeminine and cause boys to be uninterested in them.

In addition, Callahan notes that the shortage of female role models (literature assigned in school, for example, is usually written by men and about men, and textbooks still tend to portray females as the weaker, dependent sex) reinforces the conforming, dependent behavior that can be a subtle barrier to achievement for gifted girls.

Recent surveys reveal that the activity gifted girls seem to pursue most avidly is reading. When the girls surveyed were young, their parents limited TV watching and guided their daughters' reading to children's "classics," often choosing stories about women who accomplished feats of courage or intellect that girls could identify with. (Nonsexist bibliographies are available from the Feminist Press, P.O. Box 334, Old Westbury, NY 11568.)

These girls also reported an exceptionally close relationship with their parents, which points to a potentially significant factor: They were treated as intellectual equals at a very young age. "They respected what I said on the same level that they talked to their friends," said one gifted girl. Another said: "My parents always talked to me as if I were an adult. They didn't just make rules; they explained why, so it made sense."

The mother of one high-school senior said: "From early on we talked without inhibition about things kids usually don't talk about. We were just like friends."

On the other hand, too much parental pressure and involvement can create problems. Carol Copple observed preschool girls in a program for gifted children at the Educational Testing Service in Princeton. She found that young girls who were "intellectually independent and free-ranging in their thinking [were] not being pushed by their parents. But girls who were pressured to get right answers so they could move to the next intellectual level were more likely to be quite conforming — trying to figure out what the teacher wanted them to say."

Said one seventh-grader about her parents: "They have high expectations for me, but they encourage me to do things on my own, to experiment." And the mother of a college freshman responded: "We always asked her to solve her own problems. After she had exhausted all possibilities, we were glad to help."

"The main thing parents have to do," says Alexinia Baldwin, professor of curriculum and instruction at the University of Connecticut at Storrs, "is to give girls a feeling of self-confidence by building up early successes at home. Let them plan a garden, design a room or a quilt (which develops abstract thinking), invent new games, create a new recipe, or plan a route for a vacation." Baldwin also stresses the importance of carpentry and electrical and plumbing skills for girls, and the need to share experiences with fathers. "They should go camping or build a playhouse together," she says.

Of course, gifted girls need the same cultural and intellectual stimulation as gifted boys — visits to museums, concerts, the theater; access to creative materials at home; information on subjects that interest them. They also need special encouragement to be scientists and engineers, says Max Fogel, former director of science and education for Mensa (a society for people with high IQs), because many girls still perceive these as masculine occupations and avoid development in these areas. Experts agree that problem-solving skills should be taught at an early age. For girls, involvement in some aspect of financial planning is particularly useful — managing an allowance, even helping with the family budget.

Bias in the School

Schools continue to reflect the sex bias of the culture in administrative staffing patterns, curriculum materials, and teacher attitudes — despite antidiscrimination laws. "Teachers can be hostile toward the gifted of both sexes," says Fogel, "but they seem to be more prejudiced against girls than boys." In one program for gifted adolescents, teachers gave their lowest ratings to female students who were analytic and preferred nonconventional approaches, while boys exhibiting the same characteristics received the highest.

Adolescence can present particularly serious conflicts for gifted girls as they begin to hide their intelligence in order to attract boys. Studies show that girls perform well in all-girl or neutral situations, but shy away from competition with boys (who often become even more competitive around girls at this age). Suzanne Schneider, a Philadelphia psychologist, thinks that fathers play an extremely important role for gifted girls at this time. It is up to the father, she believes, to validate both his daughter's sexuality (making her feel that she is a desirable member of the opposite sex) and her competence. Mothers of gifted girls say that they point out women who are successfully combining careers and motherhood and encourage their daughters to begin career plans early. Mothers, teachers, and other women who manage to integrate their working lives with their private lives are especially important as role models for adolescent girls.

But most girls are not lucky enough to find such encouragement and role models, particularly in the sciences. Although girls perform as well as or slightly better than boys in math until the age of eleven, their interest in math and science drops off in junior high; girls' test scores at this stage begin a steady decline. A large sample of seventh-grade girls scored an average of 31 points below boys on a recent Scholastic Aptitude Test (SAT) for math, conducted by Johns Hopkins University's Office of Talent Search and Development, as part of its nationwide search for youngsters precocious in math.

High-scoring girls not only feel their femininity is threatened, says Lynn Fox, of Johns Hopkins, they also "fail to see science and math as having socially useful applications." She continues: "We've found these girls have fewer theoretical interests than the high-scoring boys, so we've created a special summer program to show them how these subjects can be used to solve human problems (in architecture, engineering, psychology). Women scientists who [speak about] their fields become role models for the girls." Fox believes that career education of this type is particularly important at the junior-high-school level to keep mathematically and scientifically gifted girls from withdrawing from these fields and to allow them to plan a comprehensive high-school program.

Patricia Lund Casserly, mentioned earlier, reports that high-school girls in advanced-placement courses often attributed their academic success to teachers who recognized their giftedness when they were eight or nine, helped them develop their skills, and inspired them to do something significant with them. The mother of a gifted writer says: "My daughter was turned on to writing in sixth grade by one of those magical teachers. All through high school she has sent stories to her for comments."

For gifted girls who haven't found that "magical teacher," parents may want to look outside the classroom at a variety of special programs. In her study, Casserly discovered several ten- and eleven-year-old girls who had been tutored in math "for fun" or who had taken science courses at university museums and laboratories. In some instances the girls had helped graduate students collect data for doctorates. Speaking for a group involved in a special science project, one girl said: "We didn't start off as scientific 'geniuses.' Our parents sent us because they thought we weren't challenged in school, but before long we were hooked." (Chapter 12 suggests math and science activities for preschoolers.)

Are Gifted Girls Prone to Eating Disorders?

It would seem that gifted girls are especially susceptible to eating disorders, on the basis of two separate studies reported in the *Journal of the American Academy of Child and Adolescent Psychiatry*.

In the first study, which involved 600 private-boarding-school and day-school girls aged twelve to eighteen, 18 percent of the students admitted to having at least one symptom of an eating disorder. Many reported having more than one. Robert L. Hendren, a specialist in adolescent psychiatry at the University of New Mexico who administered the questionnaire, stated that the schools involved in the study are of high quality with rigorous academic standards. He said the parents of these children are mostly professionals.

The girls' reported methods for controlling their weight included self-induced vomiting or bulimia (12 percent); starving themselves or anorexia (7.4 percent); and taking laxatives (2.3 percent). Hendren said the results were "similar to those of previous studies of young upper-middle-class American women, and emphasized not only a high incidence of eating disorders among this population but also an early age of onset."

The second study examined thirty hospitalized female adolescent anorexics to determine how they differed psychologically from mentally healthy high-school girls of the same ages. According to William J. Swift of the University of Wisconsin School of Medicine, what separated the anorexics from the healthy high-school students was the anorexics' high level of self-attack.

A majority of them (50 percent) agreed with the statements "I vengefully punish myself" and "I take it out on myself." And 60 percent affirmed the statement "I let my own sickness and injury go unattended even when it means harming myself."

An unexpected finding of this study was that both groups shared the same level of self-restraint; but for the mentally healthy students this was set within a context of self-love, while for the anorexics it was a matter of self-hatred.

Running through both studies is the issue of self-concept. Children or adults who exhibit symptoms of eating disorders tend to have severe psychological problems. The composite of personality traits for such individuals tends to include low self-esteem, hypersensitivity to the opinions of others, loneliness, and confusion about one's feelings — all of which can begin to develop within the first few years of life.

Gifted girls may be especially vulnerable to eating disorders in the absence of psychological support systems at home and school that acknowledge their academic and intellectual propensities as well as their femininity. Hendren says that sometimes peer pressure and societal values (for example, "success means being thin and beautiful") lead bright young women on the path to eating disorders as misguided "solutions" to their problems.

While a case should not be made that giftedness necessarily implies a poor self-concept that leads invariably to eating disorders, gifted children can be highly self-critical and hard on themselves. These are the same characteristics present in most anorexics, albeit in an extreme form.

For more information on eating disorders, you may write the American Academy of Child and Adolescent Psychiatry, 3615 Wisconsin Ave., N.W., Washington, DC 20016.

Specific Ideas for Helping Gifted Daughters

Your daughter has been born into a world whose expectations are colored by gender — many times to the detriment of her special gifts, especially if they fall within the math and science areas. What parents do with their children as toddlers and preschoolers often determines whether the problems discussed for elementary-school students and adolescents will emerge or not, and, if so, to what degree.

Carolyn Callahan believes that most of the blame for the fact that the overwhelming number of adults who are considered to be gifted and creative are men rests on the social and intellectual environment created for girls at home, in school, and in the environment in general. She suggests that parents can do the following to cut down the negative influence of environmental experiences and give gifted girls an equal chance to develop their talents and achieve in life:

- Encourage and allow girls to manipulate mechanical toys, explore electronic devices, and try other such things at the same age at which boys do.
- Be sensitive to what your child of either sex is watching on TV and how women are portrayed. Are they constantly seeing women portrayed as "dumb blonds" rather than intelligent problem solvers? As soon as they are able to understand the basic concepts, discuss the dual roles today's women are shown to embrace — as dependent and subservient wives and mothers, whose main daily activities are still cleaning the house and preparing dinner, on the one hand, and as independent professionals and heads of households, on the other.
- In eventually answering the question "How can I be both feminine and professional?" expose girls to successful professional women — in the home and community, on TV, and in movies and books — as role models.

Make sure your child's school — including preschool — and teachers are not assigning classroom tasks on the basis of sex-role stereotyping (for example: girls correct papers; boys wash blackboards). Make sure the school is providing activities that allow her to practice visual-spatial problem solving from a young age, such as working on puzzles; activities that emphasize the impact gifted girls can have on their own success, and that build confidence in their ability to control what happens to them, like teaching them to choose what clothes they wear and what subjects they study; activities that encourage girls to establish personal goals;

activities that reflect and promote equivalent standards and opportunities for boys and girls; and coed athletic activities in which boys and girls can play together and enjoy the same sports.

Deirdre V. Lovecky, a clinical and child psychologist from Providence, Rhode Island, suggests several parenting strategies to help gifted daughters achieve their dreams:

START EARLY   Adolescence is much too late to begin building an identity that allows your daughter to see herself as an achiever. In fact, you must begin in infancy to allow girls to explore, to manipulate the environment, to learn to try and to risk failure without giving up, to learn to do for themselves rather than asking parents, and to learn to combat all the media messages that show boys as participants and girls as observers and consumers.

EMPHASIZE MASTERY   Perfect performance is not necessary for success. Praise your daughter for attempts that do not succeed but that show real effort and thought. She also needs praise for persisting rather than seeking the easiest solution, and for learning the value of a mistake. Understanding what success means is also important. It does not necessarily mean high grades, but rather the ability to see herself as able to achieve, and to have an internal sense of what is required and an inner knowledge of her own power to master and change things.

ENCOURAGE THE FUTURE   Your daughter needs help in learning to develop and maintain visions of herself doing worthy and important things in the future. You can encourage dreams. They can help your daughter see possibilities in real-life situations. Having a dream about what can be done allows practice of a role without too much risk and opens up possibilities that might never have been noticed before.

DEVELOP ROLE MODELS   Parents who are positive role models are those who make active choices, who at times put their own needs first, and who engage in some activity defined as fulfilling. Mothers who are homemakers may have the most difficult time with this, as it is easy to lose yourself in the endless caring for the needs of others. Yet, if a mother is to be a positive role model, she needs to think about what behaviors and values she is modeling. It does little good to tell your daughter to value individual achievement and have a dream for the future if your own actions belie this. Unfortunately, the message that may be received is that it is fine to be gifted when you are a child, but not when you are an adult. This does not mean that all women need to be successful in careers outside the home, but rather that they need to insist on time and respect for their own interests.

Fathers are role models for gifted daughters, too. If the father treats his daughter as if she doesn't count except as caretaker to his needs, she may be unable to see herself in any other role, particularly with males. For gifted girls to see themselves as achievers in a competitive world, fathers need to take pride in and encourage intellectual and athletic achievements of females.

Beyond those general guidelines, Barbara Kerr, associate professor in the department of counselor education at the University of Iowa, and author of *Smart Girls, Gifted Women,* offers these specific recommendations for the toddler and preschool years:

- Dress your little girl for active play, rather than for watching on the sidelines. Dress her in bold, bright, very washable colors rather than pallid pastels.
- Choose nonsexist toys and encourage her interest in toys that allow manipulation of objects and active problem solving. Don't discourage quiet time, but simply make sure that other options are available.
- Avoid day-care centers or preschools that segregate girls and boys. Find out the attitudes of the child-care workers toward sex roles and look for child-care facilities that have men as well as women teachers.
- Be sure that day-care centers or preschools have plenty of books and allow time for reading them, as well as allowing individual time with puzzles, musical instruments, or art work.
- Take advantage of any preschool program that interests your gifted girl — Suzuki lessons, karate, story hours.
- Take your preschool girl to your place of work and explain your work, as well as that of all the people she sees.
- Try camping, exploring, museum hopping, and travel with your daughter. Gifted young girls usually thrive on adventure and novelty.
- Make sure your gifted young girl has a private, special place. She doesn't need to be pushed into social relationships.

- Try to find an older girl who is intellectually oriented and self-confident to be a companion for your preschooler once in a while.
- Support your daughter emotionally even when she is difficult.

And, says Kerr: "Let her know you are delighted by her gifts and talents. Always be honest about what you know about her abilities; don't hide the fact of her giftedness from her."

SNIPS, SNAILS, AND PUPPY DOGS' TAILS . . .

What little boys are made of? Or what little boys are made to be?

The question is: Are we really so conditioned by custom and experience in our male-dominated society as to believe that boys have everything going for them — that they're the lucky ones, the benefactors who do not pay handsomely for the "privilege" of their gender?

Some apparently feel this way. Gina Ginsberg Riggs, executive director of the Gifted Child Society in New Jersey, for one. She doesn't believe that gifted boys have a unique set of problems that can be differentiated by sex. She thinks that as the majority voice in our country, males in general have no "special needs."

Others would disagree. Betty Siegel, president of Kennesaw College in Marietta, Georgia, says it is much more difficult to be an elementary-school-age boy than it is an elementary-school-age girl. Recently she asked an audience how many women were "tomboys" when growing up. Many raised their hands. She asked the men in the group how many were "sissies." There were chuckles . . . but guess how many hands went up.

The Gifted Connection

Sex-role stereotyping and cultural conditioning affect both boys and girls, and do so differently for each sex. That much is evident. This section explores the problems of a subpopulation of males — that is, the problems that elementary-school-age and preadolescent boys experience as a function of their giftedness. The behavioral patterns, remember, begin during the toddler and preschool years. Some of these problems will be the same as any boy's, only more intense; some will be unique to the gifted per se.

Who Wears the Pants, Anyway?

Both boys *and* girls wear the pants, if we take Siegel's finding seriously. Unlike girls, though, boys can't also wear dresses or play with dolls — not without considerable ostracism. This isn't to suggest that you dress your son in a skirt and buy him a Barbie; but this example is emblematic of restrictions that our society, for the most part, imposes on boys. What's limited are boys' self- and role-identities, as well as their right and capacity to express emotions. And this can have devastating effects on their development and behavior.

For example, gifted boys who are raised in a family environment that reinforces primarily "macho" values, roles, and relationships may be especially at risk. Alexinia Baldwin says that highly creative or sensitive youngsters can suffer extreme frustration as a result of having to conform to the predominant societal image of male toughness. James Delisle of Kent State University in Ohio suggests that gifted boys can develop "personal insecurities" as a result of this. And Bruce Shore of McGill University in Montreal says that boys interested in art, dance, or nurturing roles are particularly "punished" for being different.

Who is Macho Man? Tough, competitive, insensitive, aggressive, self-reliant, logical, nonemotional — these are some of the characteristics of the macho male. Gifted boys who are made to feel they must conform to this stereotype against their natures are subject to internal conflicts that can cause them to reject aspects of themselves, aspects of their giftedness, in the absence of a supportive environment that validates and nurtures who and what they are. This is tantamount to self-alienation, which at the same time gives rise to guilt, feelings of inadequacy, and poor self-esteem.

Don't Be a Crybaby

Hand in hand with the macho male goes the supreme dictum: "Boys don't cry." They're taught to suppress feelings, to tough it out, to hide their vulnerabilities, to be "strong." In short, boys, in general, are not given permission to express their emotions; for gifted boys in particular, this can be especially limiting to the development of their creativity and their intuitive side. According to Signe Lundberg, a Philadelphia-based psychologist, "a whole array of possible talent areas are either precluded as a result, or, if they exist, destroyed." And there are psychological costs as well.

Hardly a week goes by that the media doesn't report an incident of a seemingly stable man going berserk. Clearly, some male violence in our society can be attributed to a culturally conditioned inability to vent and work through bottled-up emotions appropriately. The lid simply blows. Moreover, because gifted boys have a deeper appreciation and understanding of life's complexities than their nongifted counterparts, they will tend to have empathy for others. Lundberg says they may therefore be more apt to strike out against *themselves* in a variety of ways. This can range from a deprecating self-concept, to substance abuse, to depression, to suicide.

"Mommie, Dearest"

The issue of emotionality runs deep and has its roots in a child's early bonding with his mother and father. Research coming out of the burgeoning "male-studies" field describes the importance of a bonding-separation process with each parent. Sociologists generally acknowledge that in our modern world, as opposed to primitive societies, boys don't separate cleanly from their mothers, and they don't bond adequately with their fathers.

The elements of this process are complex. First of all, to the extent that the macho male is devoid of a genuine emotional side — short of the one he is taught to deny — boys grow up believing that girls and women are the sole arbiters of feelings and of judgments based on feelings. "We fail boys by not giving them the emotional apparatus they need to cope with growing into manhood and for dealing with adult roles," Lundberg states. One possible consequence of this culturally reinforced notion that feelings are essentially a feminine domain is that boys may develop only "half" a self.

The importance of developing and understanding one's feelings is echoed by Howard Gardner in *Frames of Mind:*

> The less a person understands his own feelings, the more he will
> fall prey to them. The less a person understands the feelings, the

responses, and the behavior of others, the more likely he will interact inappropriately with them and therefore *fail to secure his proper place within the larger community* [italics added].

Second, it seems that boys do have emotional needs that only get satisfied through bonding with their mothers — the need for physical closeness, protection, assurance, unconditional love, acceptance, and approval. It's not that fathers shouldn't also be there in these capacities for their sons. It's that they either cannot — don't have the ability to be nurturing — or are unavailable to do so, either physically or psychologically. Problems arise around puberty when a boy traditionally is supposed to separate finally from his mother and bond with his father. Most boys, emotionally, have no place to go.

The possible conflicts and confrontations for a gifted boy as a result of tensions surrounding bonding and separation with his mother are numerous and varied. Consider the gifted boy's intense and often earlier-than-normal need for autonomy and independence clashing with a dominant mother's inability to let go — her caregiver instincts preventing the transfer of power and responsibility her son so badly needs. (In a *Roeper Review* article on "Suicidal Behavior and Gifted Adolescents," a mother wondered in retrospect whether she had *overprotected* her son.)

Consider the pushy "stage mother" type who's bent on developing her gifted son's talent and providing every advantage and opportunity to do so — but against his wishes. Or an aggressive-mother/passive-father combination in which an artistic boy's somewhat effeminate traits are denied by his mother — possibly along with his talent — in deference to cultivating more masculine traits that his father does not or cannot display as role model.

According to Sandford Reichart, professor emeritus at Case Western Reserve University in Cleveland and vice-president of the Education Design Center, in families with dominant mothers the problems gifted boys face center around trying to meet her expectations, knowing her disappointments, and knowing how to ingratiate oneself in her eyes. "With the increased levels of sensitivity and perceptual analysis that so many gifted boys possess," Reichart says, "their being tuned in to the mother's needs often results in distorted personality development, overcompensating behaviors, insecurities about sexuality, and ambivalence toward male authority roles."

It is situations like these that can cause sex-role uncertainty and confusion in a gifted boy; resentment, hostility, and guilt toward his mother; and a particularly traumatic adolescent identity crisis.

Where Does Dad Fit In?

Nowhere . . . and everywhere. That's where Dad fits in.

Nowhere in the sense that in a traditional family, the father usually functions as provider and authority figure — sometimes even as mentor in a formal way — but from a distance, *emotionally disconnected* from his son.

Everywhere in the sense that the relationship a gifted boy has with his father can determine whether and in what direction the former will develop his talents and sense of masculinity.

Much has been written about the effects of "father absence" on social development and academic performance, with somewhat conflicting findings (see chapter 2). Far more subtle but no less important than a father's physical absence, though, is the impact of a father who is not present emotionally or psychologically for his son. A gifted boy in particular may be acutely aware of this and ask himself explicitly: "Why isn't he there for me when I need him?" Internalizing this lack within the relationship, the youngster may conclude it is his fault, his inadequacy and failure as a son, that's keeping his father at bay.

When sociologists speak of the American male's difficulty bonding with his father, they mean this lack of emotional intimacy. It is the longing for answers to existential questions, writes Harvard psychologist Samuel Osherson in *Finding Our Fathers:* "How does Dad deal with failure and success, with the conflicts of choice, and ambivalent wishes and dreams in his life? How does Dad deal with mother and women?"

If bonding is a problem, so is separation. The usual adolescent rebellion period may be more intense and painful for a gifted boy than his nongifted counterpart, as his burgeoning self-identity is wrapped up in the development and expression of superior abilities as an extra dimension.

The direction a gifted boy chooses at this juncture in his life is likely to be heavily influenced by the kind of relationship he has had with his father — good, bad, or in between. This much seems natural enough. But it's the emotional intensity that's noteworthy.

In a survey of highly creative and successful entrepreneurs, Arthur Lipper III, chairman of *Venture* magazine and *Gifted Children Monthly,* discovered that most of the men who responded had a love- or hate-relationship with their fathers. "They had to prove something to somebody," Lipper says.

Just as with Mom, bonding and separation with Dad can take many forms. Consider the gifted boy who has come to idolize his father and perceives him as the model of success he fears he can never become. Whether or not the father actually has voiced expectations that his son will follow in his footsteps, the son may spend much of his life — as a child and adult — trying to prove his worthiness to his father. This can occur at the extreme cost of not developing gifts and talents of his own choosing that might lie in other directions.

Or consider the highly divergent thinker, the kid with off-the-wall ideas. Imagine the sparks that would fly if his father was an authoritarian type who valued conformist thinking and behavior above all else — to the detriment of his son's creative spirit.

Or consider the overly dominant or controlling father — he sometimes lives vicariously through his son — who sets up extraordinarily high standards of performance and achievement because his son has been identified as gifted and who demands that the son work up to his potential in every possible area. Never mind the stress. Never mind the boy's own interests or his need to control his own life.

It's not difficult to imagine in such cases that a gifted boy could come to resent his father, as Lipper observed of many entrepreneurs. A gifted boy who feels squelched by his primary role model may shut out his father in retaliation, seek a surrogate male to replace him, or look inordinately toward his mother as a safer place to test the limits of conventional thinking and the powers of his giftedness.

Whatever the specific dynamics of the father-son relationship in a given family, problems will inevitably arise if a gifted boy feels trapped and paralyzed by his own abilities, on the one hand, and the Sisyphean burden of paternal disappointment, on the other. As Osherson states: "In that way fathers become our superego, critically judging us for letting them down. If mothers become life-giving earth in the unconscious of men, then fathers become wrathful, judgmental gods."

The Great Imposter

Undue parental pressure to perform and achieve can turn gifted boys into paralyzed perfectionists — youngsters so desperate to get things perfect that they can't act at all out of fear of failure. Perfectionism, as noted in chapter 7, is a problem for gifted children in general, but may be more so for gifted boys raised in an environment that stresses competition, achievement, and success.

Perhaps because boys aren't permitted to develop the same capacity for emotion (to give it or receive it) as girls, perhaps a result of their emotional disconnectedness from their fathers, gifted boys seem to be especially susceptible to perfectionist tendencies. It's as though their sense of self-worth and means of obtaining love and affection are inextricably tied to their accomplishments. This is a pity and a tragedy, because very often these youngsters end up feeling anxious and depressed, unworthy and inferior, guilty of fraud, burned out, and lonely.

My Alter Ego

The ancient Greek philosopher Zeno of Citium, when asked "What is a friend?" responded, "Another I." This doesn't mean an identical self so much as someone who is capable of reflecting back a person's strengths and worthiness as a human being. Gifted boys who are self-alienated perfectionists find it difficult to make friends, as they tend to alienate and turn off others.

A study published in *Gifted Child Quarterly* compared the self-concepts of gifted boys with those of gifted girls and found that giftedness is an advantage for elementary-school girls, but not for elementary-school boys. Gifted boys tend to have lower self-satisfaction than gifted girls *and* nongifted boys, when you measure the discrepancy between their ideal self and perceived actual self.

Problems with peers for gifted boys are exacerbated by the traditional male ideal, on the one hand, and, on the other, the reality of most elementary-school classrooms — even gifted programs. An aggressive, self-reliant, individualistic profile of "achievement via independence" is not usually tolerated, say researchers Roger C. Loeb of the University of Michigan and Gina Jay of Penn State.

They suggest that because early education is "feminized" by a "predominance of female teachers," who may tend to value above all else conformity and obedience, "academic success, and particularly when it results in being labeled 'gifted,' may foster feelings of self-doubt, weakness, and lack of control in the young boy."

Unless participating in gifted programs becomes part of the successful-male image, Loeb and Jay state, negative peer pressure will continue to be part of growing up gifted. As Jane Navarre, associate professor of education and director of gifted education at Ashland College in Ohio, observes, "The stereotype of the 'nerd' haunts the academically-able gifted boy and he isn't respected unless he's also athletic."

Another dimension of the feminized classroom involves the different developmental schedules boys and girls are on. In short, boys tend to mature more slowly than girls — particularly in the verbal and reading areas, which figure heavily in the early identification of giftedness.

The problem here, according to J. Kent Hollingsworth, school psychologist for the Bogota, New Jersey, public schools, is that bright and active boys may be designated hyperactive, distractible, or disorderly. Their giftedness may go unrecognized as a result. The developmental lag in the acquisition of school-readiness skills usually prevents them from being considered for grade-skipping, acceleration, or early entrance to kindergarten, options Hollingsworth says are highly appropriate for some gifted boys.

I Wanna Be Cool

Negative peer reactions to gifted boys include ridicule, name-calling, bullying, and ostracism. Sometimes this happens because others feel threatened by the gifted child's superior abilities, sometimes because he is just different. Because gifted boys want to be accepted into a peer group, it is not uncommon that they will hide their talents, their giftedness, just as gifted girls often do. In fact, Signe Lundberg says this is a more serious concern for gifted boys, as they enjoy a narrower norm of peer acceptance. Navarre concurs. And in James R. Delisle's book *Gifted Children Speak Out*, one ten-year-old Kentucky boy comes right to the point: "Sometimes I don't feel like I fit in, so I hide that I am gifted."

Negative peer pressure and perfectionism are two of the root causes of underachievement as well — two reasons gifted children *choose* not to achieve — according to Joanne Whitmore, dean of the College of Education at Kent State University and author of *Giftedness, Conflict, and Underachievement*. Whitmore found in her studies of gifted boys that most who underachieve do so "because they are either unmotivated to do the assigned tasks, or motivated not to try."

They rebel, turn off, say no. Often this "choice" comes after years of accumulated parental pushing and pressure to achieve that started during the toddler years. Alas, the opposite of what was intended occurs. Perhaps this is not all that surprising. Merle B. Karnes, professor of special education at the University of Illinois, notes that gifted boys are more apt to rebel than girls, more apt to question authority, more apt to be the troublemakers in a class.

And perhaps end up as juvenile delinquents. A University of Denver study of 300 juveniles in a suburban court system, as reported in the *Journal for the Education of the Gifted*, found that underachievement is the one thing most delinquents have in common — gifted or not. Still, there doesn't appear to be evidence that underachievement alone is sufficient to cause delinquency. Say Kenneth Seeley and Anne Mahoney, who conducted the study: "Bright children who get in trouble appear to come from particularly unstable homes. . . . As a child's perceived environmental support decreased, delinquency proneness rose."

"The Child Is Father of the Man"

Gifted boys have problems all their own, but with proper parenting these are not insurmountable. Summarized below is the collective wisdom of the sources quoted or paraphrased earlier. Many of these experts responded to a questionnaire soliciting their input and advice for parents.

- Temper Macho Man. Let your son know it's OK — indeed, necessary — to feel and express emotions for the sake of communication, intimacy, creativity, and feeling whole (Lundberg).
- Fathers: share your emotional life with your son — your dreams, aspirations, fears, and insecurities. Be a model for accepting both success and failure in life (Osherson).

- Teach boys about sex-role stereotyping and expectations, as well as the limitations these preconceptions place on both boys and girls. This will help prevent boys from developing a narrow perspective, and from specializing too early in math/science areas (Navarre, Hollingsworth).
- Educators: implement ways (such as mentorships) for recognizing the full spectrum of exceptional abilities in the classroom, and for destigmatizing boys interested in aesthetic pursuits (Baldwin).
- Defeminize early education by providing more male teachers, thereby helping to build academic striving and educational excellence into the masculine ideal (Loeb and Jay).
- Don't push boys too much, too soon, because of their slower developmental schedule (Hollingsworth). With boys, beware of grade-skipping; if anything, have them start school on the late side (Ginsberg Riggs).
- Encourage boys to accept their strengths as well as their limitations. Teach your son to respect himself and his abilities — and stress that neither should be abused (Lipper).
- Permit and encourage early, autonomous, and self-directed learning based on your son's interests and choices, not on adult agendas (Whitmore).
- Help choose and support your child's friendships with peers of similar abilities and interests (Shore, Karnes).
- Give your son unconditional love, regardless of his accomplishments. Try to keep separate your pride and his sense of self-worth (Delisle).

The Enriched Environment— "Inside" and "Outside"

D AVID ELKIND, Tufts University professor and author of *The Hurried Child* and *The Miseducation of Children*, has stated that the major "advantage" any parent can give a child — right from birth — is an enriched environment. This does *not* mean flash cards or reading instruction at age two, but rather surroundings that resemble an "intellectual broth," a dynamic mixture of stimulating ingredients, full of aromas and flavors that pique the senses.

Rather than imparting specific skills or knowledge at too young an age, the object is to surround children with experiences that they will internalize within the fabric of their very beings. It is more a matter of assimilating family life-style and perspective than absorbing arbitrary facts — which are often tossed at the child prematurely, before he or she is developmentally ready to perform certain mental tasks.

From an environmental point of view (since we can't do anything about our genes), giftedness is born, encouraged, and allowed to develop through a process that structures a child's cognition as well as social and emotional growth. Indeed, the structures of this development themselves bubble forth from that cauldron called home, family, and environment. This chapter is about cooking up that intellectual broth, and it begins with a discussion of how environment affects brain cell activity.

THE BRAIN AS "MUSCLE"

One of the most exciting areas of research for those concerned about gifted children is the study of the human brain/mind system. From it we are gaining a better understanding of how a child becomes gifted and, in fact, what giftedness actually is in a biological sense.

The new data are showing that as we can exercise our bodies to make them more physically fit, so can we exercise our brains. And the data are also encouraging parents and educators to rethink approaches to nurturing learning and to devise more effective strategies.

While each of us has a unique, highly complex genetic program built into our cells at our very beginning, a person will not become highly intelligent unless he or she is given opportunities to use these inherited programs. Intelligence does not grow in a vacuum. From conception on, parenting is the most important factor in developing giftedness.

(The following two sections, "Biological Brain Differences" and "Help Children Integrate Thinking," were prepared by Barbara Clark, author and professor at California State University in Los Angeles.)

Biological Brain Differences

New research shows that there are biological differences in the brain of the highly intelligent child or adult and that we should take these into consideration as we plan activities.

Gifted children are children whose brain/mind systems are developing more rapidly, in more and complex ways. Some of these differences occur shortly after conception, some during the first few weeks after birth, and others throughout the first three years. At no point in the life span does a human brain stop growing and changing. When the environment during the first few years provides appropriate stimulation, brain development is accelerated and advanced, and differences are measurable.

What are some of the biological differences that are influenced by environmental conditions and important to the learning process?

- The neurons, or nerve cells of the brain, become chemically richer, allowing for more complex patterns of thought.

- The neuroglial cells, which provide nutrients and support for the neurons, increase in number. Consequently, neuron activity accelerates, and neurons develop more interconnections.
- As children are given a stimulative environment and these chemical changes occur, the brain becomes more integrated and synchronous, allowing heightened concentration, focused attention, and in-depth probing and inquiry.

Giftedness, therefore, is a biologically-rooted concept, a label for high-level intelligence resulting from the advanced and accelerated integration of functions within the brain. These include physical sensing, emotion, cognition, and intuition.

Help Children Integrate Thinking

The kinds of activities suggested below will enhance the brain physiologically and increase its integrative capabilities.

1. *Provide complex and challenging experiences for your child in a responsive environment.* In the process of developing intelligence, young children have a great need for a responsive environment. People and objects in the environment can promote growth if they are meaningful or useful to the child.

   Gifted children often complain that they are never really challenged or stretched mentally. Brainteasers, puzzles, and open-ended happenings can be fun to play around with for both you and your child, and can provide interest and challenge. Inventing new games or new ways to play old ones and discovering real and workable solutions for family or neighborhood problems give a child a sense of worth and participation.

   All learning requires a period of time for the learner simply to encounter materials within the environment. Arrange a space in the playroom or in your child's bedroom where a large quantity of materials are always accessible. This will make true inquiry possible. Low shelves around the room filled with a large variety of books and materials displayed are far better than a toy box or drawers. Decorate with small, child-size tables and chairs, child-proof phonographs, chalkboards, and the like. (See the next chapter for suggested equipment.)

Time Involved: Children up to the age of three may need guidance. With four- and five-year-olds, allow large blocks of uninterrupted time.

Materials Needed: In addition to the books, art supplies, writing materials, and play materials in the child's room, set up a theme each week or so. For example, you might focus on magnetism one week, making available appropriate materials — magnets, paperclips, and other materials to illustrate what a magnet will and will not pick up, a compass, and so on. Help your child pick themes he or she is interested in, too.

Parents' Function: Provider, resource person, facilitator.

Procedure: After setting up guidelines for movement, care, and use of materials, let the child explore freely.

Sharing: Take time to discuss outcomes and what the child discovered, to admire what he or she produced, and to question and extend the learning.

You and your child can discover other challenging experiences on family outings, explorations, and vacations. Use every opportunity to extend your child's knowledge of the world.

2. *Teach your child ways to relax in order to reduce tension.* Relaxation is an essential first step in optimizing learning. The human brain literally shuts down as anxiety, tension, or fear increase. As it moves toward relaxed awareness, it processes information faster and remembers it longer. Relaxation allows the limbic area of the brain to function more effectively and enhances the interaction between the right and left hemispheres through the corpus callosum. Through the continued use of relaxation, an individual can create a more balanced and coherent use of brain energy. (For relaxation techniques, see chapter 4.)

3. *Help your child learn physical focusing or centering.* Centering, as effective for intellectual and emotional balance as for physical endeavors, is the ability to relax, focus energy, and move with your own natural rhythm. This approach allows the brain to operate in a more balanced and integrated way. It has the same biological advantages as relaxation does for balance and coherence within the brain. (Children as young as four — and in some cases three — can manage this exercise.)

Time Involved: Five to ten minutes regularly when needed.
Materials Needed: None.
Parents' Function: Guide.

Procedure: Have your child stand comfortably balanced on both feet, and give the following instructions in your own words, as you might do for relaxation:

> Imagine being filled halfway up inside with pure white sand . . .
> with any movement the sand will shift . . . now lean forward
> with your full weight on your toes, letting the sand shift just a
> little . . . lean backward with all the weight on your heels and
> let the sand shift again . . . lean forward again and notice the
> sand shifting . . . now back again . . . now lean forward again
> and stop when the sand is exactly even, neither forward nor
> back . . . the weight is exactly balanced . . . shift your weight
> to the right foot . . . feel the sand shift to one side . . . now
> shift to the left foot and imagine the sand shifting again . . .
> now right . . . now left . . . stop when the weight is neither right
> nor left, but exactly balanced between front and back, right and
> left . . . if you are now standing with your weight exactly bal-
> anced between front and back, right and left, you are centered
> . . . allow your knees to unlock and bend slightly . . . notice
> the feeling of being balanced and centered . . . notice how
> positive and relaxed you feel.

Sharing: Encourage a discussion of how this exercise feels, and when it might be useful — for example, just before a test or other stressful situation.

4. *Use imagery when playing or working with your child.* Encourage your child to develop imagery as a tool for improving
thinking and problem solving. Not only is imaging one of
the highest intellectual processes unique to humans, it en-
riches the play of the child and is marvelous fun. Use of
imagery activates the prefrontal lobe of the brain and the
intuitive processes as well as allowing further integration of
the total system.

Time Involved: Variable amounts of time each day.

Materials Needed: Books, puppets, drawing and writing
materials.

Parents' Function: Guide.

Procedure: Read to your child, tell stories, and allow your
child to finish stories you start. Using puppets (paper bag or

finger puppets are easy), make up plays or retell stories. Using costumes, sound effects, and voice changes, "pretend" a story. Read poetry aloud and encourage your child to write a poem. Take fantasy journeys to places real (perhaps to the doctor's office to prepare the child for a coming visit) or imaginary. Discuss dreams and encourage your child to illustrate a remembered dream. There is no need to interpret the dream.

Sharing: Just share the sights, the colors, and the feelings. Stretching the imagination is easy and can provide a lot of enjoyment as you build skills that will be important in future planning and in creative pursuits.

While the four areas of activity and the examples offered are an important beginning for enhancing your child's use of his or her brain, there are many ways to provide the necessary stimulation. Each child's brain — like each snowflake — is unique. What stimulates and nurtures one child may not work for another, even in the same family. It is more important that you provide a rich array of materials, activities, and events and allow each of your children to become involved with what is appropriate to his or her needs and interests. The child is the best judge of what, how, and when.

ARTISTIC FAMILIES REVEAL THEIR STYLES

What is family life like when children are talented and have a passion for the arts? It is hectic but wonderful reports the *Christian Science Monitor*. The newspaper, in publishing a series of interviews with parents and children who have achieved success in the visual and performing arts, gave an anecdotal picture of life in the high-drama lane. Throughout the comments ran an important message for parents of preschoolers: Nurturing for the arts begins early!

As a composite, parents in such artistic families tended to be

- extremely supportive of their children's interests, and fiercely devoted to allowing their children to seek and determine their own interests;

- proud of their children's accomplishments from the very beginning, when often all the kids showed was interest (talent per se had not yet emerged);
- enthusiastic about the arts (such enthusiasm permeated the family — younger children seemed to catch the fever from older brothers and sisters); and
- artistic themselves, perpetually looking for different ways to express their creativity.

How Four Families Promote Creativity

- "I wanted them to be what they wanted to be," commented Shirley Smith of Norwood, Massachusetts. Of her four children, one became a choreographer who founded her own performing-arts school at the age of twenty-one, another is a music educator, a third is a singer-composer. A multitalented youngest child hasn't yet entered the professional world, but the future looks very bright. "I'm a firm believer that from a very early age, if you see any promise in children at all, expand it. Let them do everything."
- The John Pearson family in Oberlin, Ohio, surrounds itself with the products of both the children and parents. Paintings and other carefully framed examples of the children's work cover much of the walls. Art items conceived and made by the parents — beautifully crafted and displayed doll houses, dolls, mechanical figures, and toys — complement the children's work.
- The experience of the David McCoy family in Dallas illustrates another commonality among these families: opportunities outside of school for their children to find outlets for talents. Young David and Dawn McCoy are "regulars" with the Teen Children's Theater. Their father commented that "our role is to make sure that when they get to a point where they need to make a commitment . . . they would have the same kind of support from us that they would if they were going to be in the world of business."
- Another Dallas theater family, the Wayne Meachums, has learned that the arts help children in regular schools, too. Having to deal with disappointments, successes, and hard work gives them more maturity in school than they otherwise might have. "It's been one of the best complements to their education that we could ever have provided for them," Wayne Meachum observed.

Hamming It Up: Nurturing Dramatics

When you ask your daughter to get the peanut butter jar from the cupboard, does she do it while singing the lines from the latest television commercial for the product? Has your son seen one particular movie more than five times, and can he quote entire scenes from it? If you answered these questions with a somewhat exasperated yes, don't despair. It may mean that you have a child who is talented in the dramatic arts.

But wait, you may be thinking, this is the child who is always lost in the chorus in the school play. That doesn't matter. Many accomplished actors report being overlooked for parts in school productions, perhaps by harried teachers who were searching for students who could be counted on to memorize the lines quickly. Actually, an affinity for the dramatic arts can be displayed well before school age anyway. A preoccupation with television may not be all bad, and a talented preschooler can mimic commercials word for word.

Fostering your child's natural ability need not be left to an acting coach or dramatics teacher. You can nurture acting talent by employing some relatively simple strategies.

MAKE IT PART OF YOUR CHILD'S LIFE   Use games to make tedious, routine chores into fun ways of exploring dramatics. One game you can play as you prepare lunch is simply to ask, "What if you had to make a commercial for this food?" The results can be hilarious.

• A good game that can be used during car trips is Pass the Story. Have someone begin by telling just one line of a story, and then pass it around the group, with each person adding just one new line.

• Pretend is another game for car travel or anytime children complain that they're bored. Tell the participants who their characters are and what the situation is, and then let them improvise a scene. For example, you might say, "Katie, you sell balloons at the zoo, and Jon, you're a boy who loves balloons but doesn't have any money. You have to try to talk the balloon seller into giving you a balloon."

• Another game for young children is Mirror Image. Pairs of players face one another. One child is designated the leader.

The follower must mimic the leader's actions like a mirror image.

• Sharing dramatics with their friends is also fun for children. Birthday-party games based on acting exercises tend to be very popular because everyone can participate and there are no losers. Young children ages three to seven enjoy moving and pretending to the instructions of records specifically designed for that purpose. You can usually borrow these from your local library.

COSTUMES, PROPS, AND OTHER TOOLS OF THE TRADE These can include items as expensive as a video camera; however, the simplest gadgets often generate the most enthusiasm. For example, a costume collection can help the young actor identify with a character; and when the costume is of the child's own design, it becomes doubly inspirational.

Garage sales are a gold mine for costume seekers. Look for old wigs, gawdy jewelry, boots, and hats. To decorate the newfound items, collect a boxful of felt scraps, gold braids, bottle caps, and other assorted safe doodads. These can be glued onto belts and boots for a medieval or futuristic effect.

Also, don't throw away worn sheets, swim caps, brooms, or nylon stockings. Sheets, of course, can be used for everything from capes to togas. A swim cap can become the base for glued-on-yarn "hair," or can be colored with a Magic Marker to make a bright green snake's head. Broomsticks are great canes and nylon stockings can be cut off and used for the heads of bald characters.

A simple makeup kit can also be assembled and kept in an old lunch pail. Scout discount stores after Halloween to find bargains on such gruesome items as scar wax, fake blood, and nose putty. In addition, old cosmetics can often find their way into the makeup kit. Inexpensive paintbrushes work well for makeup application. Baby oil is an inexpensive makeup remover. Of course, professional makeup items can be purchased from specialty companies.

Another relatively inexpensive tool is an audiocassette recorder. Challenge children to seek out and record sound effects. They can also use it to make their own radio plays, following a prepared script or one they've written.

Don't forget your public library. In addition to collections of plays and books about play production, the library probably has records with movement exercises and perhaps some sound-effects records. Also, the library may lend audio- or videocassettes of classic plays. Some libraries have "toybraries" from which puppets may be borrowed. In addition, public libraries often sponsor special puppet shows or improvisational troupes for children.

Developing your child's appreciation for theater need not entail a trip to Broadway, and you don't have to seek out an agent to get your child started in dramatics. Instilling a lifetime love for the theatrical arts *does* mean making dramatics come alive through creative activity and positive viewing experiences.

MUSIC ENRICHMENT PRODUCES GIFTEDNESS

Music is no mere frill. In fact, it may be the "silver cord" that binds all the elements of superior intellectual development, including the artistic and the physical. Researchers from several disciplines — neurology, education, psychology, linguistics — are building up evidence that early music training can stimulate superior intellectual development.

Emily P. Cary, gifted-and-talented-resource teacher for the Fairfax County, Virginia, public schools, describes a number of research findings and their practical applications in an article in the *Roeper Review*. Here are a few:

- The quality and quantity of music heard before age three have as much effect on an understanding of music later as the amount and quality of early parental reading have on a child's language development. Manny Brand, head of the music department at Southwest Texas State University, has found that making good music available to a young child, even just as background, leads to musical awareness very early — for example, infant's babbling will occur in various pitches, often while moving to rhythm.

- Music can and should be integrated into the preschool, kindergarten, and primary curriculum to help students learn traditional skills, such as putting syllables together. For example, Grace Nash, a music researcher and consultant, recommends that kindergarten teachers have children play marbles or shell peas in time to music to increase their vocal skills. Singing, says Nash, advances intellectual development by combining verbalization and creative movement to a rhythm. Nash believes that children who are denied this experience of a multisensory and mixed-media approach to learning can't coordinate their bodies, minds, and voices.

• Music can be used for "guessing" or "discovery learning" in the classroom. This is a technique of encouraging students to create new sounds from "found" objects or from their own voices. This teaches them trial and error, risk taking, and problem solving, and eventually helps them to develop their own musical forms with "odd and wonderful connections."

Cary concludes that "learning begins in the womb — perhaps at the moment of conception — and that the home enriched by music is more likely to produce gifted children than is the unmusical home."

Mothers Nurture Future Maestros

Picture an expectant mother, relaxing in an easy chair with her favorite music on the tape — and the earphones wrapped around her middle. A weird idea?

Not so, according to music educators. Donald Shetler is following the musical development of infants who were "serenaded" by soothing music while they were still in the womb. Some of the children are as old as three now. Although Shetler says it is too early for conclusions, his preliminary observations indicate that these children "imitate accurately sounds made by adults . . . and appear to structure vocalization much earlier than infants who did not have prenatal musical stimulations."

Shetler, writing in an article in *Music Educators Journal,* says many mothers and adult musicians tell him he is on the right track, and he has been encouraged by professionals in medical and audiological research, as well as obstetricians and pediatricians.

NURTURING A LOVE OF MUSIC IN VERY YOUNG CHILDREN Begin with lullabies, says Brand. During lullabies, he says, "the combination of singing, rocking, cuddling, looking and smiling provides the kind of sensory stimulation that enhances mental development and produces such powerful effects on the infant."

Another music researcher, E. E. Gordon, suggests that recorded music for the young child should have a steady tempo, sections with frequently changing dynamics, contrasting timbre, and, most important, pleasing tone quality. You can try playing classical music around the house. Typical children's records with story-telling components are least beneficial, he says.

A third approach recommended by Brand is informal singing with babies — when feeding, changing, and dressing them — accompanied by rhythmic movements with the baby's hands, arms, and legs.

Brand notes that during these early experiences it is not important that an infant be attentive; the purpose "is the unconscious absorption of music." Parents should "musically nourish" their children from birth, Brand advises.

When Should Music Lessons Begin?

Three-year-old Julie takes Suzuki violin. Billy, a few months older, goes to Hochstein School of Music in Rochester, New York, for a program based on the Orff-Schulwerk method. Today there are many options for children to get involved in music, even at the preschool level.

But when should a child, especially if he or she appears to be gifted, begin music lessons? Several music teachers, talking about the timing of introducing a young child to formal music training, agreed that timing for starting music lessons depends very much on each individual child. The following questions can help you decide whether or not your child is ready.

• *Is your child interested in taking music lessons?* When to begin music lessons is more of an emotional thing, according to Joyce Perkins, a former president of Greece Performing Arts Society in Rochester. "Among students for private music lessons, there are two groups: those who are sent over by parents, and those who asked their parents if they could take music lessons. The younger ones are usually prompted by their parents. As long as the child is willing, it usually works out."

Starting music lessons ties in with whether a child is old enough to be able to master the skill introduced. If the music lesson is too difficult, the child cannot do well, may feel bad about himself or herself, and may not have the incentive to go on. For this reason, Perkins thinks that second or third grade may be a good time to start traditional individual music lessons.

Carmen Tan, who was trained as a concert pianist, likes to see children get involved earlier, however. "Some children are ready during their kindergarten year or first grade. Suzuki violin or piano starts as early as three years old or younger," she points out.

For preschoolers, the kind of arrangement made is important. Look into the opportunities for early learning before any decision is made. Learning music by the Suzuki method requires a parent's dedication to taking lessons and practicing alongside the child. There are also frequent concert performances. As a parent, you have to ask yourself if you are prepared for the commitment of intensive involvement. Some music educators also feel that the early reliance on rote is detrimental.

There are less structured music programs, such as the Orff-Schulwerk method, that start with three-year-olds. In them you see line-space, as in written music, marked on the floor, and children playing rhyme games much the same way they do in nursery school. Try to make an appointment to visit such a program with your child. What is your child's response? What is yours? Talk to parents with children enrolled in the program when possible. The less-structured music experience may appeal emotionally more to the young, although for children with exceptional talent, early involvement in more-intensive training may be an advantage.

• *Does your child know how to read and count yet?* In taking traditional music lessons, a certain degree of reading and counting ability is necessary for sight-reading the written music. Most children begin to develop these abilities by the time they enter elementary school. However, don't fall into the trap of relying solely on the child's reading and counting ability when deciding on music lessons. Other factors should be taken into consideration.

• *How good is your child's ear?* Children differ in their development of listening skill as related to music. Some excel in sensing rhythms, tones, and pitches, as well as identification and discrimination of music. Sometimes, however, listening skill is tied to whether a young child pays attention or not.

• *Is your child old enough to sit still for music lessons?* Most lessons last about thirty minutes. A young child may be talented in music or may have learned how to read and count at an early age, but the child may not have the patience to sit through what seems an endless session and be attentive enough to follow the instruction.

• *Does your child have good finger coordination?* "In addition to innate ability, finger coordination has a lot to do with a child's interest and, therefore, a child's concentration," James S. Giorgianni, a piano teacher, points out. Of course, practice plays an important part in developing finger coordination. Still, consider the degree of your child's fine-motor development.

• *How does your child react to practicing?* With a child taking music lessons, the greatest difficulty on the part of both the child and the parent is practicing. Practicing requires a great deal of self-discipline. Is your child cooperative? In some households, practicing becomes a daily hassle. No matter how interested a child is in music, the question may still arise: How do you get your child to practice?

First, try to develop a regular practice schedule. Involve the child in the decision-making process by asking him or her to choose the practice time. If necessary, post a visible schedule on the refrigerator. Clear away temptations such as TV. When the job is well done, encourage the child in some way — a hug, a kiss, an occasional batch of cookies, a special privilege, or a little favor. Be available as a supportive audience to your child if the youngster expresses such a desire.

Do not overcriticize your child. Keep a respectable distance, giving the child time to learn. Don't make the practice time a confrontation or a power struggle between you and your child. A child needs to develop a certain degree of maturity or self-discipline in practicing the music.

• *Is the teacher the right one for your child?* Whether a young child should take music lessons depends to a certain extent on the availability of a good teacher. A sensitive teacher will try to establish a rapport with each child. When teaching a very young child, the teacher may adopt a simpler approach — for instance, starting with a small section of the keyboard near the center of the piano, instead of with an extensive group of notes on the scale, as he or she would for older children.

Don't force your child to take music lessons. Take time and consider all the factors. Get to know your child's interests and abilities before a decision is made. Interest him or her in music as much as you can. Many children are better off waiting for music lessons until they enter school. Regardless of whether or not they take lessons, experiencing music is important to young children. Remember that a young child learns the appreciation of culture, history, aesthetic values, rhythm, and math skills through music.

The youngster's understanding of music, as well as his or her potential and ability in playing it, is a product of both nature and nurture.

THE GIFT OF MUSIC: SUZUKI OR NOT?

The Suzuki method is one of the most acclaimed and, at the same time, criticized programs of music instruction for children. Is it an appropriate technique? Here, an advocate and a critic present their views.

YES: Suzuki Is a Method for Developing Character

Beverly Tucker Graham is a registered teacher trainer for the Suzuki Association of the Americas, and president of the Suzuki Association of Colorado. She notes that most traditional music teachers will not accept a beginning student — even a gifted child — until age six or seven. However, the Suzuki method is, indeed, designed for beginning preschoolers, and is available for piano, violin, viola, cello, harp, and flute. Graham says:

Shinichi Suzuki was fascinated by the way little children learn to speak their native language through hearing and repeating the mother tongue. Suzuki determined that children can use this same method to develop abilities in many areas.

WHEN TO BEGIN   Suzuki believes that ability development begins at birth. A parent who wants to develop a child's love and interest in music should begin playing music recordings during infancy. It is also recommended that parents play the recordings of the Suzuki repertoire if they are possibly interested in enrolling their child in a Suzuki program when the child is ready for formal lessons. The Suzuki tapes are played as background music for the child. The more a student listens, the more quickly he or she learns to play the pieces.

Most children, particularly those who have been listening to the Suzuki tapes, are ready to begin formal lessons between age three and four. Contact a Suzuki teacher when your child is one-and-one-half to two years old in order to observe the teacher and to get on a waiting list, if necessary.

THE TEACHER   There is no certification process for Suzuki teachers. However, the Suzuki Association of the Americas does offer teacher-training units of study. It is important for you to inquire as to how many units of study the teacher has completed, and what other credentials he or she has. Observe the teacher's work with students to determine the atmosphere of the studio and the quality of the students' playing, and talk with the parents of other students in the program.

Children initially learn pieces through a process of ear and imitation. By listening to the tapes, observing other students' lessons, and imitating the teacher, the young student learns to play the pieces he or she has been hearing. The student moves in small steps, mastering one idea before another is added; there are no preconceived ideas about how quickly the "average" child should be progressing.

THE PARENT   Either the mother or the father attends all lessons, taking notes on the assignment to be covered in the daily practices. Many teachers have the parent learn to play some of the beginning pieces. The parent then assumes the role of home teacher, practicing daily with the child and setting a positive tone for learning. All practice sessions and lessons are geared to the child's attention span; a young child might have several short practices during the day.

Suzuki-trained students continue to build their repertoire. Unlike the pattern of traditional lessons, Suzuki students do not drop a piece once they are able to play it. Rather, they continue to play all the pieces they have learned. Through the old pieces, the students develop their playing ability and an ease for performing publicly.

READING MUSIC   Contrary to popular myths, Suzuki students *do* learn to read music. When basic skills are well established, the teacher introduces music reading. Again, this follows the pattern of learning a language — children learn to read and write *after* they learn to speak. The teacher introduces music reading when appropriate, and the parent works daily with the child to develop reading skills. If introduced properly, music reading is not a problem for Suzuki students; they learn as easily and eagerly as traditionally trained students. An advantage Suzuki students exhibit is the ability to memorize very quickly the pieces that they learn through reading.

While the Suzuki method was initially designed for the pre-school beginner, it can be successful with a child of any age. Keep in mind that the Suzuki philosophy encompasses much more than simply teaching a child to play a musical instrument. It is a philosophy of child development and parent/child relationships.

Through the Suzuki method, a child gains self-confidence, self-discipline, and concentration, in addition to the skills needed to make music. Though the level of achievement is often very high, it is not a method designed specifically for producing prodigies and future concert artists. It is a method for developing character and human potential through the use of music.

NO: Suzuki Produces Handicapped Musicians

Janet Brady is an assistant professor at the State University of New York at Binghamton, where she teaches violin and chamber music. A Suzuki critic, she begins with some anecdotes about former Suzuki students:

• Eighteen-year-old Paul walked into his audition for the university symphony expecting the worst. He had sufficiently prepared a movement of Bach, but he knew that sight-reading would also be a part of his test, and he was weak in that area. After an excellent rendition of Bach, the auditioner placed a piece of music on the stand for Paul to sight-read; quarter notes, eighth notes, and rests swirled in front of him. Having no plan of attack, he dove in and played a confused version of the printed page.

• Fourteen-year-old Brant would leave his present traditional teacher with assignments of études, scales, double stops, and repertoire and go straight home to his mother, expecting her to provide guidance, structure, and motivation for his daily practice. He was unable to work on his own; if his mother had a busy week, Brant would not have a well-prepared lesson.

• Twelve-year-old Elise was a talented young violinist. Her music-reading skills were acceptable, her practice habits were slowly developing, but she had a serious problem related to the heavy emphasis placed on playing by ear: if she misread a rhythm or a note in the initial learning stages of a piece, that mistake would be cemented in her daily practice, becoming for her a part of the piece. At her next lesson on the piece, she would be unable to correct it.

Paul, Brant, and Elise are examples of the kinds of problems that many instructors are seeing among string students whose initial training was with the Suzuki method. These problems are not isolated, singular events; they recur frequently enough to enable string teachers to pinpoint specific procedures in the method that hamper students in the long run.

WHERE DO PROBLEMS BEGIN? It is not hard to understand how well-meaning parents are attracted to the Suzuki system. It is indeed a most impressive sight to see a row of tiny three- and four-year-olds playing the "Twinkle" variations from memory. But it is just this exclusive use of rote learning of the Suzuki repertoire that creates future reading problems.

The student relies so heavily on playing by ear that when music reading is introduced (usually too late), his or her violinistic abilities are well beyond the child's reading skills. Placing a piece of music that the student has learned by rote in front of him or her does not teach the child how to read that music; using flash cards to match fingertips with notes on the staff likewise does not do the job. Sight-reading must be taught as an organic part of a developing familiarity with the instrument; it cannot be tacked on at a later date.

A careful appraisal of Suzuki teaching procedures reveals other problem areas as well. The heavy burden of responsibility that is placed on the parent in the early years usually backfires because the young musician is not given the tools to work successfully on his or her own.

Finally, because there is no system of certification in place for properly trained Suzuki teachers, it is difficult to ensure that the teacher your child gets is qualified as either a good Suzuki specialist or even a good musician. A teacher may go to a short Suzuki workshop, return home, and begin teaching three-year-olds to play "Twinkle," without having had sufficient training to carry the students much further.

SOME ALTERNATIVES I think the most important thing we can do for our children is to provide an environment in which music is appreciated for its beauty and for the joy that it gives. Children respond to music from infancy; there is even research showing response of a fetus to musical sounds. If the home is filled with music from early in your child's life, he or she will absorb much of what is heard and will develop an appreciation of differing styles, an awareness of tonal possibilities, and a feel for rhythms.

Educators debate the best age to begin actual music lessons on an instrument. Obviously, the Suzuki method encourages very early beginnings, with most students starting at age three or four. By the time they reach age ten, many have tired of their intense involvement with an instrument and express a desire to move on to something else. You can avoid this attrition by waiting until a child exhibits certain qualities of readiness to begin instruction. Does he or she show an interest in learning to play an instrument? Sing well? Have an attention span long enough for lessons and practice sessions?

Do not be tempted by charming theater or promises of quick results. Instead, look for a way to give your child an appreciation of the values of music, while building the type of instrumental foundation that will ensure a continuing success in the art, whether as an avocation or as a career.

PRESCHOOL IS NOT TOO YOUNG FOR MUSEUMS

Jana Pantazelos, museum volunteer and former fifth-grade teacher, relates her experiences with her toddler and museums, and passes along some good ideas:

> When our son Nicholas was born, my husband and I felt we had to give up our weekly culture treks to the city. Somehow, museums didn't seem to fit in the agenda of two new parents trying to cope with diapers and drool. Those lazy afternoons in art and science galleries were put on hold and were sorely missed. But not for long.
>
> We were determined not to deprive ourselves of these enjoyable and enriching excursions. And, more important, we wanted to introduce our son to these experiences as soon as possible.
>
> When Nicholas was backpack age, we carried him through museums; when he was stroller age, we wheeled him through; and

when he was a toddler, we chased him through. But, at every age, we made sure it was fun. We never lectured, and we never stayed too long.

Parents who are art lovers and museum fans want to share with their child the same joy and enthusiasm they feel. By doing a little planning and choosing appropriate exhibits, your child will soon be at home in museum surroundings.

Start Young and Have Fun

When Nicholas was almost three we took him to a special museum show. Our regional museum had mounted a beautiful exhibition of restored carousel animals collected from around the world.

He loved the colorfully decorated animals and scampered from horse to lion to ostrich calling their names and giggling with excitement. The museum had thoughtfully placed several animals aside especially for kids to touch, and Nicholas joined the throng of youngsters surrounding the gaily painted steeds.

He had just started preschool that fall and was beginning to enjoy sharing experiences with his new friends. On the Monday after his museum visit, he took the exhibition catalog and our Polaroid snapshots to school. He enjoyed the enthusiastic response of his teacher and schoolmates. The next time we said we were going to the museum, he looked forward to it as much as we did.

Look for Variety

The natural-science museum was next on our agenda. Children have an affinity for animals and nature. And, of course, there are dinosaurs! Children love these fascinating "monsters" of prehistory, and the gargantuan reconstructed skeletons at the natural-science museum are sure to delight and amaze.

Planets, stars, and space are other topics that kids easily get enthusiastic over. Nicholas loved the planetarium show and the mobile-like model of the solar system at our academy of sciences. These celestial entertainments are still favorites of his.

The huge, swaying Foucault pendulum was another attraction that held a special fascination for him. He stood at the railing watching the slow-motion swing of the pendulum as it tumbled one peg after another. He didn't quite grasp that this was evidence of the earth's rotation, but it was a good start. Now, at age eight, he tells *us* how it works!

From science, we moved on to art. This is my first love, and I found that Nicholas was drawn to sculpture even before we consciously introduced him to museum pieces. Children are attracted to large, imaginative objects, and the outdoor sculptures and statuary we encountered in shopping malls and parks invited Nicholas's curiosity and inquiring fingers. We talked about the shape, color, and form of the objects, which ranged from undefinable abstracts to historic commemorative statues.

Abstract art is not foreboding or mysterious to children. They are more receptive to art in all forms than are many adults. They have no preconceptions, harbor few prejudices, and enjoy the basic elements of abstract art with little explanation. They often take the lead in the enjoyment of these pieces. The strong colors and undefined shapes of nonrepresentational art appeal to them on a basic level.

Enhancing Museum Visits

Here are a few ideas and activities to spark your museum visits. They are not complicated, do not require a lot of preparation, and take little extra time. The bonus is that you will find they increase the entire family's enjoyment of your museum excursions.

• *Look for special exhibits with "kid appeal."* That wonderful exhibit of carousel animals was the perfect introduction for us. Over the years, other exhibitions came along that we enjoyed as well. Examples of what to look for include puppets and marionettes, clothing from different historic eras, circus artifacts, election memorabilia, American quilts, early drawings of the Peanuts gang, and knighthood armor. These were all popular with families in our area, and more museums are organizing exhibitions with special family appeal. They realize that their futures depend on cultivating a new generation of museum-goers.

• *Limit the visit to about forty-five minutes, and know where you are going.* Capitalize on your child's interests — whether horses or boats or Indians — so that he or she can show off. A good place to begin is the museum's information desk, where you can ask for recommendations on a few (no more than five) paintings or objects your child would enjoy. By focusing on just a few things at a time, instead of an overview of the museum, you can look forward to more special moments to share in the future. Don't worry about your own lack of knowledge about art; your enthusiasm is enough of a message to your child that a museum is a wonderful treasure.

• *Play gallery games.* Try "treasure hunts" for color, shape, line, or object. For example, choose a color and have your child look for it in paintings; look for triangles, circles, and squares in abstract paintings and sculpture. Encourage your child to imagine the sounds or smells in a painting — a flower in bloom, a fresh ocean breeze.

Another game involves visual memory. Have your child study a painting, then turn away and answer questions about it: What color are her eyes? What time of day does the painting suggest?

Try a category game using museum postcards. Choose and define two or three art terms, such as "portrait," "landscape," and "still life." Place picture postcards in the correct stack for each term. This can also be done with science terms, such as "mammals" and "reptiles" or "planet," "sun," and "galaxy."

• *Talk about the feelings that different colors evoke and why they are used in certain paintings.* For example, blues, greens, and purples are calm, serene colors used in landscapes, seascapes, and romantic works; red is an exciting, emotional color used for emphasis in realistic and abstract works.

• *Discuss the different materials used in sculpture.* Why did the sculptor choose one material over other possibilities — wood rather than metal, stone rather than clay, and so on.

• *Use storytelling with a painting to pique your child's interest.* For example, using a painting of a pastoral scene, try asking your young viewer advice on where to build a cabin. This engages youngsters in exploring and discussing the whole canvas.

• *Use museum resources.* The education director at the museum arranges programs, visits, classes, and activities for school and youth groups. The director can also suggest activities for parents and their children. Give the education office a call before your next visit.

Visit the museum gift shop. It is an unexpected resource for parents. Stop by *before* your planned excursion. There will be items your child will love, and the books, games, and models chosen by the museum buyers will provide ideas for your visits.

• *Follow up the visit immediately.* On the way home, discuss which painting or object you would want to save, if you could have only one. Also, take home postcards from the museum; let your child pick out his or her favorites — while you choose some for the next visit.

Families on the Go

The following list of hands-on museums, theme parks, and historic villages around the country features attractions especially suited to the creative nature and curiosity of young gifted children. You'll find others through the tourist bureaus of cities and states you plan to visit. Call or write ahead for information about attractions, tours, and special events.

HANDS-ON MUSEUMS

Boston Children's Museum. Museum Wharf, 300 Congress St., Boston, MA 02210 (617-426-6500).

Over 100 topics are available from its Rent-a-Kit program, including an exploration of musical instruments and their sounds.

California Museum of Science and Industry. 700 State Dr., Los Angeles, CA 90037 (213-744-7438).

Children use computer-aided design equipment to run their own bicycle factory.

Capital Children's Museum. 800 Third St., N.E., Washington, DC 20002 (202-543-8600).

Children learn about other cultures by trying their hands at traditional handicrafts like weaving and pottery making.

Discovery Place. 301 N. Tryon St., Charlotte, NC 28202 (704-372-6261).

The fauna and flora of a rain forest and a tide pool are features of this "please-touch" museum.

The Exploratorium. 3601 Lyon St., San Francisco, CA 94123 (415-563-3200).

In one sample experiment, an everyday cardboard box and light bulb are combined with mirrors, lenses, and prisms to guide students through a variety of experiments with optics.

Please Touch Museum. 210 N. 21st Street, Philadelphia, PA 19103 (215-963-0667).

Materials and activities are devoted exclusively to children under seven years old.

THEME PARKS

Busch Gardens, The Old Country. P.O. Drawer FJ, Williamsburg, VA 23187 (804-253-3350).

This park features authentically detailed seventeenth-century European hamlets of England, France, Germany, Scotland, and Italy.

Carowinds. P.O. Box 240516, Charlotte, NC 28224 (704-588-2606).

This park is made up of nine theme areas depicting different aspects of Carolina history and culture.

Disneyland. Guest Relations, 1313 Harbor Blvd., Anaheim, CA 92803 (714-999-4565).

"Adventure thru Inner Space" is a mental trip in which you are reduced in size to explore the world of the atom. Visit a replica of Mission Control before boarding "Mission to Mars." "Submarine Voyage" lets you explore underseas.

Great America. P.O. Box 1776, Santa Clara, CA 95052 (408-988-2464).

"Hometown Square" looks like a rural American town in the 1920s; "Yukon Territory" resembles the gold-rush days of the late 1890s; "Yankee Harbor" is fashioned after a Revolutionary War–era New England fishing village; "Orleans Place" simulates New Orleans in 1850.

Opryland USA. 2802 Opryland Dr., Nashville, TN 37214 (615-889-6600).

In addition to rides, this park specializes in live musical productions: country and bluegrass, Gay Nineties, gospel, and 1950s rock 'n' roll.

San Diego's Wild Animal Park. 15500 San Pasqual Valley Rd., Escondido, CA 92027 (619-747-8702).

This park, which groups animals into communities as they're found in the wild, is home to 2,300 animals representing 225 species, including 36 species that are endangered or extinct in the wild.

Sesame Place. P.O. Box L579, 100 Sesame Rd., Langhorne, PA 19047 (215-757-1100; 215-752-7070).

Sesame Place combines play with science experiments and computer games. A few highlights include "Star Lightning," "Laser Lights," and "Foot Notes."

Universal Studios Tour. 100 Universal City Plaza, Universal City, CA 91608 (818-508-9600; 818-508-5444).

Live shows explore stunts, makeup, animal acting, sound effects, and computer animation at this working movie studio.

Walt Disney World. P.O. Box 1000, Lake Buena Vista, FL 32830-5000 (407-824-4321).

"The Living Seas" simulates the life-support ecosystems of a Caribbean coral reef. "Horizons" takes visitors for a trip into the future to see a holographic telephone, magnetic levitation trains, and robotic harvesters.

HISTORIC VILLAGES

Arizona Historical Society. 949 E. Second St., Tucson, AZ 85719 (602-628-5775).

The history museum in Phoenix is one of several divisions of the Arizona Historical Society devoted to depicting the history and development of Arizona. The museum includes a 1928 Phoenix streetcar and authentic streetcar track, an early 1900s-style drugstore, a general store, toy store, a mine tunnel, and a hands-on museum. The Society's Tucson museum contains a costume hall, period rooms, a life-size copper mine, and a Spanish-heritage exhibit.

Colonial Williamsburg. P.O. Box C. Williamsburg, VA 23187 (804-220-1000).

Nearly 40 exhibitions and activities and 88 restored buildings comprise the 173 acres of Colonial Williamsburg, a city that was a major cultural and political center from 1699 to 1780. Among the attractions are several museums, 225 period rooms furnished with antiques, costumed hosts and hostesses who relate the history of the buildings, 20 craft shops, many gardens, a variety of tours, and frequent special events.

Henry Ford Museum and Greenfield Village. P.O. Box 1970, Dearborn, MI 48121 (313-271-1620).

This extensive historic complex uses artifacts, restored buildings, and demonstrations to tell the story of America's transformation from a rural to an industrial society. The museum features collections related to transportation (200 autos and much more), communication, machinery, agriculture, and domestic arts. Greenfield Village features the laboratory complex where Edison worked, the Wright brothers' bicycle shop, operating sawmills, an early machine shop, and rides in old-style vehicles.

Historic Edenton. P.O. Box 474, Edenton, NC 27932 (919-482-3663).

The town of Edenton, incorporated in 1722 as the first capital of the province of North Carolina, has a long and interesting history. The Barker House Visitor Center offers an orientation slide program and a guided tour of historic houses; or take a self-guided walking tour of three centuries of homes.

Mystic Seaport Museum, Inc. P.O. Box 6000, Mystic, CT 06355 (203-572-0711).

This maritime museum emphasizes understanding of American maritime history and its impact on the economic, social, and cultural life of the United States. Included in the 17-acre exhibit area are 60 historic buildings, 4 major vessels, more than 300 boats, a planetarium, and maritime artifacts. Also featured are demonstrations of ironworking, woodcarving, and sailmaking; a children's museum featuring nineteenth-century toys and activities; and games on the village green.

Old City Park. 1717 Gano, Dallas, TX 75215 (214-421-5141).

Fourteen acres contain 37 restored structures and their furnishings, including log houses, Victorian architecture, commercial buildings, a bandstand, a doctor's office, windmills, and an 1888 school. Craft and cooking demonstrations and special events carry out the theme of how life was lived in this region between 1840 and 1910.

Pioneer Village and Kern County Museum. 3801 Chester Ave., Bakersfield, CA 93301 (805-861-2132).

Wander through the village, 15 acres of nineteenth-century streets; visit memorabilia displays, an 1891 Victorian mansion, a log cabin, a ranch house, a church, a one-room school, a sheepherder's cabin, a dressmaker's shop, a dentist's office, and a replica of the first county hospital. Adjacent is the museum, which displays such historical artifacts as guns of the Old West, gems and minerals, ostrich feathers, and oak furniture.

Plimoth Plantation. P.O. Box 1620, Plymouth, MA 02360 (508-746-1622).

An hour from Boston, this "Living Museum of 17th Century

Plymouth" depicts life in 1627 in Plymouth colony, the first permanent English settlement in the New World. Included are a reproduction of the village, a full-scale replica of the type of ship that carried the colonists, and Wampanoag Summer Campsite, which reflects the history and culture of the Indians of that time. Museum staff perform typical daily chores and talk and act like seventeenth-century men and women.

Santa Fe Trail Center. Rte. 3, Larned, KS 67550 (316-285-2054).

This museum tells the story of the Santa Fe Trail area from the prehistoric Indian era, through the settlement period, up to 1920. The exhibits include a reconstruction of a Wichita Indian hunting lodge, period rooms depicting life in a rural home on the plains, and artifacts from pioneer churches. The outdoor museum also features replicas of a sod house and dugout, an original one-room schoolhouse, and railway depot.

Vesterheim, the Norwegian American Museum. 502 W. Water St., Decorah, IA 52101 (319-382-9681).

Vesterheim, which means "western home," includes buildings, home furnishings, costumes, artworks, tools, and toys that tell the story of Norwegian immigrants, beginning with their culture in Norway.

CULTIVATE YOUR YOUNG SPROUT

If you enjoy gardening, you probably feel a need to share the joy of this hobby with your child and encourage him or her to participate in the planting, tending, and harvesting of the family garden. You can take the process even one step further by allowing your youngster to have his or her own plot. It doesn't need to be big. A 5′×5′ space will do perfectly.

Raising a garden is a marvelous learning experience for children. Not only do they acquire practical agricultural knowledge, they also learn the satisfaction that comes from transforming an idea into reality through the labor of their own hands. Of course they're not going to be able to raise a garden all by themselves. They'll need an adult to turn to for advice, and to do the heavy work like rototilling. But you'll be amazed at how hard even a very young child will work in his or her very own garden. And you'll be delighted by the proud smile on your youngster's face when he or she is the one providing fresh vegetables for the family table.

Getting Started

The learning process begins before the first seed is sown. Help your child draw a plan for the garden on graph paper with large, one-inch squares. It doesn't have to be perfectly drawn or even drawn to scale, but the graph paper will help a youngster see the relationship of small plots within the large plot. Encourage your son or daughter to visualize what the garden will actually look like, to consider the artistic as well as the practical side of the garden (whether it will also contain flowers, a scarecrow, and so on). Explain succession planting (planning your plantings — spring, summer, and fall crops — so you get as many as three harvests from the same plot). This not only ensures the most efficient use of available space, but also gives the youngster practice thinking in the dimension of time as well as space.

Squash, melons, pumpkins, and cucumbers are always popular with kids. The large seeds are easy to plant in flat-topped hills. The plants sprout quickly enough to satisfy children with limited patience and, with a minimum of care, will produce a bountiful crop. Bush varieties are generally a better choice than vining plants because they take less room and are easier to cultivate.

Greens are another good choice. Kids love to nibble on their crops, and greens give them a vitamin-packed opportunity to do so. To avoid planting greens too thickly, try mixing the small seeds with finely powdered dirt and planting the mixture. Mix radish seeds with any slow sprouters. The radishes will sprout quickly and indicate the rows. (Incidentally, be sure your child marks everything planted. Making colorful garden markers is a fun activity.)

Plants that are unusual in some way are especially exciting for children. Ornamental popcorn is an outdoor plant of special delight; in a few weeks the kernels can be harvested and popped. Giant sunflowers are worth considering for sheer drama. Some easy and attractive plants to grow include flowering maple, impatiens, Moses-in-the-bulrushes, piggyback plant, mint, and strawberry begonia.

Further Hints

Here are a few suggestions to make gardening easier and safer for your child.

- Never use poisons.
- Do not allow very young children to use hoes; older children should have hoes that are the proper size for them.
- Wear gloves to help prevent blisters.
- Always have your child shower after working in the garden; young skin is very sensitive.
- Avoid sunburn and heat prostration by working only in the early morning and evening.
- Be sure your hose nozzle will adjust to a fine spray to avoid battering plants and washing seeds away.

Gardening can give your child a feeling for the cycles of life. Be sure to preserve at least one thing raised to eat in the wintertime — maybe a pumpkin for a Christmas pie. When you eat it, talk about the day you planted the seed, and the day you harvested the pumpkin. Encourage your child to save seeds for next year's garden to complete the cycle.

KITCHEN CONCOCTIONS: RECIPE FOR LEARNING

The children of those who love to cook are lucky: the parents' enthusiasm will be contagious, and the kids can learn by their side. Those for whom cooking is a routine task need to make more of a purposeful effort to introduce the pleasures of the culinary arts into the lives of their gifted children — boys as well as girls. Regardless of whether you are a chef or not, it is well worth the effort to give your youngster the experience of learning to cook.

Cooking involves sharpening motor, math, and science skills and thinking ahead. In addition, young cooks get a chance to be creative and to learn about nutrition. The best part is that the rewards are almost immediate, making it the ideal home-learning activity for an impatient child. (Don't let impatience compromise safety, however.)

What to Expect

Though you may not want to encourage your kids to concoct and eat too many sweets, the preparation of snacks sometimes works to ease a child into kitchen lessons. Encourage experimentation. Even if *you* always follow recipes to the letter, your child can benefit from trying something different and seeing what happens. Do not look upon inedible "failures" as a waste of time. If you are willing to try (almost) anything your child prepares, he or she will be more likely to sample foods you suggest, at home and in restaurants.

Be prepared for lots of mess during the process; ignore it until the end of the session. Include cleanup chores in the agenda. You can share the burden if it's too overwhelming, but don't let your young cook fall into the habit of leaving messes for others.

Getting Started

Visit the library and bookstore with your novice chef for some beginner cookbooks, or write away for some of those listed at the end of this chapter. When you're deciding whether to purchase a particular cookbook, study one of its recipes for a familiar dish and be sure the steps are listed clearly. A "bug" in a recipe can be as disastrous as one in a computer program.

Together, choose one or more recipes, list the ingredients you'll need to buy, and shop for them. Make certain you have on hand all the kitchen equipment necessary, including mixing implements and pans. Halfway through a recipe is no time to discover an item is missing.

If you're not confident of your own culinary skills, try to line up a resource person (uncle, grandmother, neighbor) whom you can ask for help when something doesn't work as expected.

Creativity and flexibility enter the kitchen when your child decides to substitute more healthful ingredients than the ones called for, or to change some aspect of a recipe. Kids love to make up recipes from scratch and give them amusing names. Combining foods in unaccustomed ways or using unexpected colors can be exciting, and occasionally edible.

The Science of Food

The chemistry of foods is observed when sugar dissolves in hot water, gelatin changes from a liquid to a solid in the refrigerator, yeast causes dough to rise, and a soft-boiled egg blackens a silver teaspoon (the sulfur in the egg white does it). Other scientific conversation starters include these facts:

- Most adults consume about half a ton of food and drink each year (research together in the library how much the average-size four-year-old eats).
- The small intestine, which separates what your body can use from what it can't, is about twenty feet long.
- Your stomach contains hydrochloric acid — a compound that is powerful enough to dissolve cement and that would eat away the skin on your finger if you touched it.

ADDITIONAL RESOURCES

Art

Mommy, It's a Renoir, by Aline D. Wolf. Parent Child Press (P.O. Box 767, Altoona, PA 16603), 1986.

A unique book for parents and teachers to help them begin presenting fine art to children as young as three. Complete instructions for children on how to group and sort postcard-size reproductions in a graduated series of activities.

Cooking

The Culinary Kid, by Sheila Flynn-Esquivel and Valerie Orleans. Saint Joseph Hospital Publications (P.O. Box 5600, Orange, CA 92613-5600), 1986.

Healthy and speedy recipes and up-to-date information about nutrition.

Mudlicious, by Jan Irving and Robin Curie. Libraries Unlimited (P.O. Box 263, Littleton, CO 80160-1263), 1986.

Twelve chapters of food- and literature-related activities for young children, including recipes, finger plays, art projects, songs, and story suggestions. Useful for parents and early childhood educators.

My First Cookbook, by Rena Coyle. Workman Publishing (1 W. 39th St., New York, NY 10018), 1986.

Bialosky, a toy bear, shows readers how to prepare 50 dishes. Instructions are extensive and clear, though adult help is often needed.

Peter Rabbit's Cookery Book, compiled by Anne Emerson, illustrated by Beatrix Potter. Viking Penguin Children's Books (40 W. 23rd St., New York, NY 10010), 1986.

This collection of 21 recipes is inspired by the food described in the Peter Rabbit stories. Step-by-step instructions are suitable for beginners.

Small World Cookbook, compiled by the Montessori Teachers Association of Pennsylvania (Greene Towne School, 2013 Appletree St., Philadelphia, PA 19103).

A collection of international recipes and activities for children. Each is designated by difficulty level, ranging from "fairly uncomplicated" to "more complex."

Dramatics

BOOKS

Make-Up, Costumes and Masks for the Stage, by Ole Bruum Rasmussen and Grete Peterson. Sterling Publishing, 1981.

Monster Make-Up, by Marcia Lynn Cox. Grossett and Dunlap, 1976.

MAKEUP SUPPLIERS

Ben Nye Company, Inc., 11571 Santa Monica Blvd., Los Angeles, CA 90025.

Bob Kelly Cosmetics, Inc., 151 W. 46th St., New York, NY 10036.

M. Stein Cosmetic Co., 430 Broome St., New York, NY 10013.

RECORDINGS

Educational Activities, Inc., P.O. Box 392, Freeport, NY 11520.

Gateway Records SFX Sound Effects Library, P.O. Box 5087, FDR Station, New York, NY 10150.

Gardening

Children's Gardens, by Elizabeth Bremner and John Pusey. Common Ground Garden Program (2615 S. Grand Ave., Suite 400, Los Angeles, CA 90007), 1982.

Educational activities and how-to advice are included in this complete "field guide for teachers, parents and volunteers."

"A Child's Garden." Gardener's Eden, P.O. Box 7307, San Francisco, CA 94120.

Includes 14 packets of seeds (yard-long beans, giant pumpkins, wildflowers, and so on), a how-to booklet, stakes, and string. A ready-made gift for the beginner.

Eat the Fruit, Plant the Seed, by Millicent E. Selsam and Jerome Wexler. Morrow, 1980.

A beginning how-to book that describes and pictures six fruits whose seeds produce interesting plants.

Free Stuff for Home and Garden. Meadowbrook Press (18318 Minnetonka Blvd., Deephaven, MN 55391), 1981.

The gardening sections include seed, bulb, and other catalogs, and informative pamphlets.

Gardens for All. National Association for Gardening, 180 Flynn Ave., Burlington, VT 05401.

This monthly newsmagazine contains gardening advice and how-to information, seed-swapping columns, and good ideas for gardeners at all levels.

My Garden: A Journal for Gardening throughout the Year, by Louise Murphy. Scribner's, 1980.

Monthly gardening activities and space to record observations.

2001 Free Things for the Garden, by Marilyn and Robert Hendrickson. St. Martin's, 1983.

A directory of free and low-cost booklets, catalogs, and posters for gardeners of all ages.

Window Gardens, by Lizzie Boyd. Crown, 1985.

With color photographs and an illustrated how-to section, this book tells how the water and sunlight needs of plants can easily be met in window boxes.

Music

PICTURE BOOKS

Ben's Trumpet, by Rachel Isadora. (See listing in chapter 11.)

Loudmouth George and the Cornet, by Nancy Carlson. Carolrhoda, 1983.

Loudmouth George, a naughty rabbit-child, thinks he's a virtuoso on the cornet and lets everyone know it — but his ineptitude finally gets him dismissed from the school band. A funny tale with a gentle message, wrapped around vivacious illustrations.

Max, the Music Maker, by Miriam Stecher. (See listing in chapter 11.)

Miranda, by Tricia Tusa. Macmillan, 1985.

Miranda loves to play Bach, Haydn, and Mozart on the piano, but the day she hears boogie-woogie, her music interests change — much to the consternation of her family, her piano instructor, and her teacher. She finds, however, a delightful way to satisfy everyone, including herself.

The Philharmonic Gets Dressed, by Karla Kuskin. (See listing in chapter 11.)

Pooks, by Elizabeth Isle. Lippincott, 1983.

Jaunty line drawings and a simple story marvelously reveal the affectionate relationship between conductor-cellist Mstislav Rostropovich and his small dog, Pooks, who goes everywhere with him.

Ty's One-Man Band, by Mildred P. Walter. (See listing in chapter 11.)

Travel/Activity

Families on the Go, 1259 E. Camino Real #147, Menlo Park, CA 94025.

This free mail-order catalog features over 200 travel and activity books, specially selected for families with kids, from toddlers to teenagers.

All Work and No Play
Makes Jack a Dull Boy
(and Jill a Dull Girl)

GIFTED CHILDREN need stimulating play to develop their physical, social, and intellectual skills. Studies of kindergarten children have established a significant correlation between their playfulness and aspects of divergent or creative thinking. And young children observed in "free play" with specific materials have exhibited high degrees of problem solving, goal-directed behavior, and persistence.

But parents are often overwhelmed with the sheer number of toys being produced for toddlers and preschoolers. How do you select the right ones?

In this chapter, after offering some general guidelines on what constitutes an appropriately challenging play experience, we make some suggestions for both commercial and "homemade" toys and games to use with your youngster.

Keep in mind that the age levels listed for the items are only a suggested range. You need to assess the verbal, mathematical, visual/spacial, manipulative, and physical skills of your child before making your choices.

MAXIMIZE THE VALUE OF PLAY

To help your child get the most out of play, here are some starter ideas for *your* role (from a special issue of *Practical Applications of Research*, the newsletter of Phi Delta Kappa's Center on Evaluation, Development, and Research):

- Watch your children play, and learn what they like and dis-like, their favorite themes and interests. Encourage them to talk about their play; let them know you're interested.
- Show playfulness yourself. Children learn from imitating adults. Help them by making comments and asking questions that encourage playing. Also encourage pretending for fun and learning.
- Play with your children and help them select appropriate play materials. Support them by praising their efforts at using props and materials and their efforts at role playing.
- Plan for your children's play. Provide a place of their own to play and a place for organizing materials and toys.

HOW TO HAVE (CHALLENGING) FUN TOGETHER

Mihalyi Csikszentmihalyi, a behavioral scientist at the University of Chicago, has devoted more than a decade of research to understanding "the politics of enjoyment." In his interviews with different groups of players, people came up with many words to describe the intrinsic reward involved in having fun: "timeless, immediate feedback, total involvement, lack of inner dialog, focused, centered, graceful, challenged, clear, alert, alive, awake." However, Csikszentmihalyi discovered that, despite the divergence of the forms of fun they each pursued, they could all agree on a common word to describe the experience: *flow*.

Worry, Boredom, Anxiety

The accompanying diagram is a rendition of Csikszentmihalyi's formulation. Flow is depicted as a channel. Any point in this channel represents a relative balance between risks and abilities. Regardless of the activity in question, it is most rewarding when there is some degree of risk.

When the risk is greater than the abilities, when the player feels that the challenge is simply too difficult, the experience changes to one of worry and, ultimately, anxiety. Conversely, when the challenge is lacking, boredom sets in. Interestingly, Csikszcyentmihalyi has the word "anxiety" on either side of the channel. The experience of anxiety is the same, whether provoked by worry or boredom. When we are merely worried or bored, we can still move ourselves "flow-ward" by increasing or decreasing the risk. Once we become truly anxious, however, we lose contact, we lose direction, we feel lost. Thus, boredom and worry, rather than being merely negative experiences, also become guidelines.

Most of our best, individual fun experiences are right on the edge, right on the border of worry. That's what you'll probably find when you brainstorm with your family and draw your own flow channel, as explained below.

Family fun, the kind where tots and grown-ups and everyone in between are enjoying an activity together, is a positive, transforming experience, observes Bernard DeKoven, president of Playworks, Inc., in Palo Alto, California. On the following pages, he describes how to discover new avenues for having family fun (based on his seminar "The Living Game").

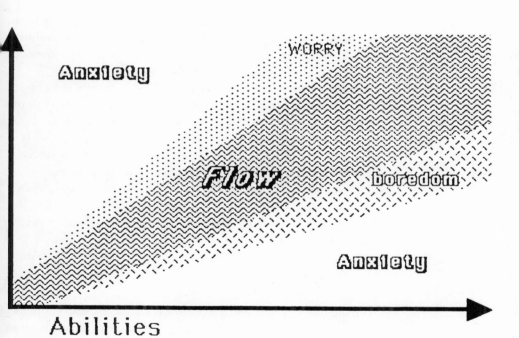

WHAT DO YOU DO FOR FUN?
An Essay by Bernard DeKoven

Get pencil and paper and gather your family around. You are going to make four lists.

1. For the first list, brainstorm all the responses to the question "What do you do for fun?" Record all the responses, like play board games, ball games, sports; play with a toy; play hide-and-seek; play house; pretend; go shopping, to restaurants, to movies; dance; sing; watch TV; eat; do a job.
2. Across from each item record a second list of how each person feels when that activity is the most fun.
3. In a third list, record which activities you do as a family.
4. On the fourth list, record how each person feels when family activities are the most fun.

Now, on another sheet, draw a big "L." Label the horizontal line "Abilities" and the vertical line "Risks." (See the accompanying diagram.)

The word "Abilities" refers to how skilled you have to be in order to do something. Clearly, ice skating requires more abilities than taking a bath. The word "Risks" refers to the consequences of failure. Again, ice skating is high-risk.

Select various activities from your first list and write each inside the "L," positioning it so as to reflect the amount of abilities the person is exercising, and the degree of risk the person is taking when the activity is clearly the most fun.

The rewards of having fun are intrinsic, they are not material or concrete. The experience of intrinsic reward as described by people who are out on a pleasant walk is the same as that described by people who find their joys on the edge of mortal peril. Remarkably, the rewards are the same. They vary only in intensity; qualitatively, the experience is the same.

Confluence

Having fun *together*, being in flow when someone else is in flow, is yet another phenomenon, one even more powerful and motivating than personal intrinsic reward. I call this experience *confluence*.

As you examine your "which-of-these-do-we-do-as-a-family?"

list, look at the words you used to describe the "flow" condition
of each activity (how you *felt* about them). Most likely these words
really could not apply to the solitary experience. Sure, you were
focused, involved, attentive. But you were also experiencing intimacy, sharing, unity, joining, harmony, understanding, communication, serendipity.

When we enjoy each other and ourselves, we have a different
kind of fun than we have when we are only enjoying ourselves.
When we are in confluence, we are each enlarged somehow by the
other. If you refer to the flow diagram, you could depict confluence
simply by widening the flow channel. The effect of confluence is
that you are able to stay in flow even though your personal risk is
actually higher or lower than your individual tolerance. You enjoy
things you would not enjoy alone. It is for this reason that confluence, the experience of having fun together, is such a great treasure.

In Sum: How To

At the heart of practically everything that is "done for fun" there
is some kind of challenge. Look again at your lists of fun activities,
or at your diagram. There may not be a goal or purpose, but there
is always some kind of "let's see if I can do this." The degree of
challenge, however, is negotiable. In other words, if it gets too
hard, we can make it easier. If it's too easy, we can make it harder.
Those activities, the ones with the broadest range of challenge,
seem to be the most likely to lead to confluence.

One of my children's favorite games was one we eventually called
"colors." We would all, at the very same moment, shout the name
of any color at all. I usually have the most fun just being as random
as possible in my choices. On the other hand, the kids would
frequently find themselves trying to guess what the other was going
to say. Thus, the object became for everybody to have said the
same color at the same time. When we did, we all won. When
somebody didn't, only some of us won.

Granted, this was a very low-risk game. One really not very far
"flow-wards" from boredom. But the risk was also richly varied.
Each of us could try to win, or try not to win, or hardly try at all.
But there were times when it was really fun.

So if you want to experience confluence more directly and

positively, if your goal is to share it with your family, you'll have the most luck trying something whose challenge is rich enough to sustain the variety of abilities that your family members have to bring to the game. No activity is too stupid. No family member is too smart. What's important is variety and the common denominator of sharing time. If the goal is to experience confluence, even watching TV, or doing the dishes, or raking leaves, or washing the car together can help you reach it. On the other hand, there are degrees of confluence that can take you each and all to a new level of excellence. To reach these, you might have to go to extremes, like giving a party, perhaps, or maybe even camping. Expand your list of "most fun, family activities." What might you try that's not on your list? The possibilities are boundless.

SOME STANDARD EQUIPMENT

"As your baby's first teacher, what do you need in the way of equipment?" asks Burton L. White, director of the Center for Parent Education. The following suggestions are from White's recommended list of standard equipment for toddlers and preschoolers. We've selected the more developmentally oriented pieces of equipment and listed them below, along with notes about each, appropriate ages, and approximate costs.

White's center is a public-service organization that offers assistance to professionals and parents concerned with the education of children in the first three years of life. It publishes a newsletter, offers training workshops, and provides speakers, consultants, and materials for conferences, projects, and programs. For more information write to the Center for Parent Education, 55 Chapel St., Newton, MA 02160.

CRIB GYM   A crib gym provides opportunities for your baby to have fun exploring the nearby world while also developing eye/ hand coordination. Several types are commercially available, but many have major flaws, so be careful in your selection. For instance, avoid those that suspend objects from strings (this tends to frustrate infants). Also, a child who sits up is too old for a crib gym, as its environment then becomes confining. Ages 6 weeks to 6 months. *About $8.*

WALKER   A walker enables your child to satisfy curiosity and practice leg extensions. (Without a walker, your child is likely to insist on being picked up and carried frequently during this period.) Safety is a paramount concern here. Supervise its use at all times — never let your baby use a walker while you are looking elsewhere! Discontinue using a walker as soon as your child can get around on his or her own. Make sure you get a well-made one. Ages 4 months to crawling (usually 7 months). *About $15.*

SURPRISE BUSY BOX   The Surprise Busy Box stimulates your baby's interest in operating simple gadgets and piques curiosity when he or she seems bored. Not many commercial toys have this much play value. Ages 7–18 months. *Manufactured by Gabriel Industries of California and available at toy stores and through the Sears catalog. About $10.*

BOOKS WITH STIFF PAGES   These provide your baby with eye/hand practice, including moving hinged objects. Don't expect much interest in pictures or stories until about the middle of the second year. Up until then books are primarily manipulative devices. Ages 7–14 months. *About $4 each.*

TOY TELEPHONE   A toy telephone enhances your baby's interest in make-believe activity. Your baby will have just as much fun with the real phone, but be careful about the danger involved. Ages 12–36 months. *About $8.*

BALLS   Balls in great variety are the most popular type of toy during your child's second year. They are great for learning about the movements of objects, for practicing throwing and chasing, for picking up and carrying, and for playing together. Get a variety of sizes, including inflatable beach balls (the bigger, the better) and soft sponge footballs. Ages 12 months and up. *About 50¢ to $1 and up.*

POTS AND PANS   These kitchen utensils feed your child's curiosity about objects and sounds. Ages 6 months and up.

PLASTIC CONTAINERS WITH LIDS   These will help your baby develop eye/hand skills. Babies enjoy removing and replacing lids on containers, so be sure the materials are not too difficult. Plastic containers also are great for water play. Empty ice-cream containers are fine (if they have handles, remove them first). Ages 7–15 months.

ASSORTMENTS OF HOUSEHOLD OBJECTS   Gather together a large plastic container with at least a dozen assorted, small, but safe objects (such as thread spools and small, unbreakable plastic doodads). With this collection your child can explore small objects and practice eye/hand skills. Toddlers seem enticed by "collections" of small items. (Caution: Don't give them objects small enough to swallow.) They'll examine these one at a time or, at other times, they'll dump them all out at once. Ages 7–15 months.

FOUR-WHEELED RIDING TOYS   Your child can sit on or straddle small, low, four-wheeled toys and move about to develop mastery of large-muscle skills. There are many good ones on the market. Ages 14–30 months. *About $15.*

DOLLS AND DOLL CARRIAGES   Validated over time, dolls and doll carriages feed your child's rapidly growing imagination. Ages 14–36 months. *About $25.*

STORYBOOKS AND PICTURE BOOKS   Books support the development of language, curiosity, and a healthy social life. By the middle of the second year, your child's language-achievement levels and social interest should be ready for storytelling — maybe a little earlier. The more, the better. Ages 18 months to 3 years (some publishers list age ranges from 4 through 8 years). *About $4 each.*

DRAWING MATERIALS   Crayons, paper, and the like are important as representational drawing emerges during the third year. These are also good practice for using writing implements. Have a large and varied supply available. Ages 2 years and up. *About $3.*

SIMPLE WOODEN PUZZLES   These toys provide a challenge to intellectual and eye/hand skills. Compile an assortment. Keep them easy enough to sustain your child's interest, and increase their difficulty as his or her skills grow. Some children get to be amazingly skillful at these, sometimes succeeding faster than adults. Ages 2–3 years. *About $4 each.*

PLAY FAMILY TOYS   Any of the Fisher-Price Play Family toy collection encourages imagination and fantasy activities that involve organization and themes. Fisher-Price toys are well made. Ages 1–3 years. *About $15.*

BRIGHT BEGINNINGS: MORE PLAYTHINGS FOR TOTS

Parents of a gifted toddler or preschooler are often tempted to buy toys that accelerate their child's skills — particularly those related to numbers and letters, since achievements are readily seen with these. But such toys are based on an adult's agenda of what and how a child should learn. Far better would be toys that entice a child into a continuing cycle of investigations and discoveries about whatever he or she is interested in and curious about.

Preschoolers learn primarily through their physical senses, so they need materials they can touch, count, take apart, and rearrange. Just as they use more than one sense in their explorations, so do they learn more than one skill from each plaything. Multipurpose toys that grow with the child's ability to probe deeper into the toy's possibilities are best. Visual-perception toys can also aid in language development; manipulative items can also be mathematical.

Some of the following examples may appear deceptively simple, but it is that very quality that draws out the gifted child's own creativity and imagination. Indeed, all the toys we recommend offer multiple learning opportunities over a long time span. These are toys that bright children will use in different ways at different stages of development.

The reviews were prepared by *Gifted Children Monthly* game reviewer Ruth Roufberg. The ages listed are the manufacturer's recommendations, but a gifted child can profitably begin to use many toys earlier, particularly with parental supervision. Prices are accurate as of 1988, although they may vary slightly from store to store and will undoubtedly rise in future years. A directory of mail-order suppliers follows the toy listings.

WOBBLY COLORS   Four balls (red, yellow, blue, and green) nestle in the scooped-out centers of four like-colored blocks, which themselves fit into a 5½-inch-square tray frame. Lots of good finger and hand manipulations as baby removes and replaces the balls, mixes or matches colors, stacks the blocks, or hides one ball between two blocks. The balls are weighted to roll in a wobbly path not too far from the reach of a beginning crawler. Ages 6 months and up. *Kiddicraft, $10.*

POP-UP TOY   Four cylindrical play people peg into a wooden block painted to match the colored figures. It's an action toy, too; baby pushes down the figures, and up they pop. Other activities are clapping the figures together like rhythm sticks, rolling them down a ramp, and eventually incorporating them into block play. Ages 9 months and up. *Galt, $18.*

NESTING SHAPE BOX   A two-part sorting box lets children learn shape discrimination at their own pace. The inner box can be turned to reveal any one of five sorting sides of increasing difficulty. When inserted into the outer box, the other sides are hidden. Start your one-year-old with two cylinder blocks and the side showing one round hole; continue in sequence until he or she is using the side with five shapes and ten blocks. Ages 1–3 years. *Educational Teaching Aids, $24.95.*

BUILDING BEAKERS   Twelve nesting/stacking containers are grooved on top and bottom so they fit in multiple ways. Sorted by color (a good way to start), they make four separate nests or towers of three beakers each. All twelve can be stacked, whether they are turned in the same or in the opposite direction. Size, color, seriation, and pattern-copying activities abound. Animal pictures embossed in the bottom of each beaker reinforce size relationships; they range from a bird in the smallest to an elephant in the largest. Ages 1–4 years. *Kiddicraft, $7.*

DUPLO BABY SHAPE SORTER   This early introduction to one of the most popular construction sets incorporates three learning activities. Fitting the six shapes into the right spot on the tray base gives practice in shape discrimination. Stacking the shapes to form a stand-up person promotes finger skills and the concept of combining parts to form a whole. The reverse side of the tray is a studded baseplate on which the individual shapes can be snapped any which way for imaginative building. Ages 18 months and up. *Lego, $9.*

JUMBO PLAYBOARD   Twenty-five fat, round, wood pegs in five colors and five heights fit into twenty-five holes in a 10-inch-square base. From random placement just for the physical challenge, children gradually progress to sorting the pegs by height or by color, eventually achieving through logic and reasoning the ultimate solution, in which each row is a solid color of graduated height. Stacking the pegs, counting them, and discovering different combinations of size equivalencies are later activities. Ages 18 months and up. *T. C. Timber, $28.*

BLOCKS   Blocks lead to discoveries about science (why things fall, what shapes roll, how to build stable structures); design (scale, pattern, symmetry); math (equivalent lengths, estimating the number of blocks needed); symbolization (using blocks to represent other objects). Ages 18 months and up. (More information about blocks, including a parents' guide, is included in the catalog *Building Block Art*, $1.56 postpaid from Please Touch Museum, 210 N. 21st St., Philadelphia, PA 19103. Unit building blocks are available from all school-supply companies.)

RECTANGULAR SORTING BLOCKS   A tray frame holds sixteen wood blocks in four colors, with each color in four graduated heights based on the cube module. As children build stairways, they effortlessly learn about fractions and multiples. The blocks are a nice size and weight for tabletop constructions, and despite their apparent simplicity, they hold rich possibilities for discoveries in math and logic. Age 2 years. *Brio, $30.*

TOTTY BLOCKS   Four plastic trays of different colors each have identical recesses that accommodate four geometric tiles. Colors can be mixed or matched either in the trays, on accompanying pattern cards, or in free-form designs. There are enough pieces to share with a friend. Ages 2 years and up. *Orda, $14.*

COG LABYRINTH   Interlocking cogwheels fit onto posts and provide fascinating sounds and motion when the gear with the handle is rotated. Figuring out why they move and how to reverse direction, designing new layouts, and predicting which way they will turn are early science experiments. The wheels are also good for stacking, stringing, tracing around, and pressing into clay. Ages 2 years and up. *Brio, $26.50.*

STACK-A-BALL   Fifteen balls in five colors fit onto five dowels of graduated height on a wood base. As children handle, count, and stack the balls, comparing the length of the dowels with the number of balls, they begin to associate the sequence "1, 2, 3, 4, 5" with both size and quantity. A lace is included for added play. Ages 3–5 years. *Chaselle, $12.50.*

PARQUETRY BLOCKS   Thirty-two square, diamond-shaped, and triangular wood blocks in the six spectrum colors lead to discoveries about design symmetry, pattern, and shape relationships. Arranging the blocks either within their tray frame or free-form develops aesthetic sensitivity. Square measures 2 inches on each side; blocks are $3/8$ of an inch thick, so steady-handed children can build upright, too. Ages 3–6 years. *Educational Teaching Aids, $14.*

FAMILIAR PEOPLE   A crepe foam rubber fit-together puzzle shows silhouettes of a cross section of society engaged in varied activities. There are babies, children, adults, the handicapped, the elderly, and even family pets. Individual bases enable the pieces to stand alone for dramatic play or storytelling. The frame measures $11\frac{1}{2}'' \times 17''$; pieces are $3/16$ of an inch thick. Ages 3–7 years. *Lauri, $10.*

THINGAMABOBBIN   This toy is simple in design, but varied and complex in its play possibilities. Toddlers will delight in putting the four color-coded dowels and four bobbins on and off the matching colors on the base. Older children will add the rubber bands and long dowels to build cars, sailboats, a gear machine, robots, and action toys. Handmade of fine hardwood with a satisfying heavy feel. Ages 3–8 years. *Learning Materials Workshop, $19.50.*

COUNTING FRAME   Long before a baby can count, he or she can gain valuable manual experiences with this ladderlike device consisting of five rods, each of which holds ten beads of a single color. As soon as a baby can hold small objects between thumb and forefinger, he or she can practice this new skill without the danger of loose beads. Whether baby slides them singly, shoves them in handfuls, or rolls them all at once with a flat swipe of the palm, he or she is developing a repertoire of finger and hand skills. Ages 3 years and up. *Brio, $22.50.*

BEAD SEQUENCES   Three wood platforms, each supporting a different configuration of wires along which colored beads move, offer a sequence of visual-tracking and perceptual motor activities. As children slide the beads along either five arches, two S-curved waves, or labyrinthine bends, their fingers and eyes are practicing all the vertical, horizontal, and curved movements necessary to form letters. At the same time, they are physically experiencing the meaning of up, down, over, under, through, and around. Ages 3 years and up. *Lakeshore; Arches, $35; Wave, $30; Maze, $45.*

100-HOLE PEG BOARD   Early random placement of pegs gives way to patterns as children discover that they can sort and place pegs according to color. The color groupings later help children visualize addition and subtraction; and the arrangement of ten rows of ten pegs demonstrates the base-10 number system. One hundred 1-inch wood pegs in ten colors fit into a 14-inch-square maple board. An activity guide includes games that can be played on the pegboard. Ages 3 years and up. *Whitney Bros., $34.95, plus $3.50 shipping.*

FUN GARDEN   Children choose from 126 interchangeable picture cards to create a picture and tell a story. They can build a cottage or barn, surround it with a garden or perhaps a lake with fish and ducks, add children and pets, put sun or clouds in the sky. Creative and imaginative possibilities are endless, for solo or noncompetitive group play. A tray frame holds twenty-four of the 2-inch-square cards, but larger scenes can stretch along any flat surface. Ages 3 years and up. *Ravensburger, $13.50, plus $2.50 shipping.*

PLAY A TUNE   In minutes kids can learn to play and sing twelve of their favorite childhood songs from this beautifully illustrated full-color book, complete with electronic keyboard. Color-coded notes and keys, which require no prior ability to read music, introduce and reinforce musical notation. Batteries are included. Ages 3 years and up. *Presents for the Promising, $14.95, plus $2.50 shipping.*

GIANT PEGBOARD   This twenty-five-hole plastic pegboard with pegs in five colors has features that make it useful for many manipulative skills beyond pegging, counting, and color matching. Pegs have holes through the center so they can be used for bead-stringing. The base also has holes through which a lace can be threaded. The pegs stack piggyback style; it requires good motor control to complete the tower before it arcs over and topples. Finally, when the base is turned over, it becomes a geoboard with 25 posts that rubber bands can be stretched around to make geometric patterns. The peg size is for children age 3 years and over. *Discovery Toys, $12.95.*

JUMBO CUISENAIRE RODS   Fifty-six rods in ten lengths range from a 2-centimeter cube to a 2×20-centimeter rod (about 8 inches). Each length is a distinctive color. As children compare, sort, group, and rearrange the rods by color/size, they come to understand counting and mathematical relationships without using numbers. The rods are later a physical representation of math functions (addition, subtraction, multiplication, and division). Reserve the smallest cube until the child is at least 3 years old. Preschool to grade 2. *Cuisenaire, $16.50.*

CREATE-A-PICTURE   More than 100 picture cards, each showing part of a house or garden, can be selectively combined to make a different picture every time. Visual imagery, composition, and storytelling all become part of the solo or cooperative play. Individual cards can be sorted into categories: house parts, fence sections, flowers, grass, sky, people, and animals. Within each group are enough duplicate cards for a homemade game of Memory or Concentration. Ages 4–8 years. *Ravensburger, $17.*

SEE BIG, SEE LITTLE   A set of two oversize lenses; one magnifies the world, the other reduces it. Together they can be arranged to invert the world, right it again, or create telescopic effects. The 3½-inch-diameter lenses are mounted into wood frames that have paddle handles. Ages 4 years and up. *Chaselle, $33.50, plus $5.03 shipping.*

PRESCHOOL PACKRAT AND PRESCHOOL PELICAN   *Preschool Packrat* is an "idea" book filled with projects in art, science, carpentry, music, creative movement, cooking, and dramatic play to challenge and motivate preschool youngsters. *Preschool Pelican* is loaded with creative learning experiences to help preschoolers perfect fine-motor control, develop large muscles, learn through the senses, improve social development, acquire language skills, and develop a positive self-image. Ages 4 years and up. *Presents for the Promising, $8.95 each.*

The Childwise Catalog

This book's subtitle, *A Consumer Guide to Buying the Safest and Best Products for your Children — Newborns through Age Five,* just about sums it up. Endorsed by the Consumer Federation of America, this 400-page paperback features:

- a brand-specific product guide, arranged by age group — with feature-by-feature comparisons;
- what to look for in secondhand items — and how to update them to today's safety standards;
- information on recalls of unsafe products;
- tips on pediatricians, travel safety, consumer discounts, and preschools;
- advice on child-proofing your home — including a checklist that covers appliances, household products, plants, and swimming pools;
- special chapters on health matters, food and diet, and protecting your child from various kinds of abuse; and
- a resource section listing free publications that offer more consumer advice.

The Childwise Catalog is published by Pocket Books and is available at most major bookstores for $6.95.

MAIL-ORDER SOURCES

Chaselle School Supply, P.O. Box 2097, Columbia, MD 21046 (800-CHASELLE; in MD, 800-492-7840).

Cuisenaire Co. of America, 12 Church St., Box D, New Rochelle, NY 10802 (800-237-3142).

Educational Teaching Aids, 199 Carpenter Ave., Wheeling, IL 60090 (800-445-5985).

Galt Toys, 63 N. Plains Highway, Wallingford, CT 06492 (800-448-GALT).

Lakeshore Curriculum Materials Co., P.O. Box 6261, Carson, CA 90749 (800-421-5354).

Learning Materials Workshop, 58 Henry St., Burlington, VT 05401 (802-862-8399).

Leisure Learning Products, Inc., 16 Division St. West, Greenwich, CT 06830 (800-243-8004).

Media Materials, 2936 Remington Ave., Baltimore, MD 21211.

Presents for the Promising, P.O. Box 134, Sewell, NJ 08080 (609-582-2065).

The following manufacturers do not fill individual mail orders, but will refer customers to retail sources in their area.

Brio Scanditoy Corporation, 6555 W. Mill Rd., Milwaukee, WI 53218 (800-558-6863).

Discovery Toys, 400 Ellinwood Way, Suite 300, Pleasant Hill, CA 94523 (check your local phone book).

Kiddicraft, International Playthings, Inc., 116 Washington St., Bloomfield, NJ 07003 (201-429-2700).

Lauri, Inc., Phillips-Avon, ME 04966 (207-639-2000).

Lego Systems, Inc., 555 Taylor Rd., Enfield, CT 06082 (800-243-4870).

Orda Industries, 272 Rte. 9, Howell, NJ 07731 (201-780-7200).

Ravensburger, International Playthings, Inc. (see Kiddicraft above).

T. C. Timber, P.O. Box 42, Jordan Rd., Skaneateles, NY 13152 (315-685-6660).

Whitney Bros., P.O. Box 644, Keene, NH 03431 (603-352-2610).

ADDITIONAL RESOURCES

Coin Games and Puzzles, by Maxey Brook. Dover, 1973.
Deal Me In, by Margie Golick. Jeffrey Norton, 1973.
Gamut of Games, by Sid Sackson. Pantheon, 1982.
Handbook of Recreational Games, by Neva L. Boyd. Dover, 1975.
Kids' Games, by Phil Wiswell. Doubleday, 1987.
More New Games and Playful Ideas, ed. by Andrew Fluegelman. Dolphin/Doubleday, 1981.
The New Games Book, ed. by Andrew Fluegelman. Dolphin/Doubleday, 1976.
Parents' Guide to Raising a Gifted Child, by James Alvino and the Editors of *Gifted Children Monthly*. Little, Brown, 1985.
Parlor Games, by Nora Gallagher. Addison-Wesley, 1979.
Teaching Toys, by Jean Warren. Warren, 1987.
Toy Book, by Steven Caney. Workman, 1972.

EPILOGUE: A WORD ABOUT TELEVISION

We all know the evils of too much television watching for children. Yet, since gifted children particularly crave novelty and stimulation, the TV set beckons temptingly to them with its offerings of words and pictures, companionship of sorts, knowledge of the unknown, and the exploration of adult situations. It's only too easy for them to get used to being entertained at will without any interaction.

The best way to turn your television into an ally for the development of your gifted child's mind and psyche is to make the process of watching an *active* one. Critical viewing is qualitatively different from passive addiction, since the viewer's own perceptions are brought to the task. You can teach your child the habit of healthy criticism and of giving credit where it's due.

Critical Viewing

A prominent group of psychiatrists, appointed by the Group for the Advancement of Society, has some definite recommendations springing from its study of the effects of TV drama on children. They suggest that parents ask themselves these questions in analyzing the programs they're considering letting their children watch:

- Does the program appeal to the audience for whom it was intended? Is it appropriate to the age and developmental level of the child?
- Does the program present racial or ethnic groups positively? Does the program present sex roles and occupational adult roles fairly? (*Sesame Street* is a good example of both.) Or does it parrot stereotypes?
- Does the program present conflict that the child can understand, and does it present positive, nonviolent techniques for resolving conflict?
- Does the program stimulate constructive activities, and does it enhance the quality of the child's play?
- Does the program separate fact from fiction? (This distinction is stressed in *Mister Rogers' Neighborhood.*) Does it separate advertisements from program content?
- Is the humor at the child's level?
- Does the pace of the program suit the readiness and developmental level of the child?
- Does the program present social issues that are appropriate for the child to view, and is there something that the child can do about them?

The group says that in "using such a checklist, parents can judge the appropriateness of particular programs for particular children. Then, as necessary, parents can assist the children, through discussion, alternative activities, and setting limits or conditions, to develop more desirable television viewing habits and to make better use of what they view."

Further guidelines that you may find helpful have been developed by the Illinois Office of Education and have been endorsed by the national PTA:

1. Start early to develop your child's good viewing habits.
2. Encourage planned viewing of specific programs instead of random viewing. Be physically active with little ones between planned programs.

3. Look for children's programs featuring young people in your child's peer group.
4. Make sure TV viewing is not used as a substitute for participating in other activities.
5. Open up discussion with your child on sensitive TV themes to offer the opportunity for him or her to raise questions that may remain unanswered in the content of these programs.
6. Explain that TV advertising is being paid for by the makers of the product being shown and that famous people say nice things about products for money.
7. Balance reading and television activities. Your child can "follow up" interesting TV programs by checking out the library books from which some of the programs are adapted and by pursuing additional stories by the authors of those specific books.
8. Help your child develop a balanced viewing schedule of action, comedy, fine arts, fantasy, sports, and so on.
9. Point out positive examples that show how various ethnic and cultural groups all contribute to making a better society.
10. Show positive examples of women performing competently professionally and at home.
11. Write to local newspapers, local TV stations, networks, the FCC, and advertisers to complain about programs that include excessive violence.

Action for Children's Television (ACT) is a national organization of parents and professionals who work to upgrade television for children and eliminate commercialism from children's TV. For more information, contact ACT at 46 Austin St., Newtonville, MA 02160 (617-527-7870).

Reading for Gifted Children:
With Eyes, Ears, and Feelings

ITHOUT A DOUBT, one of the most critical activities in the development of a gifted child is reading. Almost without exception do the biographies and auto-biographies of gifted individuals allude to the importance of reading in their early lives. Not only does reading develop and challenge cognitive skills, it opens up worlds of potential interest and in-volvement — areas in which gifted children often later excel. More often than not, children who are intellectually advanced come from homes where reading is highly valued.

But be aware: this does not mean that gifted toddlers *must* be reading before they enter school. Some may, but many others will not. Children will read when they are developmentally ready. Trying to ram reading ability down their throats too early can be harmful.

More important is to provide a rich reading environment. For example, one sharing experience that many families enjoy is a read-aloud time when everyone can join in, whether it be around the backyard picnic table, the family campground, or the family-room fireplace. Too often abandoned when children master reading skills, reading aloud not only offers the opportunity for discussion, it can also enlighten young minds whose mental promise allows early grasp of vocabulary but whose lack of experience inhibits a grasp of complex themes. Two books written especially for parents on this subject are Dorothy Butler's *Babies Need Books* and Betsy Hearne's *Choosing Books for Children*, both of which your local library may have. Or for a more personal approach in selection help, ask your librarian.

This chapter will help you approach reading the right way with your child. Included are dozens of outstanding books, both fiction and nonfiction, selected by the American Library Association; a section on art appreciation through picture books, followed by a sampling of Caldecott Medal winners; a discussion on poetry and poetic thinking; and suggested titles for dealing with two sensitive topics, sex and death.

THE MEANING AND IMPORTANCE OF FAIRY TALES

The value of fairy tales in children's literature has come under attack recently. Some critics claim fairy tales are violent and contain twisted visions of reality. But according to Bruno Bettelheim in his book *The Uses of Enchantment*, children need to be given suggestions in symbolic form (symbols of good and evil, for example) to help them deal with life's universal issues and grow gradually into maturity. Bettelheim believes that many modern stories are overly protective, that they "mention neither death nor aging, the limits to our existence, nor the wish for eternal life. The fairy tale, by contrast, confronts the child squarely with the basic human predicament."

Fairy tales give a clear message. "If one does not shy away, but steadfastly meets unexpected and often unjust hardships," as Bettelheim states it, "one masters all obstacles and at the end emerges victorious." Rather than be concerned about the effects of traditional fairy tales on the young mind, parents should be on the lookout for far more subtle influences in children's literature.

Beware of "Successism" in Children's Literature

What do Curious George, the Little Muskrat, Magic Michael, and Cue the Rabbit have in common? They are all children's story characters who are intelligent, curious, ambitious, adventurous, or imaginative and who do things a little bit differently than their peers.

Are their exceptional abilities rewarded? Not at all. In various ways their adventures into the unknown disappoint, frighten, hurt, and punish them. In spite of fun and excitement, they are finally forced to retreat to the safe, secure world they left — where success is guaranteed by obedience and conformity.

Like racism and sexism, which have been uncovered and are

beginning to be purged from children's books, this ism — successism — can also affect children — especially bright, creative kids who often walk to the beat of a different drummer. Be aware of this subtle ism that prescribes that to be successful you must conform. Discuss with your child the appropriateness of sometimes being safe and secure, but at other times taking calculated risks in order to grow or to solve problems creatively.

Speaking of sexism, the Montgomery County, Maryland, chapter of the National Organization for Women, in cooperation with the Child Care Technical Assistance Office of Montgomery College, has compiled a list of children's books — preschool through junior high — that are free of sexist stereotyping and don't reinforce "inappropriate gender role concepts." To get a copy, write to Montgomery County NOW, P.O. Box 2301, Rockville, MD 20852.

Don't Pressure Preschoolers to Read

"Reading is much too important to risk turning kids off to it," says Wood Smethurst, director of Emory University's Reading Center in Atlanta. Flash-card drills and other forms of rigorous "training," he says, will sometimes alienate children. "Flash cards in themselves are not bad, but using the cards to pressure children is. If we used flash-card drills to teach children to talk, an awful lot of kids never would."

Smethurst urges parents not to pressure their children but rather appreciate young children's natural desire to master the printed word. The role of the parent, he feels, should not be so much to "teach" preschoolers to read, but rather to provide the appropriate materials and opportunity for the natural integration of written language.

Smethurst says that you can introduce young children to reading at the same time they are learning to talk. Ideally, a parent — or sibling, or baby-sitter — should spend at least twenty minutes a day reading to a toddler. Smethurst advises that to make reading fun and enjoyable you should "hold the child close, and hold the book where they can see the words. Soon the child will come to realize that a certain book stands for a certain story, that letters stand for sounds, and that what is written can be read — and vice versa." Then you should point out certain meaningful words as you read. Finally, after your child is thoroughly familiar with the story, he or she can "read" certain words, phrases, or sentences and point them out in the text — to you!

After your child has mastered a number of words — say, at around two to three years old — you might print these on strips of cardboard and store them in a coffee can for a game. For every five of the child's words that are in the can, there should be one card with the word "bang" (or any word the child likes). You and your youngster can each take turns drawing cards from the can. If the player reads the word correctly, he or she gets to keep it; if not, it goes back in the can. Whenever a player draws a "bang" card, however, he or she must return all of his or her word cards to the can and start from scratch. The first player to accumulate seven word cards wins the game.

When your child has amassed a large number of words, by the time he or she is three or four years old, you might categorize them and ask him or her to draw conclusions about how they are alike and different (for example, "hat," "bat," "cat" — all have three letters and end the same way or rhyme; or "girl," "boy," "man" — all words for people).

Obviously, this procedure is only one way to introduce reading to a child. Many books and sets of materials are available in bookstores to help parents — for example, *Teach Your Child to Read* by R. Barker Bausell, Carole R. Bausell, and Nellie Bausell (Saunders Press, Holt Rinehart, 1980). In general, before attempting to use any of these materials, you may wish to consult a reading specialist for an evaluation.

In addition to reading to your child, playing word games, and asking him or her to make generalizations about groups of words, make sure that your child observes *you* reading. Recent research indicates that this continual observation of adults reading might be just as important as all the other strategies a parent might employ to instill an interest in reading. Also, it is very important that *both* parents be observed reading. It has been hypothesized that the reason girls in elementary school generally read more and read better is because boys perceive reading as a feminine activity — they generally see only their mothers reading.

Some other tips:

- Hang up letter strips or posters with words.
- Put messages on a blackboard.

• Encourage your four-year-old (and older kids) to write letters or keep a simple diary.

Smethurst says: "A child who is read to, and who sees that books and reading are important at home, will almost certainly be reading by first grade." He believes that reading should be an integral part of family life, one of the happy memories of home.

EARLY READING AND GIFTEDNESS

Jack Cassidy, coordinator of the graduate program in gifted education and reading education at Millersville State College in Pennsylvania, concurs with Smethurst. He found in his research with preschool gifted youngsters that 80 percent of them did not learn to read before entering kindergarten. Furthermore, those 80 percent were no less gifted than the 20 percent who did learn to read. Learning to read early should not be considered a prerequisite for being classified as gifted, nor should it even be considered a general characteristic of preschool gifted children.

Something to Grow On

The following book reviews have been condensed from the original full-length reviews that were published first in *Booklist,* a journal of the American Library Association, copyrighted by the American Library Association. The books were selected by Barbara Elleman, contributing editor of *Gifted Children Monthly,* who chose them for their complexity, advanced thinking level, and themes of intrinsic value or interest to gifted children. The books are divided into fiction and nonfiction, and are listed by ascending age level. However, the ages cited (which are given in years) are guidelines only. Appropriateness should be determined by your child's reading level and interest.

FICTION

Across the Stream, by Mirra Ginsburg. Pictures by Nancy Tafuri. Greenwillow, 1982. Ages 2–4.

A strikingly simple story line of a hen and her chicks escaping from a crafty fox works perfectly in the company of crisp, clear, full-color scenes that depict its action one step at a time. The simple shapes and strong colors are tailor-made for the younger picture-book audience, who will find the story's action tuned right to the sensibilities.

The Car Trip; First Day of School; The Checkup. By Helen Oxenbury. Dutton, 1983. Ages 3–5.

Oxenbury's deft line-and-wash drawings play out the three episodes. Comedy is always central to Oxenbury's vignettes. Both children and parents will recognize themselves in these affectionate mirror views of their own foibles.

Ellsworth and the Cat from Mars, by Patience Brewster. Clarion, 1981. Ages 3–5.

A cat from Mars gives Ellsworth a magical hat that carries him to outer space. There, some unexpected things happen, and he has his share of difficulty getting back home. Bright colored drawings add zest.

Let's Make Rabbits, by Leo Lionni. Pantheon, 1982. Ages 3–5.

A pencil meets a scissors and they decide to make rabbits, one drawing his bunny, the other cutting his creation from gaily patterned pieces of wrapping paper; from there the two rabbits take over the snippets of dialogue.

Max, the Music Maker, by Miriam Stecher. Lothrop, 1980. Ages 3–5.

Through distinctive photographs, Max discovers music in everyday sounds — an effective introduction to help preschoolers open their ears and to shape their listening skills in an inventive way.

Moonlight, by Jan Ormerod. Lothrop, 1982. Ages 3–5.

Ormerod has taken the simple ritual of bedtime and without words portrayed it in a way children can appreciate. Her realistically colored washes show shrewd observation of home life, from fruit rinds in the kitchen sink to toothpaste escaping from its tube.

Peter Spier's Rain, by Peter Spier. Doubleday, 1982. Ages 3–6.

This wordless picture book celebrates a brother and sister's experience of a rainstorm, from first drops to clearing skies. A comic-book format with various-size scene frames offers a wealth of detail, and it's Spier at his richest in color and composition.

The Princess and the Pea, by Janet Stevens. Holiday, 1982. Ages 3–6.

Stevens has stuck, for the most part, to the familiar story of the princess and the pea, but she has invented a whole menagerie of amusing animals to inhabit this kingdom; they're bound to be a group readers will adore. The soft crayon art works well to highlight Stevens's focal point, the marvelously expressive characters.

Bear's Adventure, by Brian Wildsmith. Pantheon, 1982. Ages 4–6.

A big, brown bear crawls into a balloon basket for a nap; instead he finds himself on the airways to high adventure when he lands in the middle of a big-city parade. Bright, vibrant circus colors highlight the amusing, oversize pictures.

Ben's Trumpet, by Rachel Isadora. Greenwillow, 1979. Ages 4–6.

Ben longs to have a horn of his own, but must confine his dreams to pretending until the Zig-Zag's trumpeter gives him a lesson and a chance. Art deco black-and-white drawings extend the 1920s setting.

Do Not Open, by Brinton Turkle. Elsevier-Dutton, 1981. Ages 4–6.

This simple story of a lady who finds a bottle on the shore is lifted above the ordinary by Turkle's impressive illustrations executed in vibrant color. When Miss Moody finally opens the bottle marked "Do Not Open," a truly frightening monster pops out. Children will appreciate such an appropriate conclusion; everyone will enjoy such a lovingly designed book.

First Traveler's Guide to the Moon: What to Pack, How to Go, and What to See When You Get There, by Rhoda Blumberg. Four Winds, 1980. Ages 4–6.

Though not a story, this is an amusing and inventive look at an imaginative trip into space that is strengthened with factual details about what equipment to carry, tours to take, and how to deal with weightlessness and lack of oxygen.

Good as New, by Barbara Douglass. Pictures by Patience Brewster. Lothrop, 1982. Ages 4–6.

Grady's teddy bear is almost destroyed by his little cousin; he's offered a new bear but only his old friend will do. It's up to grandfather to wash and restuff the bear, and though Grady has some anxious moments, his toy turns out fatter — and more dear — than ever.

Jed's Junior Space Patrol, by Jean Marzollo. Dial, 1982. Ages 4–6.

Jed's interplanetary travel, complete with creatures called cogs (part cat, part dog), life-size computerized robots for toys, and characters with telepathic abilities make this sci-fi story exciting from start to finish.

Night Story, by Nancy Willard. Illustrated by Isle Plume. Harcourt Brace Jovanovich, 1986. Ages 4–6.

Willard invites the reader on a metaphorical night train to dreamland, a country where "nothing lasts . . . where all is given and nothing is given for keeps." The poem is illustrated with crayon drawings that have a velvety texture and strong, quiet colors. A handsomely designed book whose glowing appearance befits its magical, slightly mysterious content.

Nora's Castle, by Satomi Ichikawa. Illustrated by the author. Putnam/Philomel, 1986. Ages 4–6.

This story of a little girl who explores a deserted castle has a leisurely, old-fashioned air about it. One day Nora sets out on her bicycle with her doll, stuffed teddy, and dog, ready for a day of exploration at the castle. Meticulous pastel drawings of castle and countryside are hushed and bucolic, as sedately self-assured as Nora's imaginings.

Ty's One-Man Band, by Mildred P. Walter. Four Winds, 1980. Ages 4–6.

Set in a black southern community, this book portrays a young boy's wide-eyed enjoyment when a mysterious peg-leg man appears and makes a one-man band with a washbasin, a pail, spoons, and a comb.

NONFICTION

Let's Play, by Satomi Ichikawa. Putnam/Philomel, 1981. Ages 1–4.

In this picture book for very young children, the point is to look — and *look* at the familiar toys Ichikawa features, first alone, and then as a part of a scene in which children play with them. The pictures are softly colored, clean-looking depictions of slightly antique interiors and fresh, rural-looking backyards.

Round & Round & Round, by Tana Hoban. Greenwillow, 1983. Ages 2–4.

A simple idea effectively executed. Hoban's crisp lesson on

becoming aware of circular shapes is crystal clear in this album of apropos photographs. Sharp, well-composed pictures show, for example, a seal balancing a ball, with rings around the seal's neck echoing the ball's round shape.

Deer at the Brook, by Jim Arnosky. Illustrated by the author. Lothrop, 1986. Ages 2–5.

Arnosky's illustrations are everything here, amplifying the sparest of texts with dramatic scenes of deer coming to a woodland brook to drink, eat, play, and nap. The full-color pictures are soft and compelling, focusing on a doe and her two fawns, which are masterfully drawn and imbued with nearly as much presence as real-life creatures would have.

Farm Counting Book, by Jane Miller. Prentice-Hall, 1983. Ages 2–5.

Capitalizing on young children's abiding interest in animals, particularly farm animals, Miller has put together a counting book that relies on large, clear color photographs that show one kitten, two lambs, three horses, four pigs, five cows, etc. But there is more than a simple 1-to-10 sequence. Subsequent pictures provide some simple logic and basic problem-solving opportunities.

On Market Street, by Arnold Lobel. Pictures by Anita Lobel. Greenwillow, 1981. Ages 2–6.

Children just learning the alphabet, as well as those already expert with letters, will appreciate this merry display of ABCs.

Dinosaurs, Beware!: A Safety Guide, by Marc Brown and Stephen Krensky. Atlantic Monthly Press / Little, Brown, 1982. Ages 3–5.

At last, a painless way to teach children safety rules (unless they hurt from laughing so hard!). Some pages feature several tips, others one large one, but in all cases the message is clearly stated and the vividly colored pictures will make that message stick in a child's head.

Shapes, Shapes, Shapes, by Tana Hoban. Illustrated by the author. Greenwillow, 1986. Ages 3–5.

In one of her more open-ended picture books, Hoban suggests on the first page some shapes to look for — arcs, circles, hearts, hexagons, ovals, parallelograms — and illustrates them with small, simple drawings. On each of the following pages is a vibrant color photograph, bordered with white. Subjects vary from a construction site to a child's open lunch box, from a shoe-store display to a manhole cover.

A Year of Beasts, by Ashley Wolff. Illustrated by the author. Dutton, 1986. Ages 3–5.

In a simple yet striking fashion, Wolff moves through the months introducing the animals that appear during the various seasons. Wolff's sturdy, hand-tinted linoleum-block prints handsomely illustrate the linkage between wildlife and humans.

Big City Port, by Betsy Maestro and Ellen Del Vecchio. Illustrated by Giulio Maestro. Four Winds Press, 1983. Ages 3–6.

"A big city port is a busy place. Boats and ships come into the port to load and unlock. It is a safe place for them to dock." So begins this picture-book rendition of a big-city port. Expansive double-page spreads lay out panoramas of liners, cargo ships, tugs, and freighters that are maneuvering in and out of the harbor.

The Philharmonic Gets Dressed, by Karla Kuskin. Harper, 1982. Ages 4–6.

The 105 members of an orchestra are imaginatively depicted showering, dressing, traveling to the concert hall, and arranging themselves on stage before an evening's concert.

Tool Book, by Gail Gibbons. Holiday, 1982. Ages 4–6.

Gibbons takes everyday tools and, through maximum use of graphics and minimum text, gives young children a fine introduction to how things work. The art, striking in its simplicity, makes use of plain perspectives and jelly-bean colors that will rivet attention.

DISCOVERING ART THROUGH PICTURE BOOKS

Introducing children — particularly talented youngsters, who are often especially sensitive to visual nuances — to art at an early age can shape the development of their powers of imagination and discrimination.

The exciting world of picture books is an ideal vehicle for making children aware of good art and exposing them to it on a regular basis. Though parents sometimes think of them within the context of literature, picture books offer true art through illustrations especially designed to be meaningful to children. They are illustrated by fine artists — who represent a variety of artistic schools and employ a wide range of styles, palettes, and approaches — and are readily available from libraries and bookstores. Most important, the books can be shared often in the coziness of the home. Children can hold them themselves and examine the illustrations at close range.

Developing an artistic awareness through picture books can begin with very young preschoolers. As they grow older, gain experience, and grow in their perceptions, you can introduce more complex and sophisticated concepts. And older children can also benefit from exploring the art in the picture books intended for younger ones.

Shapes, Details, Colors

Enjoyment of the story should come first, but at the close of a read-aloud session, you can encourage even the youngest child to look at the pictures and notice shapes, details, and colors. Counting and alphabet books are particularly good for getting started. Molly Bang's *Ten, Nine, Eight* (Greenwillow, 1983) — uniquely presented from 10 backward to 1 — uses, for example, shoes, usually thought of in pairs, as the unlikely object for number 7. Sharp-eyed youngsters will find the "missing blue sneaker," being chewed on by a cat, on the number 7's page.

Youngsters allowed to take time to look and look again will delight in these innovative touches, and it will help them be aware that pictures contain all kinds of surprises. Years later they will be ready for the detail of Brueghel and the idiosyncrasies of Bosch. Both Frank Asch's *Happy Birthday, Moon* (Prentice-Hall, 1982) and Mirra Ginsburg and Nancy Tafuri's *Across the Stream* (Greenwillow, 1982) are stories that use clear colors and simple shapes against sparse backgrounds, letting the images stand clear and unobstructed, and perhaps paving the way for the austerity of Vermeer or Hopper.

Somewhat older children will enjoy discovering nuances in a story's characters. You can help them see how they can know if a character is sad or happy, scared or silly, from clues in facial expressions and body stances that illustrators have carefully included. Rachel Isadora's *Max* (Macmillan, 1976), about a boy's visit to his sister's ballet class, Steven Kellogg's *Ralph's Secret Weapon* (Dial, 1983), concerning a boy's hilarious attempt to charm a sea monster, and Rosemary Wells's *Timothy Goes to School* (Dial, 1981), about a rabbit-child's problems in first grade, are particularly noteworthy.

Setting is often given an added dimension by the graphics. Illustrations can suggest a place that is only hinted at or perhaps not described at all in the text. Pictures of famous landmarks, styles of architecture, geological formations, and peculiarities of weather come alive under a talented artist's brush. Lead children into observing how Robert McCloskey builds his storm in *Time of Wonder* (Viking, 1957), how Uri Shulevitz gradually enlarges his pictures to parallel the coming of dawn in his book *Dawn* (Farrar, Straus, Giroux, 1974), and how Parisian scenes in Ludwig Bemelmans's *Madeline* (Penguin, 1977) add an authentic air.

Quality

Susan Baum, an assistant professor of graduate gifted education at the College of New Rochelle in New York, says picture books involve more than art. They can launch young minds into the unknown. They can expose children to unfamiliar phenomena and abstract concepts. Chosen wisely, they offer invitations to critical and creative thinking.

Writing in *Early Years,* Baum recommends three criteria to use in selecting picture books for gifted children.

1. *Quality of Illustrations:* Children between the ages of four and eight "are developmentally bound by vivid imagery," she says. It is important that the complex ideas in a book are represented in its illustrations. Are the illustrations colorful? Are they dynamic? Are they detailed enough to provide new information? Are they simple enough to eliminate confusion?

2. *Authenticity of Content:* Accurate information about complex ideas must be stated simply, Baum says. The author should have some expertise in the topic or at least have verified the content. What is the background of the author? Does the book give new information about a topic, or is it a story? Has the author consulted an expert in the field?

3. *Richness of Language:* Gifted children enjoy playing with ideas and words, and colorful verbal descriptions accom-

panying the illustrations will stimulate intellectual growth. The author must use creative language. In assessing the richness of language, ask: Will the vocabulary be simple enough for my child to understand while sufficiently complex to stretch his or her mind?

CALDECOTT WINNERS ARE PICTURE PERFECT

Each year a committee of children's librarians announce their choice for the Caldecott Medal winner. Given annually since 1938, the Caldecott Award honors the illustrator of the most distinguished picture book of the year. Though it is named after an Englishman, the great nineteenth-century illustrator Randolph Caldecott, only American citizens and residents are eligible for consideration.

The very first winner, Dorothy Lathrop, received the medal for *Animals of the Bible* (Lippincott), written by Helen Dean Fish. Lathrop's black-and-white illustrations, which interpret both Old and New Testament verses, provide naturalistic depictions of animals balanced by touches of mysticism in the settings.

Traditional literature has constantly remained a strong choice among winners throughout the decades. Folktales from various corners of the earth as well as Mother Goose stories, myths, fables, and nursery rhymes have been designated as worthy of the awards and as honor books.

The Best of the Past

A survey of the fifty years of medal winners brings to mind many well-loved books. Listed below are a sampling that have high quality and sure appeal for children of all ages; those with text should be read aloud to preschoolers who cannot yet read. (Selections, listed chronologically, were illustrated by the authors except where noted.)

Abraham Lincoln, by Ingri and Edgar d'Aulaire. Doubleday, 1939.
Popular episodes in Lincoln's life from childhood to presidency emerge through five-color stone lithographs that alternate with black-and-white pencil drawings and an evocative text.
Make Way for Ducklings, by Robert McCloskey. Viking, 1941.
Set in Boston Common, this endearing picture book details a

mother duck's determined efforts to take her brood on an outing in the park. Vitality permeates the illustrations both in the individualized expressions and in the sweeping background scenes.

The Biggest Bear, by Lynd Ward. Houghton Mifflin, 1952.

Strongly composed black-and-white pictures enliven an imaginative story of a boy who adopts a bear cub but later faces heartbreak when the bear, now full grown, must be returned to the wild.

Madeline's Rescue, by Ludwig Bemelmans. Viking, 1953.

When Madeline is saved from a Parisian river by a quickthinking dog, the pup becomes the mascot of the orphanage where Madeline lives. Contrasting yellow and black colors enhance the impressionistic illustrations, adding mirth to the rhyming text.

The Snowy Day, by Ezra Jack Keats. Viking, 1962.

The joys of a small boy's fun in the snow are creatively depicted in simple, full-color collage illustrations.

Where the Wild Things Are, by Maurice Sendak. Harper and Row, 1963.

Sent to his room for misbehaving, Max conjures up a bevy of deliciously grotesque monsters, whom he eventually overpowers. Bold colors and lines set an appropriate mood for this boisterous romp.

May I Bring a Friend? by Beatrice de Regniers. Illustrated by Beni Montressor. Atheneum, 1964.

A repetitive, rhyming text and rollicking pictures describe a small boy's invitation to tea by the king and queen — with any or all of his four-legged friends.

Sam, Bangs, and Moonshine, by Evaline Ness. Holt, 1966.

After her cat and a playmate nearly meet tragedy, a little girl learns the necessity of distinguishing between truth and moonshine, a theme subtly enhanced through fluid watercolors.

The Fool of the World and the Flying Ship, by Arthur Ransome. Illustrated by Uri Shulevitz. Farrar, Straus, Giroux, 1968.

In this old Russian tale, an ancient Czar offers his daughter's hand in exchange for a flying ship, and everyone sets out to find such a vessel. Effective watercolors and pen-and-ink drawings capture both the humor and fantasy of the story.

Sylvester and the Magic Pebble, by William Steig. Windmill, 1969.

In his brilliant artwork, Steig treats a serious situation with humorous flair as a young donkey escapes danger by changing himself into a rock and returns to the loving embrace of his parents only after a year-long separation.

The Funny Little Woman, by Arlene Mosel. Illustrated by Blair Lent. Dutton, 1972.

A rice dumpling takes a funny little woman through a hole in the earth to the underworld of the monstrous *Oni.* Lent nicely bridges the fantasy and real worlds through ingenious integration of color and black-and-white illustrations.

Why Mosquitoes Buzz in People's Ears, by Verna Aardema. Illustrated by Leo and Diane Dillon. Dial, 1975.

A lively *pourquoi* tale, set off by a mosquito's lie, is projected in stunning, stylized paintings emblazoned with African art motifs.

Ox-cart Man, by Donald Hall. Illustrated by Barbara Cooney. Viking, 1979.

Full-color illustrations, reminiscent of folk art, strengthen a seasonal tale of a nineteenth-century New England farmer, who takes handcrafts and produce to the Portsmouth Market, purchases supplies, and returns home, where the cycle begins again.

The Glorious Flight: Across the Channel with Louis Bleriot, by Alice and Martin Provensen. Viking, 1983.

Beautiful, stylized paintings with deadpan humor dramatize Bleriot's historic flight across the English Channel on July 25, 1909.

The Polar Express, by Chris Van Allsburg. Houghton Mifflin, 1986.

A young boy is summoned aboard the *Polar Express,* a larger-than-life train bound for the North Pole. Once there, he is chosen by Santa to receive the first gift of Christmas. He selects a silver bell from Santa's sleigh that can be heard by only those who truly believe. The story unfolds against deep-toned, double-page paintings that are as full of mystery as the story itself.

You can locate a complete list of the Caldecott Medal books in *World Book* and other general encyclopedias. Leaflets giving all the medalists and honor books can be purchased from the Children's Book Council, 67 Irving Place, New York, NY 10003, or from the American Library Association, Order Department, 50 E. Huron, Chicago, IL 60611.

POETIC THINKING MEANS
SEEING WITH FEELINGS

Poetry — the word strikes terror into many a person's heart. It is laden with years of memorization, threatening sheets of blank paper, and a great deal of misunderstanding. Studied, and promptly forgotten, the book of seventeenth-century English verse sits high on the bookshelf, collecting dust, superfluous to our daily lives.

This is a legacy we do not want to pass on to our children. If we can strip away the layers of fear and look at poetry in a new way, we will be able to help our children — and ourselves — enjoy a very special art form.

Poetry is particularly relevant to our high-tech world, which thrives on efficiency and economy. A poem is an efficient way of expressing feelings and sharing images. The form helps you get to the heart of the matter with no wasted words, say what you have to, and leave — but say it so that the reader can perceive the world in a different way. And the first step to writing poetry is not to write poetry at all, but to learn to think poetically.

As a parent of a gifted child, you are a jump ahead before you start because your child already sees things in different ways. And as preschoolers, kids possess expressive feelings that are still unshackled by the rules they learn to employ later. The child who sees an upturned skateboard as a bug on its back is thinking poetically. So, before the blank sheet of paper, before meter and rhyme, here are some ways to help foster poetic thinking in that young and curious child of yours. They were suggested by writer Ferida Wolff and poet Dolores Kozielski.

Provide Experiences

Expose your child to a wide variety of experiences that involve focus and connection. Newness is stimulating to children as well as adults. Go to new places; see new things. Who can resist looking straight up at the Washington Monument when seeing it for the first time? Yes, it's tall and pointy. But is that all? Focus on it.

Feel it. Then start making connections. Does it remind you of something else? A rocket, perhaps, ready for firing. Or a paintbrush shading in the gathering clouds.

Repeating old experiences can be valuable, too. Visiting the zoo for the tenth time can bring out poetic thoughts by focusing on one aspect of the trip instead of a diffuse, global scanning of the familiar. For instance, go specifically to look at how the animals move. Does the ape move as if his cage were a trampoline? Does the stiff-legged gait of the giraffe bring to mind four trees walking?

Verbal Games Improve Perception

Play verbal games with your child that will expand his or her perception of ordinary things. The game of "I packed my suitcase and in it I put . . ." is a great way to build on poetic concepts. Just as the suitcase keeps accumulating items, each added to the one before, the same thing can be done with objects.

> This is a chair.
> This is a green chair.
> This is a soft, green chair.
> This is a soft, green chair with wooden arms.
> This is a soft, green chair with wooden arms that curl into fists.

Each addition contributes something to the overall image of the chair. The direct observations can be broadened to include subjective images as well — personal feelings about the objects. For example:

> This is a soft, green chair with wooden arms that curl into fists
> and keep me safe inside.

Try word associations. Take an ordinary tree. How does its bark feel? It feels hard, bumpy, scratchy, scabby, wrinkly, like alligator skin. How do its leaves sound when the wind blows through them? They whisper, rustle, gossip, giggle, chatter, pant, complain. Use as many senses as you can. It will make the object come alive.

Make up your own games. Anything that enlarges your child's understanding of an object is good.

Animation Gives Life

Make inanimate objects move by giving them animate qualities. The gelatin mold on the kitchen counter is only waiting to stretch up on its turtlelike legs and crawl away. The piano smiles an eighty-eight-tooth smile. Walt Disney was thinking poetically when the little Chinese mushrooms in *Fantasia* danced across the movie screen. Your child may not be as well known, but his or her ability to see animate qualities in inanimate objects may be just as good. Let your child's imagination roam a bit.

Encourage Comparisons

Similes and metaphors are good friends to a bright mind. The simile, a comparison between two things using the words "like" or "as," is nothing foreign but something we use all the time.

> People seen from an airplane look like ants.
> The homegrown tomato becomes as big as a grapefruit.
> The sleeping child looks like an angel.

The metaphor, a comparison whereby one thing is likened to another as if it actually were that thing, asks for a more complete indentification of two dissimilar things, but is also commonly used.

> The old Volkswagen was a Beetle.
> Powdery snow is cotton candy.

One of the most famous metaphors in poetry is Carl Sandburg's poem "Fog."

> *The fog comes*
> *on little cat feet.*

So it does. Fog springs into our minds with all the softness and silence of a real cat; the poet's figure of speech makes us see it in a different way.

Encourage your child to compare dissimilar things. What is an orange like? An orange is like a ball, or a globe, or a scoop of icy sherbet. What do you hear from the teakettle? It is a whistle, or a bird's call, or a scream. Again, use the senses. Children are masters of comparisons when their imaginations are encouraged.

And remember — this is not a test, and there are no wrong answers.

Read Modern Poetry

The best way to get the feel of what poetry is today is to read it, by yourself and with your child. The juvenile section of your public library has volumes of modern poetry, rhymed and unrhymed, many of which are collections of poems written by young people themselves.

It is never too early to start. Even babies in their cribs can be read to. They may not know that what they are hearing is poetry, but they will respond to the sound of your voice and the rhythm of the words.

Poetry Is Life

Make poetry part of everyday living. When your child is bouncing on a horse, it is entirely appropriate to recite the poem "Hoppity" by A. A. Milne, which begins like this:

> *Christopher Robin goes*
> *Hoppity, hoppity,*
> *Hoppity, hoppity, hop.*

The rhythm of the poem and the bouncing will synchronize, delighting both you and your child. If you get caught in a rainstorm, remember "April Rain Song" by Langston Hughes:

> *Let the rain kiss you.*
> *Let the rain beat upon your head*
> *with silver liquid drops.*
> *Let the rain sing you a lullaby . . .*

By now, it should be obvious that poetry does not have to inspire dread. If some time is spent in learning to think poetically, the results can be fun, satisfying, and enriching.

A TOUGH TOPIC: SEX

Awkwardness about the subject of sex crops up often between parents and children for a variety of reasons. Some children —

the gifted ones, in particular — ask sophisticated questions much earlier than the parents anticipate. Others don't ask at all. At certain ages, a child's embarrassment will prevent his or her talking about bodies, babies, and lovemaking. Many parents find that as their kids get older, their own discomfort increases.

Whether or not you have one or more of these problems, there are books to make the telling about sex informative, interesting, and even fun. Illustrations help clarify complex biological information, and children will absorb different aspects at different ages and stages of their growth.

In selecting books for yourself or your child, look for these five qualities:

1. Language, whatever the audience (younger children or adults), should be direct in referring to body parts and sexual functions, rather than filled with cute euphemisms.
2. Naturalness of sexuality as a basic human need should be stressed at all ages. The tone should be one of acceptance, not judgment.
3. The broad range of expression of sexuality that is natural and normal — including masturbation, and affectionate touching within the family and among friends of the same or different sex — should be introduced and explained.
4. Enjoyment of sensual feelings, alone or with others, should be frankly, not coyly, discussed as a major reason for sexuality.
5. Expression of sexual feelings within a relationship containing affection, respect, and commitment should be discussed.

Most preschoolers are more interested in the birthing of a baby, not the conception. For the precocious ones who do ask about lovemaking, the first two of these recommended books present the subject sensitively:

Where Do Babies Come From? by Margaret Sheffield. Illustrated by Sheila Bewley. Knopf, 1972.

With beautiful, soft paintings, this wonderfully done book shows how bodies look and tells how a man and woman lie close together to make love. The text is direct and explicit, yet subtle. Drawings of babies in utero precede ones showing the baby's birth. The book ends by saying, "Everybody in the world started life as a baby and was made in the same way, by a man and a woman together."

How Babies Are Made, by Andrew D. Andry and Steven Schepp. Illustrated by Blake Hampton. Time-Life, 1968.

More abstract than the first because of the illustrations, this book shows the mating of chickens and dogs. The nude human form is presented but human intercourse is safely represented under the blankets. The text conveys the idea that when people create a new baby, "they are sharing a very personal and special relationship." Again, illustrations show baby in utero and being born. The limited amount of text on each page makes this a good choice for the youngest interested family member.

A Baby Starts to Grow, by Paul Showers. Illustrated by Rosalind Fry. Crowell, 1969.

A picture book. No reference to intercourse. Emphasis is on the growing fetus.

The Story of a Baby, by Marie Hall Ets. Viking, 1939.

This picture book transcends all age groups and attitudes. Found in the juvenile section of the library, it is a classic.

ANOTHER SENSITIVE TOPIC: DEATH

Here are some recommended books about death to read aloud together with your preschooler (ages 4–6). The list was compiled by Virginia L. Fortner, a learning resource specialist.

About Dying, by Sarah B. Stein. Walker, 1974.
Picture book plus adult text shows ways to discuss death.

Badger's Parting Gifts, by Susan Varley. Lathrop, Lee and Shepard, 1984.
Friends remember gifts given when Badger was living.

Bubby, Me and Memories, by Barbara Pomerants. American Hebrew Congregation, 1983.
A child's process of converting loss to positive memory.

Christmas Moon, by Denys Cazet. Bradbury Press, 1984.
Remembering Grandpa's teachings helps celebrate his life.

Everett Anderson's Goodbye, by Lucille Clifton. Holt, Rinehart, and Winston, 1983.
Everett explores feelings with mother.

The Fall of Freddie the Leaf, by Leo Buscaglia. Holt, Rinehart, and Winston, 1982.

Freddie and friends change with passing seasons.

I'll Always Love You, by Hans Wilhelm. Crown, 1985.

Preparation for death starts in natural, happy times.

Lifetimes, by Bryan Mellonie and Robert Ingpen. Bantam, 1983.

Illustrations show all living things as living in between a beginning and an end.

The Tenth Good Thing about Barney, by Judith Viorst. Atheneum, 1982.

Remembering nine good things was easy; the tenth was most important.

Math, Science, and Logic — Plus the Best Available Software for Preschoolers

N o GIFTED preschooler's "education" at home would be complete without a kindling of his or her quantitative intelligence — that aspect involving numerical concepts and reasoning skills. This chapter offers math activities you can initiate with your youngster, ways to cultivate scientific attitudes, and a sampling of elementary logic puzzles that are fun and, at the same time, can serve as models for creating others like them.

The final section is devoted to reviews of some outstanding software programs that should challenge and interest your child. In addition to the instructional and play value of each program, you'll be introducing your child to the rudiments of computer literacy as well.

PARENTS CAN IDENTIFY EARLY MATH ABILITY

Can your three-year-old classify objects by size, shape, and color, and arrange seven or eight objects in order of size? Parent observation of these kinds of skills may hold the key to early identification of mathematically precocious youngsters, says Julian Stanley, director of the Study of Mathematically Precocious Youth at Johns Hopkins University in Baltimore.

According to a report in the *Boston Globe,* Stanley and his associates think that mathematical talent can be identified in children long before they enter school, because numerical concepts can be understood without social experience. "You could earn an outstanding grade on a calculus test while you still believed in

Santa Claus," Stanley says, "but you probably couldn't be an authority on Hamlet."

Although mathematically able preschoolers learn to count and add more quickly than their peers, parents should not rely on that as a sole indicator. But because mathematically precocious youngsters truly grasp the concepts of math and can "play" with numbers, there are some other signs that parents can spot. Here is a checklist of behaviors to look for in your child as he or she grows up. A child gifted in math may possess several of these talents.

- *Ability to classify and arrange objects in a series.* A mathematically gifted three-year-old will be able to arrange seven or eight objects in order of size while most three-year-olds can only arrange three.
- *Rapid comprehension and generalization.* At six, the child may use a thermometer as a tool to add and subtract.
- *Ability to organize data and see patterns.* A precocious fourth-grader may determine the odds on any combination of rolling dice.
- *Original approaches to problems.* A gifted fifth-grader may use human body proportions to determine the lengths of different parts of the Statue of Liberty.
- *High test scores — but not always.* Tests must be carefully chosen to measure mathematical ability per se and not be tainted by other factors, such as verbal deficiency.

MAKING MATH ADD UP FOR KIDS

"Two cookies!" demands the child as she passes her first math test. It is a moment of triumph, both for the tiny student and for the parent who has patiently repeated "two shoes," "two blocks," and "two fingers." The child has become a creative mathematician who not only recognizes the invisible but important thing called "two," but who can use it in her own pursuit of happiness.

A parent doesn't have to be a math whiz to be a good math teacher for little folk, says Patricia C. Kenschaft, associate professor of mathematics and computer science at Montclair State College in New Jersey, and author of three widely used college textbooks. He or she must simply be willing to savor the child's innate joy in patterns and to share excitement in exploring them together. Early in her own children's development, Kenschaft found herself considering her priorities for them. She realized that emotionally she wanted to share her joy in mathematics with them while there was still time, and intellectually she also wanted to prepare them for a technological world.

There are many ways parents can promote their child's innate joy in patterns. "One, two, three, four, five . . . ," a toddler enjoys chanting, and relishes the admiring attention adults give to this particular chant. It can be recited before the child knows the meaning of the words, just for the fun of human interaction. Later, when the child suddenly realizes that saying "three!" may bring more cookies than saying "two," it is already possible for him or her to ask for four or five cookies without learning any more words.

Use Concrete Examples

Once your child has connected counting with the concept of numbers, there are endless opportunities for the youngster to apply mathematics to life. "Let's count the chairs in the waiting room." "Let's count the crocuses." "Let's count the cars we pass." Unless the road has too many or too few cars, this last one can keep a child happily absorbed learning ever-larger numbers with only minor distractions to the driver. It's also a good way for keeping squabbles to a minimum in driving the nursery school carpool.

If your child has been counting for a while, it takes only a little extra work to teach the concept of addition. While making conversation at dinner, why not add the number of spoons to the number of forks to get the number of utensils? (An advanced lesson would include knives.) If you are waiting in a doctor's office, your child can add the fingers you are holding up in your left hand to those in your right to get the total number of fingers you are holding up. It's lots more fun than deciding which child in the waiting room gets the doctor's only hobbyhorse. There are enough fingers for all.

Once your child knows what it means to say "two plus one is three," learning addition facts can be great sport. On long drives and on public transportation with your youngster, keep him or her entertained by seeing who can add rapidly sums like "two plus three." Later, of course, add "seven plus eight."

Little boys are given blocks more often than little girls, and teenage boys are better at spatial relationships than teenage girls.

Is there a connection? Most mathematicians believe so. Blocks are an important learning tool for both your daughter and your son.

If you can afford something special, order Stern blocks from Houghton Mifflin. The "one block" is a green cube, the "two block" is two connected purple cubes, and the "three block" consists of three white cubes in a row. The complete set is colorful and can be used to make many patterns. Teach addition by putting the blocks end-to-end.

Cuisinaire rods (see chapter 10) are more appropriate than Stern blocks for school-age children because of their lower cost, but the large Stern blocks are easier for preschoolers to hold. Keep your set of Cuisinaire rods handy for visitors of all ages. They never fail to keep guests under the age of eight occupied for a long time — and often entertain visitors well over that age!

Take It in Small Bites

Little children are eager to learn, and unless sessions are too long, mathematics will provide much entertainment for both the child and the adult, Kenschaft says. "Every preschooler with whom I have discussed numbers has shared my enthusiasm for them. This impresses me, because my conversations with youngsters often wander to that topic." As with every other activity, including sleeping and eating, it is important to recognize that there is a time to stop. Math "lessons" should cease before the child becomes restless.

Kenschaft's own two offspring gobbled up the following mini-lessons. She explained why "x times y equals y times x" to both of them while changing a diaper. Of course, she didn't use x's and y's. She asked them to think of two dogs standing in line and consider how they would count the total number of legs. There are two "fours" of legs: the right legs and the left legs. Or you can think of there being four "twos" of legs — the front pair of the first dog, the back pair of the first dog, the front pair of the second dog, and the back pair of the second dog:

Thus two fours is the same as four twos.

After the diaper was changed, she got a piece of paper and showed the child that there was nothing special about two and four; the same thing is true of three and four. Three rows of four dots each will equal the same number as four rows of three dots each:

$$
\begin{array}{cccc}
\bullet & \bullet & \bullet & \bullet \\
\bullet & \bullet & \bullet & \bullet \\
\bullet & \bullet & \bullet & \bullet \\
\end{array}
$$

The concept that "x times y equals y times x" for all x's and y's is called "the commutative law for multiplication." It is usually introduced well into the elementary grades, but Kenschaft was teaching it to kids in diapers.

Don't Make Drill a Drudgery

Kenschaft says that once they had the idea of multiplication, it was time to teach them their tables. She never spent time on drill that could be spent reading together or singing at the piano, but when they were traveling or waiting in a supermarket line, she would see who could answer "three times five" faster.

Learning multiplication tables or addition facts is not math; it is rote memorization. But acquiring these basic skills is essential for pursuing higher mathematics — the exploration of patterns, the communication of patterns through symbols and words, and the use of patterns to solve problems.

One of Kenschaft's daughter's first memories is wondering how many holes there were on the door of the clothes dryer. She began counting them. Mother showed her how she could count only the numbers of rows and the numbers of dots in each row and use multiplication to find the number much faster. The little girl was so excited that she will always remember that moment.

But I'm Not Prepared

"Not my kids," you may groan. "Not with the way I've always done in math!" Even while pleading guilty to the charge of having an unusual family, Kenschaft tells about the impact of her own third-grade teacher, Miss Weyer. Like all great elementary-school teachers, Miss Weyer chose her profession because she loved children. They still correspond and occasionally visit. Recently Kenschaft told Miss Weyer how much she had enjoyed arithmetic in her class, and Miss Weyer confessed that she herself had always hated math. "But I was determined that my little people would not notice!" she confided. "I tried as hard as I could to make arithmetic lessons fun." Indeed, Kenschaft remembers them as great fun, and Miss Weyer did her part in stimulating at least one college math professor.

You, too, whatever your mathematical background, can experience the great joy that Miss Weyer did when your children master a difficult but vital subject. If you suffer from a case of math anxiety, you know that is something you don't want to pass on to your "little people." You also know that you can count and add numbers under ten as well as the next adult. These are the intellectual credentials you need to prepare your child to face technological challenges with confidence. No matter what your own feelings about higher mathematics, it is important to share elementary number concepts with enthusiasm, tenderness, and appreciation.

Making Math a Natural Pleasure

Young children can grasp surprisingly advanced mathematical concepts if the ideas are presented in terms that kids understand, says Judy Sizemore, an ingenious parent from McKee, Kentucky. She introduced her daughter, Robin (now eight years old), to negative numbers, octal and binary number systems, topology, and other mathematical concepts through simple games and puzzles.

They started with negative numbers when Robin was four. Sizemore drew a numbered scale from −10 to +10 on a two-foot-long piece of cardboard. Then she made a deck of cardboard cards numbered in sequence from −10 to +10. They each used one of Robin's miniature cars as a playing piece and started the players at zero. They took turns drawing cards from the shuffled deck. If Robin drew a +7, she could move her car 7 spaces toward the +10. If Mother drew a −5, she moved 5 spaces toward the −10. The winner was the person who reached either the −10 or the +10 first.

IF YOU HAD EIGHT FINGERS   Robin learned the octal number system through a game called Romaluvia. She loves to play "store" and thinks Romaluvia is a fun variation. Mother and daughter pretend that Robin has won a shopping spree on the planet of Romaluvia, whose inhabitants have only eight fingers. Mother plays the role of a Romaluvian merchant, offering her daughter such fabulous buys as a "genuine pangi-pangi sweater imported from the planet of Tofu and selling for a mere 13 pennies." The catch is that Sizemore means 13 *Romaluvian* pennies (that is, 13 in base 8: 1 in the "eights place" plus 3 in the "ones place," which equals 11 in base 10) and Robin has to give her the exact change to be allowed to buy the sweater.

The binary system is a natural one for "secret codes." (In the binary system, you use only 0 and 1. The place values progress from right to left: ones, twos, fours, eights, sixteens . . .). Sizemore started by showing her daughter how to write her phone number in binary. Later, she wrote coded messages in which each letter of the alphabet was represented by a binary number corresponding to its alphabetical sequence (A = 00001, Z = 11010).

A MAGIC STRIP   Topology is a system of geometry that deals with the properties of shapes rather than their measurement. You can introduce youngsters to topology by making a Möbius strip (named after mathematician August Möbius, 1790–1868). Cut two 1½-inch-wide strips from the long side of a piece of typing paper. Bend one into a hoop and tape the ends together. Do the same with the second, but in doing so, hold one end fixed and twist the other 180 degrees before taping it. This one is the Möbius strip, and it's quite different from your first strip. For one thing, an ant walking on the plain strip would have to cross an edge to get from the outer surface to the inner surface. Not so with the Möbius strip. It has only one surface! Prove the point — to yourself and to your child — by drawing the ant's path with a pencil.

Now comes kids' favorite part. First cut your plain strip in half lengthwise with a scissors. You end up with two hoops. But what happens when you carefully cut your Möbius strip lengthwise down the middle? Try it and see.

Sizemore uses other games and puzzles to introduce Boolean algebra, modular arithmetic, and probability. What is the purpose of all this? Is she trying to make her daughter into a precocious mathematical wizard? Not at all. Sizemore says that the unfortunate fact is that most people, especially females, are intimidated by higher mathematics. By giving her daughter the idea early in life that advanced math concepts are fun and easy, Sizemore hopes to give her the confidence to go as far in the study of mathematics as she may desire.

Shapes All around Us

The preschool child is ripe for an initial exposure to geometry. When the situation permits, point out geometric shapes such as circles, squares, triangles, and rectangles in familiar, everyday objects — furniture, buildings, artwork in picture books, for example. Take advantage of opportunities to broaden your child's mathematical vocabulary by introducing ovals (and their relationship to and difference from circles), pentagons, octagons (stop signs!), and diamonds. Help your child to distinguish between squares and other rectangles and to name objects that are examples of each.

Develop creativity by challenging your child to make a variety of objects from the same basic shapes. For example, given a large triangle, a smaller triangle, a large circle, a smaller circle, and a rectangle, your child may put together these figures:

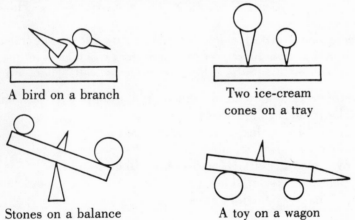

A bird on a branch

Two ice-cream cones on a tray

Stones on a balance

A toy on a wagon

Almost everyone has at one time or another made "snowflakes" by folding paper and making cuts on the folds to create symmetrical designs. What you may not realize is that this simple activity is an excellent introduction to symmetry. Have your child try to visualize what the designs he or she cuts will look like when the paper is unfolded. Introduce the term "symmetry" to your child and explain the differences between line symmetry (as in a couch), rotational symmetry (as in a square), and mirror symmetry (as in a capital T). Together find examples of each type of symmetry in familiar objects, furniture, clothing designs.

Another useful activity to make your child comfortable with geometry is visual estimation. Estimating numbers, measurements, amounts, and so on, is becoming an increasingly essential skill in order to judge the accuracy of results as we rely more and more on computerization for the actual computation. Make a game of it. Without peeking, estimate and draw *to scale* familiar shapes such as the triangle a church-key can opener makes, a hole (or button) on the telephone dial (or keypad), postage stamps, and so on. Take turns choosing the shape to draw and check your final drawings for accuracy. Be imaginative. Use coins, ice-cream cones, and the like — both for models and prizes!

DEVELOP SCIENTIFIC ATTITUDES

The young child has a highly inquisitive spirit — the premier ingredient for scientific thought. Doubtless you have been inundated with whys and hows. Why does an airplane fly? How high is the sky?

According to Rita Haynes Blocksom, an educational consultant writing in *Preschool Perspectives,* budding preschool scientists will tend to possess five other characteristics as well. They will

- explore objects with an almost microscopic eye for detail;
- take interest in science activities and tools (such as magnets);
- have a strong desire to work independently;
- collect a variety of objects — rocks, seashells, bugs — and love to sort, classify, and identify them; and
- choose books on science, nature, outer space, and the like over more commonly chosen storybooks.

Blocksom suggests that you keep these characteristics in mind as you encourage your son or daughter to explore. Give age-appropriate explanations of what your child is observing, and don't allow very young children to confuse science with magic. Science in all its splendor may be magical in many ways, involving wonder; but it also entails explanation — particularly of cause and effect. Magic involves illusion and, though also subject to explanation, connotes a more supernatural and random universe.

Balance structured activities such as demonstrations with opportunities for your child to explore related topics independently. Encourage him or her to follow hunches (hypotheses) — a basic scientific principle. And vary your approach: supplement independent work with family projects, walks, field trips, museums, books, and so on.

Things to Do

• Provide old appliances and household items to take apart and explore — alarm clocks, flashlights, radios. Remove the cord on all electrical items so they can't be plugged in, and always supervise the activity.

• Use a magnifying glass to explore hair, fingernails, and whatever.

• Take a "rock walk" to collect rocks. Back at home, examine them for differences, likenesses, and classify them in various ways — color, size, shape, and texture, for starters.

• Build a spiderarium. Use a large, clear plastic jar. Punch small holes in the lid and cover it with thin cloth or line it with a fine screen; add grass, twigs, and a few nonpoisonous garden spiders; and observe spiders spinning webs.

• Examine the various parts of a flower under a magnifying glass. Point out the stem, petals, sepals (which are small, green, leaflike structures under the petals), pistil (the central, female organ of the flower), and the stamens (the male reproductive organs surrounding the pistil).

LOGIC AND PROBLEM SOLVING

Logic and reasoning are extremely important disciplines in any area of study. Spawned at an early age and nurtured, these abilities will grow and develop into natural responses by your child. Four fundamentals of logical reasoning and problem solving that are easily adapted to other areas are organization, pattern recognition, precise verbalization, and concentration.

The following logic puzzles — taken from the kids' section of *Gifted Children Monthly* and created by Donna Lugg Pape — can help your child build his or her reasoning skills. Make enlarged photocopies of these and give them to your child. You may have to assist young children or do the activities with them. The answers are provided at the end of this chapter.

Number Wheel

On tracing paper, trace the figure at the top. In the blank, pie-wedge shapes, now trace the lines from the same-numbered wedges at the bottom to complete a picture of a pair of animals. Do it in sequence, beginning with wedge number 1. How many wedges does it take before you can recognize what the animals are?

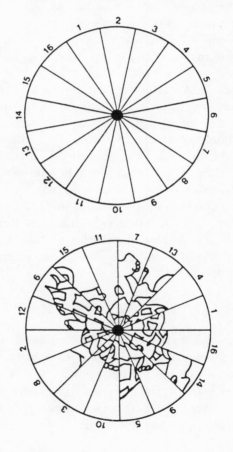

Mystery Animal

There's a mystery animal hidden here, but it's been divided into puzzle pieces. To find the puzzle pieces, color in all the spaces that have a letter from the word "animal" in them. Next, cut the pieces out or trace them on a piece of paper. Assemble the pieces to reveal the mystery animal.

SOFTWARE FOR PRESCHOOLERS

There are literally thousands of software programs designed with preschool-age kids in mind. As you might suspect, not all are tested by preschoolers. Still, there are diamonds in the rough, if you know where to look. There are imitation diamonds, too. Software for the preschooler is a big market, and it has produced a rich and varied field from which to choose. What follows are reviews by Phil Wiswell of some of the best programs in this field. Each is available for under $60. (The publisher and computer versions follow the title.)

Dinosaurs (Advanced Ideas — Apple, Commodore, IBM) uses one of the most fascinating subjects to young children these days, dinosaurs, to promote keyboard literacy and to lay the groundwork for building math, reading, and memory skills. *Dinosaurs* presents five different games in which your child's task is to match and sort objects, numbers, and letters in different and progressively more challenging ways. Kids are asked to match similar dinosaurs; types of dinosaurs with their foods; dinosaurs with how they move — on land, in water, or in the air; the type and number of dinosaurs to the depiction shown on screen; and each dinosaur with its name. Keyboard operation is simple, and children thrill to commanding the dinosaurs with easy-to-remember keystrokes.

Easy as ABC (Springboard Software — Apple, Commodore, IBM) helps your child learn the alphabet with five activities that teach letter recognition and sequence. Children enjoy the animal alphabet, among other sequencing games. Includes a manual of activities.

Facemaker (Spinnaker — Apple, Amiga, IBM) has no direct relationship to any school curriculum, but it is a wonderful introduction to the computer and how to make it do things by typing on the keyboard. Using simple-to-follow on-screen menus, your child selects items to construct a funny-looking face — ears, nose, eyes, mouth, and hair. Then your child learns how to animate the face. Pressing one key makes the face wink an eye. Another key wiggles the ears. Finally, the computer challenges your youngster to duplicate a series of facial expressions in a memory-type game. The face might frown, wink, frown, then smile, and the child must try to repeat the sequence. Your child will be delighted with the silliness of the faces and with animating them, while at the same time learning the positions of some important keys on the keyboard.

First Letter Fun (MECC — Apple) introduces your child to phonics through the beginning sounds of familiar words. For starters, apple is the "A" word. Your child is shown a boy picking an apple and feeding it to a horse. Your youngster must then choose from four letters the correct initial sound. When he or she selects "A," the word "apple" appears on the screen. An accompanying manual includes color-book pictures and stories.

First Shapes (First Byte/Electronic Arts — Apple, Commodore) uses speech synthesis and animated color graphics to grab and keep the attention of its preschool audience. And there is nothing like a talking computer to rivet the attention of youngsters to the screen. The program also uses an easy-to-love character named Ted E. Bear, who plays five different games that teach basic shape recognition. The games are all simple in concept, such as Make-A-Match, in which your child tries to find pairs of identical shapes in similar fashion to the TV game show of *Concentration*. Each game builds on concepts learned in the previous one, so there is a natural progression of learning.

Kindercomp (Spinnaker — Apple, Commodore, IBM) is a series of six prereading, premath, and pattern/shape-recognition games designed to get young children interested in both learning and the computer itself. There are simple, fun activities in which your child "draws" colorful pictures on-screen, scribbling with bright colors accompanied by sound. And there are challenges in which he or she must try to match letters, numbers, and shapes to those shown on the screen, or complete a series of numbers. Colorful, animated graphics and computer sound effects help keep your child's interest while rewarding correct responses and encouraging improvement.

The Muppet Word Book (Sunburst Communications — Apple) uses the lovable Muppet characters to teach how to recognize letters, distinguish upper and lower case, and identify consonants and appropriate word endings, among other language skills. Scoot, Gonzo, and the Muppet gang challenge your child in their own delightful way. Although the program was originally designed for school use, it has had wonderful success at home as well.

Observation and Classification (Hartley Courseware — Apple) uses four colorful activities to teach children to observe and classify objects. In one, called "Rainbow Hop," your child must select the animal in each series that does not belong. Each activity provides three levels of difficulty. You can choose the most appropriate starting point for your child as well as the speed at which the challenges occur. Other activities involve the ever-popular stickers and shape stencils.

Peter Rabbit Reading (Fisher-Price — Apple, Commodore) is a good program for a child who has learned the alphabet and is ready to start reading. The program is a very lively reading game in which the child must guide the main character — Peter Rabbit, of course — to the many familiar locations of his friends. Each of Peter's friends has a reading test for your child — simple tasks such as matching the first letter of a word being displayed as a colorful graphic, matching short words, and filling in letters missing from words. Occasionally, the program will prompt your youngster by pronouncing the word out loud through speech synthesis. Between tests, Peter walks through the woods and fields from one friend's house to another, which children find quite entertaining.

Play Together, Learn Together (Grolier Electronic Publishing — Apple) tutors your child through the basics of your Apple. It contains three dozen educational and entertaining activities designed to demonstrate your computer's capabilities. Includes a workbook for parent and child to learn together.

Rainbow Painter (Springboard — Apple, Commodore) is one of the most engaging drawing and painting programs available for young children. It contains hundreds of outline drawings of pictures in a dozen different categories. Children select an outline, then pick tools and colors from menus presented on the left and bottom border of the picture. There are hundreds of colors and patterns from which to choose, or children can create their own new colors. Tools are included to make it simple for kids to do things like fill an area with colors or patterns, draw lines with dozens of different styles, erase mistakes, and explore their creativity.

Stickybear Numbers (Weekly Reader — Apple, Atari, Commodore, IBM) teaches the concept of numbers through the use of groups of moving objects such as bears, trucks, spaceships, and ice-cream sundaes displayed on the screen with captivating color graphics. The way different pictures are displayed in combinations yields an almost endless variety to the program. There is no real game or challenge involved here. The point is simply to reinforce the concept of numbers in an entertaining way. By pressing any of the number keys, the child is presented with a picture containing that many objects. Counting forward or backward from any number of objects is done by pressing the spacebar, which adds or removes one object from the screen each time it is pressed.

Talking Teacher (Firebird Licensees — Apple, Commodore) is a prereading program that teaches alphabet recognition, alphabet sounds, and letter relationships with a novel twist — it actually talks! Children are intrigued by the nicely done, animated color graphics, and are captivated by the computer voice that prompts the child through the program and sounds out each letter. Three levels offer different kinds of challenges. Level one simply displays and sounds out any letter the child types on the keyboard. Level two displays a letter and waits for the child to type it on the keyboard. Level three displays an animated picture of a word, waits for the child to type the first letter of that word, and, like the first two levels, offers help for wrong answers.

See also *Computers and Small Fries* by Mario Pagnoni (Avery, 1987). This computer-readiness guide for parents of toddlers and preschoolers is a clearly written, up-to-date, and practical guide for parents who want to get their children started on the right road to intelligent computer use. It answers parents' most common questions about computers:

- What kind of a computer should I buy for my child?
- Which educational software programs are best?
- How do I know when my child is ready for a computer?
- What can I do now to help my child become computer-ready?

But this book does more. It tells you what keyboard alternatives are available to enhance your child's computer learning, explains how to choose the appropriate software for your child's ability, and discusses how to child-proof your computer station and computer-proof your child. It even includes a description and evaluation of the forty most popular children's programs currently available.

Number Wheel

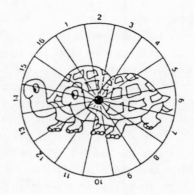

Mystery Animal

Challenging Family Activities for Preschool and School-Age Children

B EING THE PARENT of a gifted child has its puzzling and challenging moments. But parents, in general, are a resourceful group, and the best solutions to their dilemmas are often those they improvise themselves.

This chapter contains twenty-nine updated versions of the best items from *Gifted Children Monthly*'s "Idea Place" column. They are mainly the improvisations of parents of gifted children — parents who, through experience and need, have devised meaningful and enriching activities for their children. These ideas have worked for them, and they can work for you as well. Remember, though, no two situations are the same, so you may have to adapt these ideas to the needs and interests of your children and family.

The chapter is divided into five general categories that indicate the predominant focus of the activities, although in most cases there is some overlap. The ideas in the first section, "Stimulating Infants and Preschoolers," can get you started with your youngster right now. The other sections will be especially helpful as your child gets older (or maybe you have an older child already).

STIMULATING INFANTS AND PRESCHOOLERS

Visual Stimuli in the Nursery

I tried to give variety to my daughter's nursery. Babies' rooms can be appealing to adults, but not have much in their decor to interest children. I decorated my daughter's room to interest a baby. Before she came home from the hospital, I put a border around the *top* of her room. The border had a paradelike design. It started with a girl followed by a boy, each holding balloons. Behind them came a duck, a cat, a dog and some other animals. As our infant daughter lay in her crib we could often see her eyes glancing along the top of the wall near the ceiling.

I also changed the scenery in her bedroom. If I ran across a pretty piece of wrapping paper or if I brought home a bag from a store with a design I thought would interest an infant, I would lace a strip of it through the slats of her crib. Every week or so my baby daughter had new pictures to look at on the side of her crib.

I think that the experience of having visual stimuli at an early age made her more aware of her surroundings.

— *DeAnne Rosen, Lawrence, Kansas*

Color Me Stripes

The amount of sensory stimulus an infant receives in his or her early environment "can actually cause physical changes in the brain and foster growth of mental development," reports the National Association for Gifted Children. In a guide entitled *Suggestions for Stimulating the Minds of Infants,* the NAGC states that the period of a baby's growth and brain development from birth to eighteen months can be stimulated through a wide variety of sensory experiences, encompassing all of the human senses.

Here are some ideas given for expanding the richness of an infant's surroundings:

- Use multicolored sheets and bright colors in the nursery.
- Adorn the walls with bright pictures; mount objects at various distances, such as a large mirror placed strategically to allow your baby to see his or her reflection.
- Change the location of the crib from time to time to vary the view.

"Researchers have found that babies can focus on shapes and show enjoyment in seeing them," the guide states. "They like two or three bright shapes and prefer complicated patterns — diagonal stripes, and spirals as opposed to solids. Within the first month, they can follow moving objects."

From about the third month on, babies enjoy repetition of movements or actions. "These familiar patterns lead to the next stage of curiosity in exploring new objects and activities." The guide suggests playing nursery games that involve counting fingers and toes — or touching the ears, nose, mouth, and eyelids.

Ways to help nurture creativity in your infant include letting your child experiment, manipulate, and explore; and talking happily to your baby right away, listening to him or her, and taking seriously the infant's attempts to communicate with you.

— *Gifted Children Monthly*

Reading in a Flash!

When my son was three and learning to read, we couldn't find any reading flash cards at the store so we decided to make our own. Using index cards and old magazines and catalogs, he would cut out the pictures and tape or glue them on each card. Then I would print the name of the object, in both upper and lower case, on the other side of the card. He loved making his "word collection" and having his own index card file for it.

Making his own flash cards gave him excellent practice in decision making — which pictures he wanted (were they good single-word pictures and would they fit on the cards?) — as well as practice in cutting, taping, and word recognition. Also, all of the words were selected by him. Preprinted cards often have words that the child is really not interested in.

My son soon learned to read using his homemade flash cards and has since passed them on to his younger sister who is enjoying adding to the collection. She finds it easier to have the words printed on both sides of the cards.

— *Mrs. L. C. Graunke, Beaverton, Oregon*

If It's Worth Hearing, It's Worth Taping

Since preschoolers love to be read stories, I started to make some cassette tapes featuring stories that are treasured by my two-year-old daughter. The Golden picture books, for example, are easy to find at grocery stores and discount houses, and so are a multitude of others that teach the alphabet and numbers. We found such fascinating titles as *The Good Neighbor Contest, Big and Little Are Not the Same, Birds,* and *Animal Sounds.*

We have taped about sixty educational books so far. Usually I can fit the reading of three books on one tape, organized whenever possible around a single theme. I add questions and comments as I read, taking into account my daughter's attention span.

There are many things that can be learned from tapes. Children need to know their complete names, addresses, and phone numbers. This knowledge bolsters a preschooler's self-concept. They can be taught more complicated things, like the days of the week and the seasons. In addition to being a parent, I am a trained child psychologist and happen to believe also that the best learning time for foreign language, classical music, and even common sense starts before the child is two or three.

Once we started taping, the list of themes grew to include time and space relationships. I talk at about the beginning, middle, and end of the tape; and I refer to the book itself — which the child should hold as the tape is being played — and discuss concepts like open/shut, big/little, and top/bottom. Once you start, other ideas will come to you. I have included rules on health, courtesy, and safety also. These are best done in a lively manner and, if possible, demonstrated with a song. If these "lessons" can be recited cheerfully by the child, they are learned easily.

I also included a physical activity several times on each tape to make sure my daughter was getting enough physical exercise. In the library I found "finger plays" and "jump rope" chants. These not only provide a physical break, but also teach how to follow directions, sequences, coordination, and the like.

When a new tape is ready to use, I listen with her to watch how she develops her habit of participating, responding, and doing the physical activities. I also found that taping with your child present allows you to anticipate more precisely the timing required for her responses and activities.

For our preschooler, we found the tapes more challenging than a traditional nursery school. It is also a low-cost, high-quality method of learning when you leave your child with a baby-sitter.

— *Marty Smith, Fayetteville, Arkansas*

Scaled to Size!

Would you like to teach your gifted preschool child about local geography and combine it with his or her play period at the same time? By finding a large piece of cardboard from a used mattress or refrigerator carton, you can begin an inexpensive way to draw a map of your community and let the kids use it as a surface on which to play with their toy cars, trucks, and blocks.

Using watercolors, felt-tip pens, acrylic paints, or other non-smear materials, you can make a map to scale with roads four inches wide to accommodate two-way traffic for toy vehicles. Show major local landmarks that your child can identify and "build" bridges, rivers, parks, schools, houses on your street, post office, firehouse. Start by laying out the simple outlines; he or she can fill in the spaces. Explain that "scale" means to use a smaller unit of measurement for a larger one — one inch for five feet, say. As your child becomes familiar with the features of the map, you all can add more details.

Cardboard is a clean, warm surface for preschoolers to play on and the materials are so cheap that spills and other imperfections are not important. Happy motoring!

— *Jack C. Rye, Missoula, Montana*

Hide-and-Feel

Many preschool and kindergarten teachers who are interested in developing children's language and tactile-discrimination skills use a very simple game, which you can easily make at home for the whole family to enjoy. All you need is a paper sack or, if you want something more elaborate, an empty cardboard box with felt-covered openings. The openings should be large enough to allow a child to pass his or her hand through, and the felt covers should be ample enough to conceal what's inside.

Each round begins with one player placing a variety of small objects within the box. The other players then take turns attempting to identify the objects by touch alone. The difficulty level depends on the similarity of the size, weight and texture of the objects chosen; thus, the challenge can be interesting enough to involve players of almost any ability.

— *Evelyn Witter, Milan, Illinois*

Hold the Book, Pass the Notes

When my two-and-a-half-year-old started reading, he would get very excited as I pointed to the words in a book; he happily read them aloud. After the initial challenge was met, however, his eagerness seemed to wane. He didn't want to "perform." He preferred to relax and have stories read to him.

I worried how to keep up his enthusiasm for reading. I began to write little notes to him during the day such as "What do you want to do now?" "Do you want to go outside?" "Can you see the fish?" "You are a very nice boy," and so on. He never seems to tire of reading these little notes that relate so directly to him.

When I do read books to him, I never ask him to "perform," but I will stop to point out new words or old, familiar words. At times I slow down and he starts reading along with me on his own. He enjoys reading more than ever, and to my surprise, a few months ago he started writing and now writes notes to me!

— *Pamela Pacula, Mill Valley, California*

The Sunday Funnies for Serious Learning

Our love affair with the Sunday funnies began several years ago when I found myself with a gifted preschooler who was having a little trouble with her sequencing skills. Although a few sets of "sequence cards" were available through educational-supply sources, we found that they were rather unimaginative and of little value compared to their cost. Frustrated, I started casting around for ideas. The Sunday funnies caught my eye and we were off and running.

I took several of the simple comic strips, cut each one apart into its individual squares, and glued each square to heavier paper. I put the name and date of the strip on the back of each square for ease in sorting. Voilà! Our own set of sequence cards. A quick shuffle and we had a very enjoyable learning game in trying to put them back in order.

We could easily check our game by obtaining another set of funnies from the neighbors when they were finished reading them, and gluing the complete strip to stock paper. We had the bonus of having a story line in our sequence cards and we were able to discuss the meaning of the strip — why it was or wasn't funny or sad, how it presented real-life comparisons and consequences, and so on. It provided an excellent time to discuss values. Little did I realize at the time that this was just the tip of the iceberg!

As my daughter grew, so did our use of the Sunday funnies. After a while, as our collection of comic strips increased, we realized that there wasn't always one "right" combination of squares. Other combinations worked that were different from the original version. It was interesting to discuss our different viewpoints and interpretations of the comic's sequence.

Eventually we began to use the squares from past Sundays with newer, more recent squares (of the same strip) to create new story lines. At first this was merely amusing, but it soon became an obsession. Suddenly we were writing and/or drawing our own endings to simple strips. We began cutting out single-panel comics and their captions for a simple matching exercise, and then found ourselves purposely wedding the wrong captions to different comics for the different connotations. We began to read the adventure serials every Sunday and devise our own endings. We discussed the different appealing and appalling attributes of the different comic-strip characters and eventually created our own heroes and villains.

As my daughter grew older and became interested in comic books, I took a few apart and cut off the page numbers. She enjoyed trying to put the shuffled pages back together to make sense.

In the future, I suspect the editorial cartoons will provide some interesting areas to explore.

Meanwhile, I have another gifted daughter, a preschooler, who is just discovering that the daily black-and-white strips are great for coloring, and that the whole newspaper provides material for a great scavenger hunt. I go through the paper first and look for several easily identifiable photographs, drawings, advertisements, extralarge letters that stand out, and so on. I make a list of these, and then she scours the paper to find the hidden items. It looks as though my old friend the newspaper will continue to be a valuable educational tool in our house.

— *Lorraine O. Strom, Bay Saint Louis, Mississippi*

Unpuzzling Puzzles

Gifted children as young as three years old often are bored with simple puzzles of 9, 12, or 15 large pieces. Yet puzzles of 50 to 100 pieces are often too complicated.

The day a new baby joined our family, my husband gave our daughter, Catherine, who was not quite three years old, an extra bit of attention and a new puzzle containing 100 pieces. We found a way to help her do this complex puzzle all by herself.

First, we completed the entire puzzle together and pointed out to her the different hues and shades — the blue background of the left side of the picture, the shaded pink on the opposite side. I slid the finished puzzle onto a sheet of poster board and made a frame out of the four sides of the puzzle, fitting and gluing the border pieces in place. Next, I took each remaining piece and outlined its proper place on the board with a pen. When Catherine later dumped out the inside pieces and attempted to do the puzzle, she was able to do it independently, using only the outlining of the inside pieces and the colors of the frame pieces as her guide.

— *Janice M. Watrous, Bristol, Tennessee*

A Gifted Baby Needs Room to Write

At eighteen months, my son was able to recognize letters and numbers. By the time he was two years old, he could read street signs and prices off labels at stores. He could sound out letters and read a little at two-and-a-half. Problems arose, however, when he tried to transfer all the things in his head to paper. The fine motor control he needed to paint letters on pieces of paper was simply not developed enough. He was terribly frustrated until we gave him large pieces of water soluble chalk and sat him down on the sidewalk; there he could use the full range of his arm. He promptly and happily printed his name, did number problems, and drew pictures, as well as printed out the letters of the alphabet — all before he was three years old.

— *Nancy Monestero, Omaha, Nebraska*

Try Saying Yes

When my daughter was two, she asked for a knife to cut her sandwich. Naturally, I said: "Little girls can't use knives, honey. When you're older you can try." I then made sure I put the bread knife in the sink, out of her reach, when I left the room for a few minutes. When I came back, she was attempting surgery on her sandwich with a sharp steak knife.

"Where did you get that?" I screamed.

"From the dishwasher," she replied.

Rather than view this situation as disobedience requiring punishment, I tried to look at things from her point of view. Here was an extremely bright and resourceful child, reaching out to explore the world. *She* felt ready and intensely interested in learning a new skill. I was not responding to her request. Just because *I* thought she was too young to use a knife didn't mean anything to her. Looking back, I know I should have said yes, rather than no. I should have given her a dull butter knife and a soft piece of cheese to experiment with, instead of risking a dangerous accident.

The day she asked to use scissors, I tried to be more responsive. First I hid all the scissors in the house. Then I bought her a pair of quality safety scissors and gave her a magazine to cut up. She sat there for hours at a time, practicing cutting. Within three days she could cut out coupons, manipulating the scissors in the correct, adult manner.

— *Carol Saunders, Port Chester, New York*

A Toddler Is Always Right

Though my kids were most definitely not right when they bit me, or clubbed a friend with a toy, I always held firmly to this "rule" in the educational arena. For example, both my children confused *m* with *w*, and *b* with *p* and *d*, as many children do. Some parents will calmly correct their children, seeing the importance of learning basic information properly. However, I found that, although an eighteen-month-old toddler does not *need* to know the alphabet correctly, he or she does need to know that learning is a positive, rewarding, pleasant experience.

So when my one-and-a-half-year-old son used to run around the huge floral *M* imbedded in a hillside at the University of Maryland screaming, "Double-oo! Double-oo!" I would say, "Good for you! How smart to see a *W* is an upside-down *M!*" or "Yes, and this kind of *W* is called an *M!*" The key, then, is to find something right in all their attempts, to make learning feel good, while gently leading to new understanding.

— *Cathleen Ann Steg, Fairfax, Virginia*

How Do You Get Apple Juice?

It was an icy, cold day in January, the day before my daughter Judy's second birthday. We sat together in the kitchen drawing pictures of her upcoming birthday party. Little cups of apple juice decorated her pretend party table.

"Apple juice is best," she said very seriously. Looking up from her drawing, she asked with a puzzled look, "Mommy, where do we get apple juice?" Hoping to be an enlightening parent, I went through a somewhat detailed explanation of peeling apples and taking out seeds and squeezing to get the juice.

Her big, brown eyes looked somewhat resigned as she said: "No. No. No. *How* do we get apple juice?"

Fishing around for an answer, because I thought I might not have understood the question, I said, "At the supermarket?"

"No. No. No," she cried, one tear slipping down her silky cheek. "*When* do we get apple juice? Where? How? Why?"

Totally bewildered because I knew I didn't understand the question, I tried various answers. Each one brought more tears, a few sobs, and lots of no-no-no's.

Finally, she held me tight and pressed her nose to mine. She took a deep breath and patiently said, "Judy knows how you get juice out of the apple, but *not how it got in*."

Judy is now fourteen years old. Her brother, Michael, is almost eleven. They both ask impossible questions, but then again I ask a few, too, and sometimes they know the answers. "Hey, Judy, how *does* juice get into the apple?"

— *Jan Mercer, North Brunswick, New Jersey*

Trials and Tribulations

Try to believe that all is not lost when your eighteen-month-old child discovers that throwing raw eggs down carpeted stairs makes a "bigger splash" than simply dropping them on the floor, or when he or she prefers rubbish to toys and disassembles *everything*.

Attempt to control your temper when, at the age of about two, he unbuckles all three "child-proof" safety straps on his car seat while you are driving on the freeway; when he transforms a small carton of juice into a squirt gun; when he refuses to accept conventional game methods and insists upon devising his own rules; and when he is determined to convince you in July that Santa Claus just came and gave him the cookie he took from the cupboard. Yes, these are more likely indicators of giftedness than signs of obnoxious behavior.

Pay no attention to the unwarranted accusations of "pushing your child" you will receive from well-meaning friends and relatives when your two-and-a-half-year-old child proudly demonstrates that she can add and subtract in Spanish; when your three-year-old informs his aunt, "You are wrong! The sun does not set — we do!" and then provides a lecture on gravity; and when your four-year-old rejects your neighbor's offer to read *Winnie-the-Pooh*, stating that she would prefer the encyclopedia.

Allow your youngster to develop at his or her own pace, and try not to have unrealistic expectations (too high or too low). Secure appropriate education when the time comes and be a strong advocate for your child. Trust your instincts — do not allow anyone to coerce you into believing: "Your child is not as bright as you think — he will be completely satisfied with the standard grade-level curriculum."

Learn about the idiosyncrasies and vulnerabilities of exceptionally able youngsters; attempt to increase public awareness of the emotional and educational needs of this highly sensitive group of kids. Find companions with similar interests and abilities for your child. Appreciate your youngster's insatiable curiosity and answer those never-ending questions; nurture his or her often frustrating and messy but valuable creativity; encourage continuation of your child's innate and compelling desire to learn; and set aside time for "just plain fun." Have patience, maintain a sense of humor, and learn stress-management techniques.

Above all, instill in your toddler a strong feeling of self-worth; and unconditionally love that precious gifted child with whom you have been blessed!

— *Susan J. Nilson, Seattle, Washington*

Look, Mom, Black and Decker!

As a very young child, my son, Peter, now six, would refuse to sit still for any length of time, which posed a problem when it came to feeding him. Exasperated with chasing him around the room with a spoonful of food to get him to take a mouthful (which I am embarrassed to admit I actually did), we discovered that he would sit at the table if we gave him a magazine to leaf through while being fed his meals. His favorite magazines were *Time* and *Business Week*, and he particularly liked the company logos that accompanied the advertisements. He would point to the logos between mouthfuls and my husband and I would dutifully tell him the name of the company.

Sometime after he was feeding himself, around the age of two, he and I went to the local hardware store and, as I was paying the cashier, Peter came running over to me from the display window a few feet away, all excited. He pulled me over to the window, and much to the surprise of the cashier, who thought Peter had spotted a toy in the window, he proudly exclaimed: "Look, Mom, Black and Decker!" There in the window was a power drill with the Black and Decker logo on it!

— *Susan Tryforos, Glen Rock, New Jersey*

COMMUNICATION AND LANGUAGE ARTS SKILLS

Communication Builds Emotional Health

As the parent of a gifted child, nurturing your child's emotional health is one of the most important tasks you will ever have. The way you communicate, both verbally and nonverbally, is crucial in the development of your child's unique personality and emotional stability.

The following communication techniques, derived from experience with my gifted son, are very effective if you persevere, day by day, and trust yourself, seemingly against overwhelming odds.

• Plan at least ten or fifteen minutes together each day to talk about the day's happenings. If you are on a tight schedule, visit while you do a chore together or during mealtime. This communication time is very important and should be done on a consistent basis.

• Encourage the discussion of successes, failures, and concerns in an atmosphere free of ridicule or harsh criticism. Be quick to listen, but slow to judge. Likewise, accept your child's constructive criticism of you. If you can learn to do this, no matter how painful it may be to admit your faults, you will be amazed at how much you can grow and change for the better. In return, you will find that your child will be much more willing to accept your discipline and constructive criticism.

• Respect your child's privacy and need for space and expect the same in return. Regularly scheduled quiet times when there is no talking, TV, or music can help create a peaceful atmosphere in your home and allow your child to develop as a creative thinker.

• Encourage the expression of opinions and open debate on different topics. Even when these opinions may offend you, keep the lines of communication open at all times. This practice, great around the dinner table, will help train your child to express ideas in a positive manner, verbalize thoughts, and develop a strong sense of identity.

• Ask for forgiveness when you make a mistake or do something that hurts your child, and expect your child to do likewise. A willingness to "forgive and forget" will help prevent suppressed guilt feelings and seeds of resentment that may eventually cause emotional upheaval.

• Be alert to your child's nonverbal behavior as a clue to hidden problems. When you suspect a problem, ask what is wrong and help your child to verbalize problems when possible. Identifying a problem is often half the battle in solving it.

• Show your love with positive remarks, hugs, and genuine affection every day. Touching is an important part of communicating and making your child feel loved and also helps develop his or her self-esteem.

• Don't be afraid to take a stand on what you consider to be right and wrong and communicate your values through your actions. By your example, you will help your child develop character and a strong set of values and beliefs.

— *Judy Nichols, Tampa, Florida*

And This Week's Surprise Subject Is . . .

Each week one member of our family researches one area of interest and presents this topic as the "surprise subject of the week." First, we try to guess what it's about. For example, "Is it about airplanes, microscopes, lasers, seashells?" — narrowing the subject down from general to more specific categories. Then the "presenter" shares it with us. It can be oral or written and there are no rules. However, the family member must impart some knowledge in some interest area.

In addition to building research skills and giving our children practice making presentations, it's a great way for our family to spend some productive time together. We usually try this during the weekend, somewhere away from the television, telephone, and computer games. Very often the discussion takes off on unusual tangents, which makes the exercise more and more fun.

— *Karen Demetriou, Saginaw, Michigan*

Saying Good-bye . . . and Hello

I still remember how, just before the used-furniture men came to haul it away, I secretly and solemnly kissed, then pulled a splinter from, the leg of the first sofa I ever knew. It was something by which to remember that faded "veteran," and I have that sliver of wood still. I was seven then — the age of our daughter as we planned our move last summer. To help all of us say a fond farewell to our house and neighborhood, and a positive hello to the new area, we made a personalized "moving book" patterned after *Goodbye, House* by Ann Banks and Nancy Evans (Harmony/Crown, 1980).

Long before the hectic last weeks of packing, we purchased a scrapbook and began listing, together, things that made our house special to us. Where did we like to curl up to read? Where was our daughter's favorite place to play or hide? (She could reveal the secret now.) Where did we usually have our family conferences or mother-daughter talks? Where was homework done?

Our daughter took and collected snapshots of her friends and mounted the pictures on pages with each child's address and list of personal favorites (books, hobbies, animals, school subjects, sports, names of pets, jokes).

At the same time that we were making a record of the life we were leaving, we started finding out about the new area. We helped our daughter write to the chamber of commerce, asking that information about the new city and its attractions be sent to us.

We talked about the "new start" aspects of a move. (Did she want to drop the nickname she recently acquired?) We helped her think about her strong points as a potential friend of the children she would meet. What about her riddle repertoire and that awesome stuffed-animal collection? She might look forward to sharing these and other things with her new friends.

It was a time to take stock, to appreciate where we'd been and what we were at the moment, then to join together confidently to plan more growth in a new place. The early attachments, friendships, and meanings that gifted children attribute to their world can be so strong that it helps to deal with this kind of "breaking away" openly and concretely. In addition to the organizational and creative skills the project nurtured for our daughter, the moving book chronicled our journey, both the emotional and physical one.

— *Suzette Smith, Columbia, South Carolina*

Share the Newspaper with Your Children

Gifted children, by nature, have greater awareness of the world about them, and they can find the daily newspaper a source of entertainment as well as a challenge. With gentle parental guidance, even a toddler can learn to read the paper. A systematic way to introduce or include the newspaper in your child's early life might be to focus on the following aspects:

- *Photographs:* Your local newspaper has fresh artwork every day. Show your child the picture of the fuzzy twin bear cubs at the zoo or the gala fireworks display the family attended. Read the caption to your preschooler. It is usually short enough for his or her attention span.
- *Headlines:* They are big and bold, making them easy reading for young ones. Once your child masters reading a few headlines, he or she will want to attempt to read every headline in the paper.
- *Weather Report:* This is short and easy to find. Some newspapers run weather maps and national trends. Your child can pick up map-reading skills and a smattering of geography this way, too.
- *Calendars:* Most papers run listings of weekly or daily happenings. This is a good way to learn about your town or city, and by studying the listings, children can choose favorite places to go or things to do.
- *Ads:* Children are drawn to the artwork and enjoy comparing the prices of favorite toys, records, or bikes.

• *Charts and Graphs:* Children who enjoy math are often fascinated with charts and graphs. Find a "pie chart" and explain how it is used to depict statistics ("a big word for numbers") visually. Have your child make one of his or her own — say, on "How I'd like to spend my day."

Besides building reading skills and interest in a larger world, newspaper reading can provide a springboard for discussion, especially with more mature children, on every imaginable topic. Pictures of starving or displaced children, stories about family tragedies or triumphs, can initiate family interchange that is both sensitive and sophisticated.

As an added bonus, you might familiarize your child with journalism basics. Explain the difference between an editorial and a news story, between a feature and a column. Show him or her the dateline (where the story originates) and the byline (writer of the story).

Of course, the newspaper must not be "taught" — a gifted child may "turn off" if he or she thinks you are lecturing. Let your child's interest and maturity dictate the degree to which you "share" the paper together.

If your child observes that you enjoy the paper on a daily basis, and is allowed to "grow into" reading it on a gradual basis, you may have to settle for the comics while he or she finishes reading the front page.

— *Judy Wax, Birmingham, Michigan*

Using Enchantment

Our highly creative son was very self-critical and lacked confidence. My husband and I tried praise, patience, and positive experiences, but our efforts to bolster his ego met with minimal results.

One day at the library I found *The Uses of Enchantment* by Bruno Bettelheim. In this book, the author states that the reading of fairy tales can help a child "bring order into the turmoil of his feelings" and assist him or her in "finding meaning in life." These ancient stories, Bettelheim continues, speak to "a child's budding ego and encourage its development."

I checked out several fairy-tale collections to read to our son. Through these delightful stories, he learns how various heroes and heroines solve the problems that life presents. Although many of the main characters are intially considered simpletons or weaklings, by the end of the tales they prove their worth by being smart enough and creative enough to outwit the opposition. For us the most successful of these tales have been "Clever Gretchen," retold by Alison Lurie, and "The Wonder Clock," by Howard Pyle.

Our son greatly enjoys these stories. Often he will refer to one, comparing an incident in his own life with that of the story character. And as the months have passed, there has been a slow but continual improvement in his self-image. By finding our own use for enchantment, our son is gaining self-confidence, becoming braver, and learning to laugh at life a bit more.

— *Linda Gresser, Cincinnati, Ohio*

CRITICAL THINKING, COMPUTATION, AND ANALYSIS

Use "Think Starters," Not "Think Stoppers"

The words we use can be powerful determiners of the depth of thinking that occurs at home. Those words can be "think stoppers" or "think starters" for our gifted children.

Some words stimulate thinking; others eliminate the need for it. "Put your toys in the chest" requires only that your child understand a simple direction and follow it. "Company is coming; everything in your room should be clean and neat" requires that your child determine and take appropriate actions.

Remember, just because your child has special abilities in an area does not guarantee the presence of decision-making skills or the initiative for taking responsibility. These things need to be nurtured so your child's abilities can blossom fully. With a young child, this nurturing can begin with the mundane situations that take place around the house. As our children develop, they will transfer these skills to other areas, including those in which they have exceptional talent.

To help your child become a responsible, active thinker, you might, as a general rule, try these approaches:

1. Present the child with specific, descriptive information at his or her level of understanding: "It is time to put your toys (or clothes, and so on) where they belong."
2. If your child does not respond, follow up with a question:

"Where can you put your toys so that you will be able to find them later?"

3. If your child remains unresponsive, ask, "Do you need help deciding what to do?" This way, your child becomes responsible for seeking help in making decisions and acting on them. Eventually, your youngster will begin to make decisions on his or her own, without prompting from you.

Check yourself on the following common situations to see whether your words are "think stoppers" or "think starters":

- Two children are arguing over a toy.
  Think Stopper: "Sue, let Bill play with it now; you can have it second."
  Think Starter: "It looks like you both want to play with the same toy. Can you decide on your own what to do, or shall I help you?" (If the children cannot decide, go ahead and step in.)

- Your child says, "I'm bored."
  Think Stopper: "Call John and see if he can come over and play."
  Think Starter: "What might you do that you haven't done for a while?" (You may need to suggest some general activities from which your child can choose.)

- Your child can't figure out how to do something and says with frustration, "I can't do this."
  Think Stopper: "Here's how to do it: first you . . ."
  Think Starter: "Which part is giving you trouble? Let's try to figure it out."

Using "think starters" with our children helps develop flexibility, creativity, and resourcefulness — all ingredients of gifted behavior.

— *Pam Balis and Madeline Hunter, Los Angeles, California*

From Scorekeeper to Navigator

From early on, it was quite apparent that my son, Chuck, was highly gifted in the area of math. I was constantly searching for challenges for his mind. As I look back, some of the best ideas came right from him. When I'd take him to the junior- and senior-high basketball games, he'd sit in back of the scorekeepers and watch them keep the book. When he was six years old, he asked me to buy him a score book for Christmas. That year he took his score book to all of the games.

I wrote in the names of the players from both teams and he did the rest. He kept a perfect book, showing shots taken, shots made, foul shots, players going in and out, the score after each quarter, and so on. Soon he insisted on knowing what the percentage column was all about. After an explanation, he proceeded to figure out each player's shot percentage.

We had the support of Chuck's first-grade teacher in this endeavor and she was delighted when he brought the book to school to share with his classmates.

From the time he was four, Chuck insisted on having his own map when we took a family vacation. He would follow the route, estimate the mileage, and involve the whole family in guessing the population of cities we were passing through. It wasn't long before he was planning the entire trip by himself. I would give him the final destination and how many miles we wanted to cover each day. He planned some of the most beautiful trips imaginable. He figured out where we would spend the night and how much the expenses would be.

The biggest problem was Chuck's desire to go directly through the downtown area of the big cities. He liked to see the design of the different urban areas. Often we would find ourselves turning off the interstate and taking the business routes through towns and cities.

By the time Chuck was eleven, he had planned trips to Ridley Park, Pennsylvania; Yakima, Washington; and around Lake Michigan through Canada. Right now Chuck is thirteen and he's working on a winter vacation trip to Florida.

— *Anne Anderson, Plainfield, Illinois*

How Did It Work?

Instead of throwing broken appliances away, our family takes them apart to see how they work. We have disassembled an electric clock, a radio, a blender, our old washing machine, a depth finder for locating fish, and a typewriter.

This activity is great for teaching kids about such things as tubes, motors, leverage, and tools. It also stimulates their curiosity and satisfies their sometimes destructive urge to mess with things.

If we are working on a small appliance, I put a sheet on the living-room floor, supply the tools — large and small screwdrivers, a small wrench, wire cutters, and whatever else is appropriate — and let the children attack it at their leisure. We work on larger appliances, such as the washing machine, in the garage. Since I don't know a lot about electronics myself, we look things up in Reader's Digest's *Fix-It-Yourself Manual* for information about the appliances' internal machinery.

— *Maria Kaino, Kailua, Hawaii*

CREATIVITY

Move Over, Superman!

A discussion of the process of imagination is a good place to begin encouraging creativity in your gifted child. For example, explain to your child that "there is something inside your mind that you can't see, but it helps you to think of things that no one else can think of; this is called your imagination." Help your child grasp the meaning of this concept by bringing your youngster's attention to his or her own creativity in a positive and reinforcing way. The following activity will encourage creative and imaginative behavior in your child:

Children are fascinated with superheroes on television. Here is an excellent way to approach the subject of creativity as it relates to your child's interest. Ask your child, "Is Superman real or is he make-believe?" You should discuss that Superman doesn't really exist but was conceived by someone's imagination. The creators of Superman, in other words, gave him his special powers, his identity, and his form.

Ask your child to create his or her very own special superhero, one that no one has ever seen on television or heard of before. Allow your child "thinking time" to sit with eyes closed and just imagine. Your child then can tell you about his or her superhero and what that superhero can do that is so special.

Next, your child is ready to give the imaginary hero a name, tell a story about it, and draw a picture of it. The use of pictures is extremely important in encouraging creativity, since many ideas have their origin in visual images. A simple crayon and piece of paper can express thousands of words for a creatively gifted child. If you wish, you may want to tape-record your child's description so that you can play back the comments and discuss them together.

— *Susan Rotner and Laura Siegelbaum, Rockville, Maryland*

Put Circulation into Circulation

Has this ever happened to your child? While studying the human body, he or she laboriously drew diagrams of the heart, lungs, and so on, then put the drawings into a notebook — and never saw or thought of them again. Instead of filing away those diagrams, you can give your child a chance to wear them — on T-shirts!

You'll need some tracing paper, fabric crayons or iron-on transfer pencils from your fabric store, and an electric iron. (Fabric paints for coloring-in the diagrams are optional.) First the chosen diagram should be simplified as much as possible without damaging scientific credibility. Then follow these steps:

1. Draw the design onto tracing paper.
2. Turn the tracing over and retrace the lines with a special transfer pencil. (Note: When you "print" a transfer, everything comes out in reverse.) Check the specified procedures that come with fabric pencils, crayons, or paints to ensure washability.
3. Place the tracing color-side-down on the shirt.
4. Press it slowly with a medium-hot iron. Check to see if the lines are transferring before removing paper.
5. The diagram can now be painted with fabric paints for a bolder effect, or left as is.

The heart, lungs, kidneys, and other assorted internal organs all make fascinating T-shirt designs, especially if you attempt to locate them as close as possible to their true positions. Of course, this idea is not confined to parts of the human body. Any of your child's creative and artistic drawings can be adapted for this unusual medium.

— *Lynne B. Baines, Washington, Virginia*

Children Create Their Own Environment

Children love to play in big cardboard boxes, and the sturdy wardrobes used by moving companies are great for construction projects. If you haven't moved lately, you can purchase the oversize boxes from a local moving company. We kept four from our last move, and after nine months and untold renovations, they are still going strong. The children needed help to cut out the doors, windows, mail slots, skylights, with a sharp knife; then I set them loose with paints, crayons, old wallpaper sample books (which most stores will give you free), fabric scraps, yarn, nylon net for screens, paste, and usable trash items (such as egg cartons and bottle caps).

We now have our own "town," including a spaceship, secret tunnels, a hideout, a little home with appliances drawn on one wall and tieback curtains, a post office, and even a train made from smaller boxes. We are so enthusiastic about the creativity our children are showing that we plan to buy a couple more "houses" from the moving company for the kids' birthdays.

— *Mary J. Conaway, State College, Pennsylvania*

Happy Birthday, Mr. Beethoven

Our family makes a point of celebrating the birthdays of persons who have made significant contributions to civilization. We make a special dessert and share interesting facts about that person's life. If the person is a composer, we play his music during dinner. The children consider it a festive event, and we all learn something new and gain a greater appreciation for the person's life.

— *Nancy Roehm, Stelle, Illinois*

OUTSIDE-THE-HOME ACTIVITIES

To Catch a Butterfly

If your gifted child enjoys learning about nature, you can set aside a little time each week to plan nature walks and other projects together. Using the four seasons as your guide, there are unlimited nature activities year-round. Here are a few for spring and summer:

• March is the "wakening month" and in many wooded areas, your child may be able to catch a glimpse of a small, furry animal, such as a badger or chipmunk, just coming out of its winter sleeping place. Or you might choose a field and catch a glimpse of the migrating birds. Some of the best known are the robin, the bluebird, the cowbird, the red-winged blackbird, and the Canada goose. Then, there is the March butterfly — the mourning cloak. Wildflowers of this month are adder's-tongue, trout lily, arbutus, skunk cabbage, hepatica, spring beauty, and wake-robin.

• In April, nature is fully awake for the approaching warmer days. Butterflies are everywhere: cabbage species, busky-wing, comma, sotty-wing, zebra swallowtail — all just emerging from their cocoons.

• In May, as you stroll through the woods, look for little mauve-winged blooms among the mosses. This flower, fringed polygala, holds a secret all its own. Tell your child that it doesn't matter if he or she picks this flower, because it has a crop of underground blossoms among its roots, and these are seed bearers, too!

• In July, if you come upon a sassafras bush, you will want to dig out a bit of the fragrant, delicious root to chew for its spicy flavor. You might want to offer a piece of it to your child as July's contribution to the never-ending wonders of nature. This is also the time to hunt for a hummingbird's nest. It is no bigger than an English walnut and is a rare and difficult object to find. It looks like a knot on the limb of a tree.

— *Evelyn Witter, Milan, Illinois*

Programs for Saturday Scholars

What alternatives to Saturday television are available to children? The success of Saturday workshops for children of all ages indicates that these programs are meeting some of the needs of bright children. Unfettered by a prescribed school curriculum, these programs are providing gifted children with activities at an appropriate level and pace. They offer an environment that allows gifted youngsters to experience relationships with others like themselves on an intellectual, artistic, and emotional level.

Parents and other advocacy groups have successfully initiated and administered these kinds of programs for years, and groups interested in developing a Saturday program should consider the following questions:

• *What physical facilities are available?* Can classes be held in a school, on a college campus, or in a public building such as a library or museum? This will, in part, determine what form the program will take.

• *Who will be the instructors?* Saturday programs have successfully used school personnel, university faculty, practicing professionals, and parents as teachers. The selection of the teachers, and their expertise and interests, will shape the course offerings of a program.

• *What funds does the group have at its disposal?* With expenses itemized in a budget, parents can determine how much tuition is needed to cover costs for instruction, supplies, and possible building rental.

• *What format should be used for identifying the participants to be enrolled in the program?* Some groups have based their plans on state or school-district guidelines for gifted programs. Other programs are based on self-nomination by the children. Parent groups can save a great deal of planning time by adapting the forms and procedures used by other such programs in existence. This information is available from parent advocacy groups for the gifted as well as from other sources.

— *Ann Robinson, Macomb, Illinois*

Local Shops Provide Knowledge and Fun

As the parent of three advanced boys, I find that there is extreme competitiveness among them. I also find the constant manipulation of my time very tiring. Reading materials and conferences concerning the gifted many times don't address these concerns, for they assume that there are unlimited time and financial resources. Another presumption is that there is only one child to be stimulated and two doting parents whose lives revolve around extracurricular activities for their offspring. And this is not always so.

For those who have similar problems, let me share some practical ideas. Visit your local shops (television repair, camera shop, jeweler, furniture refinishing, bank, and so on). Independent small-business persons are usually friendly and have a good knowledge of their equipment and pride in their talents. They usually welcome questions and often allow children to become involved in their operation to some extent.

If you choose manufacturing plants, for example, it is preferable to take children to smaller companies, where everything is not closed off and highly technical. Careful checking of the yellow pages of the telephone directory can provide an enormous variety of possible experiences, be it a glass-making or chocolate factory, the local newspaper, or a motorbike store. This is the real world, and the experiences can be adapted according to the interests and the ages of your children. Such outings may spark new ventures and widen reading areas. They can be arranged to suit your own schedule, and they seem to lessen competitiveness among children.

There will still be those times of boredom when "good reading" isn't even the solution. Hobbies are good independent activities and also help to alleviate boredom. Visit the local lumberyard or building site, where they often give away scraps of wood and other materials that can be used for hobbies and projects.

It is said that gifted children detest routine chores. (My lads are positive proof of this!) They have very logical arguments against these mundane tasks. So I balance one thing with another. For example, a "Beasts Banquet" was planned where each son invited one friend. They planned the menu, did the shopping, and prepared the food. Afterward, they washed mountains of dishes without a single complaint!

— *Veronica Zarowny, Streetsville, Ontario*

Select Bibliography

The following resources have been selected to supplement the topics covered in *Parents' Guide to Raising a Gifted Toddler*. Although by no means exhaustive, this list offers a broad range of texts that can serve as background materials or can occasion additional reading on subjects of particular interest. (Also see the "Additional Resources" listings at the end of many chapters.)

Adderholdt-Elliott, Miriam. *Perfectionism: What's Bad About Being Too Good?* Free Spirit, 1987.

Allen, Steve. *How to Think* (record album). Gifted and Talented Publications (P.O. Box 134, Sewell, NJ 08080), 1982.

Allison, Christine. *I'll Tell You a Story, I'll Sing You a Song*. Delacorte Press, 1987.

Alvino, James, and the Editors of *Gifted Children Monthly*. *Parents' Guide to Raising a Gifted Child: Recognizing and Developing Your Child's Potential*. Little, Brown, 1985.

Barrett, Susan L. *It's All in Your Head: A Guide to Understanding Your Brain and Boosting Your Brain Power*. Free Spirit, 1985.

Becker, Wesley C. *Parents Are Teachers*. Res Press, 1971.

Bettelheim, Bruno. *The Uses of Enchantment*. Knopf, 1976.

Bloom, Benjamin S., ed. *Developing Talent in Young People*. Ballantine, 1985.

Bradway, Lauren Carlile. *Quick Check of Children's Learning Styles*. Beeby-Champ Publishing, 1987.

Brown, Sam, ed. *Bubbles, Rainbows and Worms*. Gryphon House, 1981.

Burke, James. *The Day the Universe Changed*. Little, Brown, 1986.

Butler, Dorothy. *Babies Need Books*. Atheneum, 1980.

Clark, Barbara. *Growing Up Gifted*. 2nd ed. Merrill, 1983.

———. *Optimizing Learning*. Merrill, 1986.

Coffey, Kay. *Parentspeak on Gifted and Talented Children*. Ventura County Superintendent of Schools (535 E. Main St., Ventura, CA 93009), 1976.

Coles, Robert. *The Moral Life of Children*. Houghton Mifflin, 1986.

Cumming, Robert. *Just Imagine: Ideas in Painting*. Scribner's, 1982.

Davis, Gary A., and Rimm, Sylvia B. *Education of the Gifted and Talented*. Prentice-Hall, 1985.

Delisle, James R. *Gifted Children Speak Out*. Walker, 1984.

———. *Gifted Kids Speak Out*. Free Spirit, 1987.

Delp, Jeanne, and Martinson, Ruth. *The Gifted and Talented: A Handbook for Parents*. Ventura County Superintendent of Schools (535 E. Main St., Ventura, CA 93009), 1975.

Dunford, Jill W. *Teach Me, Mommy*. Writer's Digest Books, 1984.

Eberle, Bob, and Stanish, Bob. *CPS for Kids: A Resource Book for Teaching Creative Problem Solving to Children*. DOK Publishers, 1980.

Ehrlich, Virginia Z. *Gifted Children: A Guide for Parents and Teachers*. Prentice-Hall, 1982.

Elkind, David. *The Hurried Child: Growing Up Too Fast Too Soon*. Addison-Wesley, 1981.

———. *The Miseducation of Children: Preschoolers at Risk*. Knopf, 1987.

Feldman, Ruth Duskin. *Whatever Happened to the Quiz Kids: Perils and Profits of Growing Up Gifted*. Chicago Review Press, 1982.

Felker, Roberta M., ed. *A Parent's Guide to the Education of Preschool Gifted Children*. National Association of State Boards of Education (444 N. Capitol St., N.W., Washington, DC 20001), 1982.

First United Church Nursery School. *Celebrate!* Rainbow, 1987.

Galbraith, Judy. *The Gifted Kids' Survival Guide*. Free Spirit, 1983.

Gallagher, James J. *Teaching the Gifted Child*. 3rd ed. Allyn and Bacon, 1985.

Gardner, Howard. *Frames of Mind*. Basic Books, 1983.

Gifted Child Society. *The Private Sector: New Answers to Old Budget Questions*. Gifted Child Society (190 Rock Rd., Glen Rock, NJ 07452), 1983.

Gillis, Jack, and Fise, Mary Ellen R. *The Childwise Catalog*. Pocket Books, 1986.

Ginsberg, Gina, and Harrison, Charles H. *How to Help Your Gifted Child: A Handbook for Parents and Teachers*. Monarch Press, 1977.

Goertzel, Victor, and Goertzel, Mildred G. *Cradles of Eminence*. Little, Brown, 1962.

Hall, Eleanor G., and Skinner, Nancy. *Somewhere to Turn: Strategies for Parents of the Gifted and Talented*. Teachers College, 1980.

Healy, Jane M. *Your Child's Growing Mind*. Doubleday, 1987.

Hearne, Betsy. *Choosing Books for Children*. Dell, 1982.

Hechinger, Fred M., ed. *A Better Start: New Choices for Early Learning*. Walker, 1986.

Hipp, Earl. *Fighting Invisible Tigers: A Student Guide to Life in "The Jungle."* Free Spirit, 1985.

Kaufman, Felice. *Your Gifted Child and You*. Council for Exceptional Children (1920 Association Dr., Reston, VA 22091), 1976.

Kerr, Barbara. *Smart Girls, Gifted Women*. Ohio Psychology, 1986.

Khatena, Joseph. *The Creatively Gifted Child: Suggestions for Parents and Teachers*. Vantage, 1978.

Krueger, Mark. *On Being Gifted*. Walker, 1978.

LeShan, Eda. *When Your Child Drives You Crazy*. St. Martin's, 1985.

Lipman, Matthew, and Sharp, Ann M. *Philosophy for Children*. Institute for the Advancement of Philosophy for Children (Montclair State College, Montclair, NJ 07043), 1980.

Mitchell, Patricia Bruce, ed. *An Advocate's Guide for Building Support for Gifted and Talented Education*. National Association of State Boards of Education (444 N. Capitol St., N.W., Washington, DC 20001), 1981.

Montessori Teachers Association of Pennsylvania, compiler. *Small World Cookbook*. Greene Towne School (2013 Appletree St., Philadelphia, PA 19103), 1987.

Moore, Linda Perigo. *Does This Mean My Kid's a Genius?* McGraw-Hill, 1981.

Osherson, Samuel. *Finding Our Fathers*. Free Press, 1986.

Pagnoni, Mario. *Computers and Small Fries*. Avery, 1987.

Parke, Ross D. *Fathers*. Harvard University Press, 1981.

Pellowski, Anne. *The Family Story-Telling Handbook*. Macmillan, 1987.

Perino, Joseph, and Perino, Sheila C. *Parenting the Gifted: Developing the Promise*. Bowker, 1981.

Pirz, Therese Slevin. *Speak French to Your Baby*. Chou-Chou Press, 1981.

———. *Speak Spanish to Your Baby*. Chou-Chou Press, 1985.

Renzulli, Joseph S. *The Enrichment Triad Model*. Creative Learning Press (P.O. Box 320, Mansfield Center, CT 06250), 1977.

Richert, E. Susanne; Alvino, James; and McDonnel, Rebecca C. *National Report on Identification: Assessment and Recommendations for Comprehensive Identification of Gifted and Talented Youth*. Educational Information and Resource Center (700 Hollydell Court, Sewell, NJ 08080), 1982.

Rimm, Sylvia B. *Underachievement Syndrome: Causes and Cures*. Apple Publishing (W6050 Apple Rd., Watertown, WI 53094), 1986.

Rogers, Fred. *Mister Rogers' Plan and Play Book*. Family Communications, 1983.

Rosen, Marcia. *Test Your Baby's I.Q.* Prentice-Hall, 1986.

Saunders, Jacqulyn, with Espeland, Pamela. *Bringing Out the Best: A Resource Guide for Parents of Young Gifted Children*. Free Spirit, 1986.

Sisk, Dorothy. *Creative Teaching of the Gifted*. McGraw-Hill, 1987.

Smith, Kim Stevens. *Stress Management in Gifted Education*. ERIC Reports (3900 Wheeler Ave., Alexandria, VA 22304), 1984.

Snowball, Marilyn. *Preschool Packrat*. Learning Works, 1982.

———. *Preschool Pelican*. Learning Works, 1982.

Striker, Susan. *Please Touch: How to Stimulate Your Child's Creative Development through Movement, Music, Art, and Play*. Simon and Schuster, 1986.

Strom, Robert D. *Growing through Play: Readings for Parents and Teachers*. Brooks/Cole, 1980.

Thoman, Evelyn B., and Thoman, Browder. *Born Dancing*. Harper and Row, 1987.

Torrance, E. Paul. *The Search for Satori and Creativity*. Creative Education Foundation (437 Franklin St., Buffalo, NY 14202-1301), 1979.

Torrance, E. Paul; Weiner, Deborah; Presbury, Jack H.; and Henderson, Morgan (with the assistance of over 5,000 children from 16 countries). *Save Tomorrow for the Children*. Bearly Limited (149 York St., Buffalo, NY 14213), 1987.

Trelease, Jim. *The Read Aloud Handbook*. Penguin Books, 1985.

Vail, Priscilla. *Smart Kids with School Problems*. Dutton, 1987.

———. *The World of the Gifted Child*. Walker, 1979; Penguin, 1980.

Webb, James; Meckstroth, Elizabeth; and Tolan, Stephanie. *Guiding the Gifted Child*. Ohio Psychology, 1982.

White, Burton L. *Educating the Infant and Toddler*. Lexington Books, 1988.

———. *A Parent's Guide to the First Three Years*. Prentice-Hall, 1980.

Whitmore, Joanne. *Giftedness, Conflict, and Underachievement*. Allyn and Bacon, 1980.

Williams, Robert A.; Rockwell, Robert E.; and Sherwood, Elizabeth A. *Mudpies to Magnets*. Gryphon House, 1987.

Wurtman, Judith. *Managing Your Mind and Mood through Food*. Rawson Associates, 1986.

Zdenek, Marilee. *The Right-Brain Experience: An Intimate Programme to Free the Powers of Your Imagination*. Corgi Books (Tansworld Publishers, Ltd./Century), 1983.

Index